365+
WAYS
TO SAVE
THE PLANET
AND YOUR
MONEY
AT THE SAME TIME

LOTTIE DALZIEL

murdoch books
Sydney | London

Contents

Introduction

Sustainability is at a pivotal point. We know that time is running out to turn the tide on climate change, but, simultaneously, many people see making sustainable changes as luxuries they simply cannot afford. However, the truth is that saving money and the planet can go hand in hand with the right strategies. One key element is making a conscious return to a simpler way of life, where getting back to basics is the focus. It's about doing what's possible within your means, step by step, little by little, and making small but meaningful changes that, when combined, add up to a significant positive environmental impact.

It's not hard to see where the misconceptions about sustainability have come from. Many of the commonly marketed 'solutions' to climate change, like driving electric vehicles and buying expensive organic produce, are prohibitive to the average person. But living sustainably need not be the preserve of the wealthy. I want to help us reframe our thinking to see living sustainably as something that is, by its very nature, simple, affordable, frugal – and available to anyone. Consuming less, making your own and repurposing existing items were common practices for our grandparents, and they are things that we need to return to in order to collectively achieve the goal of sustainability.

Addressing climate change can feel so big and beyond the individual that it's easy to see it as someone else's problem – the responsibility of big business to change their operations, or governments to improve their policies. These things should happen, of course. But, in actual fact, everyone can participate in a global effort to save our planet no matter what their financial situation. To move the needle on climate action, we need everyone to pull together, and I'm going to show you how you can take actionable steps to immediately reduce your environmental impact without breaking the bank.

It's important to recognise that making sustainable swaps in your life is a gradual process. It's a good idea to set realistic expectations from the get-go and manage your mindset, because the changes you need to make take some time to learn and implement. It is nearly impossible to live perfectly sustainably every day. I've been on this journey for almost a decade and I am still learning. So, instead of perfection, it's easier to focus on making small improvements every day. Some days this might look like simply remembering your reusable coffee cup. Other days, it will be purchasing an eco-friendlier appliance. It's about progress, not perfection.

I do want to acknowledge that some sustainable options are just more expensive, but this is why it's important to have a strategy. Making cuts and consuming less in some areas of your life frees up budget for others. It's not about making more money to spend more. It's about mindfully allocating what funds you do have for the things that are going to make the biggest impact. This might mean making up-front investments on some sustainable items to save money further down the track, which is a recurring theme in this book.

One of the biggest and most important principles of sustainable living is using what you've already got and only consuming what you absolutely need. Allowing these two principles to guide your decision-making – and spending habits – is a great jumping-off point for saving both money and the planet. But let's get this straight: living sustainably and saving money isn't easy. If it were easy, there would be no need for this book. It requires effort, determination and grit, but I have dedicated my life to making it easier for people like you so we can all get on with the urgent task at hand.

Halting climate change is not a 'one and done' thing; it requires a multi-pronged effort – seven days a week, 365 days a year. Feeling overwhelmed at the thought? Don't be! I'm going to show you how you can make over 365 simple, small and cost-effective changes that will see you living a more sustainable life, while simultaneously saving the planet and saving you money.

Here are a few of my favourite affirmations that I hope will help you reframe the way you think about living sustainably. Write them down and stick them somewhere you will see them all the time:
- Focus on what you can control, not what you can't
- Small steps make the biggest difference
- Aim for progress, not perfection
- Actions speak louder than words
- Something is better than nothing
- Don't be afraid to ask questions
- Think globally, act locally

'We have access to almost anything with just the click of a button, making it too easy to mindlessly overconsume.'

One of the biggest things I hope you'll learn in this book is that much of the challenge surrounding sustainability is due to our society's culture of consumption. There are a couple of drivers for this – firstly, convenience. We have access to almost anything with just the click of a button, making it too easy to mindlessly overconsume. Secondly, we are bombarded with advertising that encourages this overconsumption from the moment we wake up, whether it's from television or social media ads, billboards or bus stops.

This has led to an economy that is based on the promise of infinite growth on a finite planet. But our growth – and consumption – cannot be exponential. It cannot go on forever, because we are working within the constraints of a planet that has limited resources. It is up to everyone to start learning the skill of living more sustainably on a sustainable planet, where resources are conserved and regenerated instead of depleted.

I wish I could tell you that I've found the mythical money tree that also sequesters carbon and gobbles up all the world's plastic, but that's a pipe dream. What I can show you is how you can nourish both your bank account and the planet at the same time with practical, affordable solutions. Put simply, I want to show you how you can live more, with less.

About me

For those of you who don't know, I'm Lottie. I am the founder of Banish, one of Australia's leading education platforms that teaches people how to live more sustainably. Before turning green I was a journalist, working for some of the biggest publishers in Australia to help them simplify complex issues and studies for large audiences.

I've been on a journey to live more sustainably for almost ten years, which sounds like quite a long time, but, for me it has been an absolute whirlwind. In 2018, I made an extremely long list of New Year's resolutions. One of them was to run a half marathon, another was to become fluent in Spanish and another one was to do better for the planet. (Hint: only one of them stuck.)

I didn't really know what I meant by 'do better for the planet'; I certainly didn't have a list of strategies and affirmations ready to go. All I knew was that I was increasingly reading news headlines about global warming and seeing devastating pictures of birds with plastic in their stomachs. I wanted to take immediate action, but I had no idea where to start, and the task felt utterly overwhelming.

Small changes, like swapping single-use plastic straws for reusable ones, was just the tip of the iceberg, and I quickly became aware of how much I didn't know about living sustainably. There was plenty of information for people who wanted to increase their efforts, but not much for someone at the very beginning of their journey. So, I thought why not use my skills as a journalist to help inspire action, educate and empower others to start reducing their waste, one step at a time?

I was going on the journey myself, so all I needed to do was write about it. I started documenting it on social media and connecting with other Aussies who were also keen to reduce their environmental footprint. It helped to meet like-minded people who empathised with the process, especially during times when I felt disheartened, overwhelmed and upset by the enormity of it. Through this, I also discovered amazing small sustainable Australian businesses that were doing the right thing for the planet but didn't have the time, the money or the know-how to connect with larger audiences.

So, I created a platform where I could teach people how to live sustainably and also connect them with Australian businesses that were making big strides towards addressing the climate crisis. And so, Banish was born. I could never have anticipated what it would eventually become, but I am so proud of what I've achieved and the impact I've been able to make.

And then there's BRAD (Banish Recycling and Disposal Program). Its aim is to stop people from having to send items to the wrong pit (landfill) and, instead, send them to the right BRAD pit ... get it? BRAD is a beast ...

Three years into my sustainability journey I was practising everything I was preaching and teaching; I was composting, making swaps, saving and recycling what I could. But I would still look inside my bin at the end of each week and see items that were destined for landfill – things like medical blister packs (aluminium and clear plastics), bottle-top lids (plastic), coffee pods (aluminium). I was overwhelmed by frustration that my intensive efforts were still not enough to keep this waste out of landfill, so I set to work and researched what I could do differently.

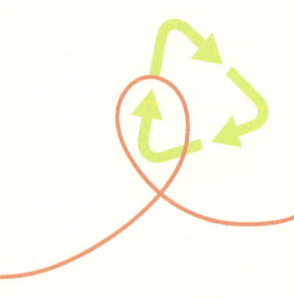

With Banish, I wanted a way to give back to the community that was meaningful and empowering and, importantly, educational. So, I came up with a service to recycle hard-to-recycle items and provide people with a way of disposing of them responsibly. People could pool their items together to make larger bundles that could be recycled traditionally once they reached a certain weight. For example, 15 kilograms (33 pounds) of plastic beauty products, and 50 kilograms (110 pounds) of aluminium blister packs.

I honestly had no idea how many people would get on board with a program like this, but the outcome blew me away. What started as a handful of households sending me a few shoeboxes of recyclable items in November of 2020 quickly snowballed into over two hundred parcels by February the following year. As someone who was determined to find a way to banish these hard-to-recycle items, the concept felt genuinely exciting to me, but I didn't expect so many other people to care about it, too.

During this time, I was documenting everything on social media. I had a couple of complete strangers reach out to me and say 'Hey Lottie, I see that you're sorting all of this rubbish in your backyard. I'll come over this weekend and give you a hand.' I have to admit that I felt weirded out by it at first, but I was living with roommates at the time who weren't too impressed by the boxes that were piling up in our laundry and garage, so I said yes.

The weekend sorting sessions began. It wasn't all smooth sailing; we had to pause it if it was raining, as it was an open garage, and the boxes arrived at such a rate that we couldn't sort them quickly enough. Six months later, I moved the operation to a small storage unit at a self-storage centre.

The boxes never have slowed down over four years later. I am continually blown away by the fact that this many Australians want to recycle with us. In April 2023, we moved into our first physical site at Central Station in Sydney. We also now have a team of over seventy volunteers each month who come to sort and separate each of the different waste streams by hand so that we can keep this program in operation.

BRAD is by far one of the most challenging things that I have ever created. He pushes me and tests my limits, but running this program is also one of my most rewarding achievements to date. It demonstrates at a large scale the impact that a grassroots movement can have on the environment and how, collectively, the actions of individuals can make a big difference.

I think it's helpful to remember that no matter how hard it can feel to make sustainable improvements in your life, you are not alone. You are not the only one taking action for change. The best advice I can give you? Surround yourself with people who are doing the same thing. And remember that every step, no matter how small, is a move in the right direction.

I'm a big believer in being the change that you want to see in the world. It's one thing to talk about it or share something online, but it's a whole other thing to actually do it. It can be scary and it can be confronting, but that usually means it is worth doing.

When I first made that New Year's resolution, I had no idea that a simple wish would grow into an enormous positive vehicle for change. I didn't anticipate being here writing this book, but I'm so proud that every day I get to help teach people how they can do better for the planet.

The core principle of sustainability is consuming less. Buying (and consuming) less, by definition, saves money, and so the two are inextricably linked. People put living sustainably and saving money in two different baskets, but, after reading this book, I hope you'll be able to see that when you have one, you have the other.

'BRAD is by far one of the most challenging things that I have ever created.'

But before you close the book thinking I'm going to tell you to live like a monk, I want to emphasise that consuming less does not mean living less. In fact, I would argue that it means living more, because once you start recruiting time, attention and money towards the things that really matter to you, your life becomes richer. Living more mindfully, with intention and making conscious reductions to your environmental impact, will improve your wellbeing.

When you think about it, saving the planet and saving money actually have a lot in common. Mostly, their values: frugality, getting back to basics, consuming less and spending mindfully. They also require the same mindset, behaviours and priorities, though they are applied differently. The Venn diagram below is a great way of visualising this crossover:

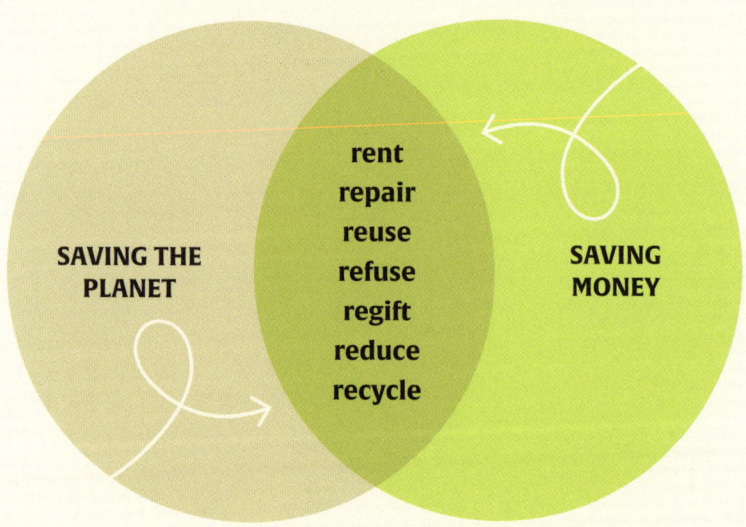

How to use this book

I have written this book like a menu. You can pick and choose what topic you're going to tackle first, starting with what feels right for you. The more changes you make, the more you'll save – both environmentally and financially. Don't bite off more than you can chew, though. Start small and take it in manageable chunks.

I'd also like to address the fact that this book isn't about going 'zero waste' or 'plastic free'. While I commend people who can stuff a year's worth of rubbish into a single jam jar, I don't think this is realistic for the average person – and I'd much rather you kept it realistic with smaller, meaningful changes, than became overwhelmed by the task. This book also won't make you millions (unless you become a professional thrifter and flipper; more on that in How to shop and sell secondhand, page 158). What it will do is make saving money and saving the planet a whole lot less daunting.

A word of warning, though: this isn't a cosy Sunday read. This book is designed for doing. You're not here just to cross off another title on your list, or simply shelve it on your perfectly coordinated rainbow bookshelf. I encourage you to take in the information and put it into action. It doesn't matter if it takes you a few rereads, highlighting it, dog-earing the pages, adding coloured tabs – whatever you need to do to really digest and apply it to your life.

At the start of each chapter, you'll find a savings scale. This is designed to give you a sense of what savings you could make depending on how many changes you make, and whether you want to take an easy, medium or hard approach. Use it as incentive to scale your actions and make some seriously savvy changes!

All amounts given in this book are in Australian Dollars unless otherwise stated.

At the end of each chapter is a list of actionable steps. Think of them as key takeaways that turn aspirations into actions: things you can do right then and there to implement what you've learned in that chapter.

To start with, we're going back to basics and diving headfirst into the sustainability essentials – you know, the stuff you weren't taught at school (but really should have been!). Once you have a grasp on basic terms, jargon and concepts, you'll be set up for success!

Inside, outside and out in the world

Living more sustainably is an holistic task, and one that can be achieved with gradual, often simple, changes in every part of our lives. This book will walk you through what you can do to start your sustainability journey right now, with everything from tips for reducing kitchen waste, to mindfully choosing new beauty products, and suggestions for how to talk about the changes you're making with your loved ones.

1. Before we tackle the task of living more sustainably, it's important that we understand the lingo – and **exactly what sustainability means** by today's standards.

2. Food waste is of the biggest contributors to climate change, so it's number one on our sustainability hit-list. Here you'll find **smart strategies for shopping, cooking and eating** to keep excess food out of landfill.

3. **Plastic really ain't so fantastic.** It's time to learn why, how to recycle it and how to stop using (and eating) so much of the shiny stuff without putting a serious dent in your bank account.

4. We'll also look at what you can do to **reduce your energy consumption** and plastic waste in the kitchen, and make the most of your existing appliances.

5. While we're in the kitchen, let's see what we can do to **reduce the expensive, plastic-bottled cleaning agents** and toxic chemicals, too.

6. Then, in the bathroom, we'll cover a bunch of **DIY recipes, tips and tricks** for creating a cleaner, cheaper and more sustainable beauty routine.

7. Hand in hand with beauty, **fashion is another area where you can make some savvy savings**. From diving deeper into sustainable textiles to shopping smarter for secondhand fits, your wardrobe will never look the same again.

8. And while we're on the subject, **secondhand doesn't mean second best.** We'll discuss everything from how to snag the best buys to how to sell your wares for more.

9. Let's not waste your energy doing unnecessary things to save energy. **Power up your savings and power down your spending** as you slash your utility bills – and environmental footprint.

10. Work, work, work. **It's time to turn your office green.** I'm talking indoor plants, bins and taking the stairs. Plus, is carpooling better than catching the bus? Let's find out.

11. Now, let's take this thinking outside; **you're about to grow a green thumb.** I love gardening and it honestly isn't that hard. Plus, there are major savings to be made by growing your own vegetables.

12. And when you're ready to get away? Don't worry; that overseas holiday is still a reality. Even though air travel is a controversial topic in sustainability circles, **I'm not going to clip your (airline) wings.** Life is here to be lived and the world needs to be explored. I'll just show you how to do it on a budget and with as little impact on the environment as possible.

13. For all of this to work, you need to feel supported by those nearest to you. **Let's look at how you can talk to your family and friends about your sustainability journey** – and possibly even bring them along for the ride.

Ultimately, to me it's logical that someone is more likely to participate in the agenda of living sustainably and preventing climate change if they are taught affordable ways to do it. I want to show you that getting back to basics, planning ahead and being more intentional with your spending, behaviours and choices are the keys to both saving the environment and saving money. I am honoured that you have picked up this book, and excited for the journey you are about to begin. Let's get started.

1.

Sustainability essentials

Have you heard?

* Recycling 1 tonne of paper or cardboard saves 30,000 litres (8000 gallons) of water.

* 90 per cent of Australians participate in some degree of sustainable practices.

* 75 per cent of UK residents recycle or compost their household waste.

* 77 per cent of global citizens want to learn how to live more sustainably.

Sustainability 101

The term 'sustainability' is relatively new and forever changing. It's one of the reasons I ask each guest on my Sustainability Further podcast what sustainability means to them. My personal definition is also always shifting according to societal changes, but to me it means the ways in which we can leave our planet better than we found it, and in a state that can sustain itself and its inhabitants for many years to come. Hopefully by the end of this book, you will have your own meaning for the term and decided what your own journey will be into living more sustainably.

Sustainability means something different today than it did even twenty years ago in response to developments in our culture, economy and technology, which means we need to constantly review how we define and, more importantly, how we go about the 'task' of living sustainably.

One of the biggest present-day misconceptions about sustainability is that it is expensive and difficult to execute. But I want to show you that living sustainably is not only affordable, but simple, too. It is no longer the sole responsibility of large corporations and governments to make changes to their environmental and social targets to move the needle on climate change. In fact, it's the cumulative effect of every individual's contribution that is going to save our planet – and I'm going to show you that you don't need to drop a lot of money in order to achieve it.

With this book, I want to arm you with achievable, actionable steps you can take to make significant environmental and financial savings. Before we dive in, let's lay the foundations by looking at some common sustainability terms.

The nine Rs of waste

'Reduce, reuse, recycle.' I can still hear the jingle in my head. But, just to make things more confusing, these days there are no longer only three Rs of recycling, but nine! Our waste hierarchy has evolved alongside us, and recycling is no longer the bronze-medal winner. As you'll see below, recycling should be seen as one of our last resorts, not our first go-tos.

The link between waste reduction and our budgets is simple. Consuming doesn't just cost us money but our planet's resources, too, so when you make your next purchase or dispose of something, use these nine present-day 'commandments' of waste as your guiding light.

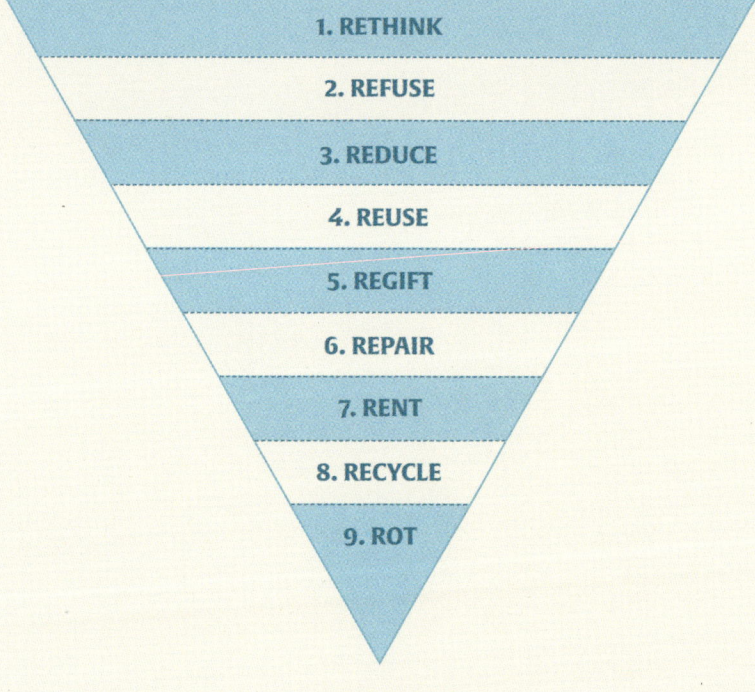

1. RETHINK
2. REFUSE
3. REDUCE
4. REUSE
5. REGIFT
6. REPAIR
7. RENT
8. RECYCLE
9. ROT

Notice how far down in the hierarchy recycling is? You love to recycle, I love to recycle – everyone does! – but this is 'old think'; the definition of recycling has expanded. Sure, putting something in the right bin might trigger those feel-good endorphins, but the bigger high comes from pausing to think before you make a purchase in the first place. Now, I'm not suggesting you don't buy anything – just that you need to think more about the front end: do you really need it at all? Could you buy less of it? Could you buy it secondhand? Would someone else get some use out of it? Starting with these questions moves you towards thinking about waste *creation* and away from thinking about waste *disposal*.

Greenwashing

Greenwashing is when brands or marketers make false or misleading claims about a product's environmental credentials, and it's everywhere these days.

This could look like using terms such as 'eco' or 'green', saying an item is recyclable when it can't actually be recycled, or using trustmarks (see page 23).

I've been caught in pretty much every greenwashing booby trap there is, from buying from organisations I *thought* were sustainable, to purchasing stainless-steel straws that came individually wrapped in plastic, to switching to soap bars that contained palm oil, to purchasing products that leached microplastics. And, most recently, buying a product I was assured would last a lifetime only to have it break after two uses. So, if it makes you feel any better, this sustainability landscape can be very difficult to navigate, even for me!

Saying that, I'm better at avoiding these traps than I used to be, so here's a bit of a guide to the most common confounding terms, so you can go in eyes peeled.

The words 'eco-friendly', 'clean', 'green' and 'sustainable' are thrown around by marketers to make products appear environmentally friendlier. However, these terms are just words that don't hold any promises and they aren't backed up by any actual sustainability credentials.

For example, your neighbour – let's call her Lauren – decides to make her own home-cleaning product. She purchases some pretty glass bottles online, throws on some minimalist branding and calls it Loz's Low-Waste Wash. Inside the bottle is a concoction of bleach, purified water and synthetic fragrance, and ta-dah! Thankfully, governing bodies are starting to crack down on bigger businesses that use such misleading words, but little old Loz is, as yet, unregulated.

As a rule of thumb, I always suggest that you do a quick search before making a purchase from any company. And don't wait to start until the thing you need is running low, because revealing a company or product's actual environmental values and practices can be complicated and time-consuming. To help speed up the process, here are a couple of trusted certifications to look out for, as well as some whacko words with very opaque definitions.

Australian Certified Organic (ACO)

An important thing to note straight away is that there's a jolly big difference between 'organic' and 'certified organic'. In Australia, there are just six organisations that can deem a product 'certified organic'. The most common certification is Australian Certified Organic (ACO). The equivalent certification in Europe and the United States is COSMOS.

On the other hand, 'organic' is a claim *without* the official backing. Businesses may have used organic or chemical-free practices to grow or make their product, but they have not been through the official channels to have it certified organic. The certification process is expensive, which means that not all businesses can afford it. However, if purchasing organic is a priority for you, I would suggest sticking to certified organic products only.

Cruelty Free International

Home to the leaping bunny certification, Cruelty Free International deems that no ingredient or subsidiary has ever been tested on animals. They will only certify a whole brand at a time, meaning that even if one small ingredient in one product is tested on animals at some point in the production process, the brand will be deemed ineligible.

Also, even if a product is vegan, it doesn't necessarily mean that it has not been tested on animals. Confusing, right? That's why you always need to look for the certification.

'As a rule of thumb, I always suggest that you do a quick search before making a purchase from any company.'

Australian Made

Look for the Aussie-made stamp: a green triangle with a yellow kangaroo, which means that a product has been grown and/ or created in Australia. Pay close attention to the percentage of Australian-made ingredients; it could be as little as 7 per cent (!), so always read the fine print, folks!

Natural

The words 'natural' and 'naturally derived' are thrown around *a lot*, but what do they even mean? That at some point an ingredient or component originated in nature? I mean, most things do. These terms don't really make sense, so proceed with caution.

Compostable

Although more and more brands are transitioning to using 'compostable' packaging, sadly – and ironically – it's still not as simple as throwing your packaging in your compost bin. In Australia, there are two main standards to look out for: home compostable (Australian Standard AS 5810–2010, UK/Europe OK compost and TÜV AUSTRIA, and in the US, ASTM D6868), and commercially compostable (Australian Standard AS 4736–2006, UK/Europe Standard BS EN 13432, and in the US, ASTM D6400). The difference? Industrial facilities treat compost at much higher temperatures, meaning that they can break down more difficult products than your regular compost bin. If you spot the home compostable symbol or code on the packaging of an item, that's your green light to put it in your backyard compost bin, but be aware that materials will still only break down under optimal conditions, such as in a warm environment and the right percentage of organic matter (see page 210).

For a product to comply with the industrial compostable standards, at least 90 per cent of the product should biodegrade in a 180-day period in their conditions, in addition to not having a toxic impact on earthworms.

For the home compostable certification, the standard period is twelve months, and the product should contain at least 50 per cent organic material.

Biodegradable

I harbour a special kind of hate for the word 'biodegradable'.

Technically speaking, a 'biodegradable' item claims to be one that can be broken down in nature by bacteria or microorganisms alone, whereas simply 'degradable' items are those that can be broken down into smaller pieces – we don't know when or how long it will take.

My bugbear? It's hard to pin down exactly what a 'biodegradable' item actually *is*. How long does it take to break down? What conditions does it need to do so? How do these considerations vary from product to product? Blanket definitions like this are always more nuanced than first meets the eye.

Biodegradable items are also definitely *not* recyclable (throwing a biodegradable coffee cup in your recycling bin is as pointless as throwing in a banana peel), but they also aren't compostable, because, more often than not, they're made from bioplastic, meaning that they need to go to landfill. How sustainable is that? *Cough cough*.

Recycled vs. recyclable

Ah, here we go again! A quick jumble of letters and we have two very similar words with two very *different* meanings.

'Recycled' means that a product is made from recycled materials. We don't know which ones, we don't know in what quantity (unless it specifies 'made from 100 per cent recycled materials'), and we don't know where those materials came from. To add another layer of complexity, if something is made from 'recycled materials' it doesn't necessarily mean that it is recycla*ble*. I know.

So, what's 'recyclable'? Recyclable simply means that an item can be recycled at the end of its lifespan. To really trust this claim, don't look for the traditional chasing arrows recycling symbol. Instead, look for back-up in the form of the Australasian Recycling Label (ARL). The ARL is an Australian labelling scheme that guides people on how to dispose of a product. You'll see one of three symbols: a solid chasing arrows triangle, which indicates curbside recycling; a tiny rubbish bin, which indicates landfill, and a white chasing arrows triangle, which means that an extra step needs to be taken in order for the item to be recycled, such as return to store or scrunch.

Tip

Traditionally, plastic is made from fossil fuels and takes forever to break down. Bioplastics, on the other hand, are a relatively new addition to the plastics market and are made from plant sources, such as linseed (flaxseed; the 'bio' bit). Problem is, their properties are so similar to traditional plastics that it still takes forever for them to break down. Bioplastics also can't be recycled, whereas traditional plastics can (if they make it to the right facility).

In the UK, look for the On Pack Recycling Label (OPRL). You will see either a green or black label, which guides users on how to recycle a product. At the time of publishing there isn't a guide for residents in the US, other than the plastic resin identification codes.

Trustmarks

Not as obvious as words like 'eco', 'green' or 'sustainable', trustmarks are design elements used in branding that give consumers the *impression* that a product is planet friendly. These might include images of planets, leaves, plants, and the colours green or brown. These sneaky tactics work on the consumer's subconscious beliefs and associations to appeal to their environmental conscience without actually meeting any standards whatsoever.

I'm going to sound like a broken record by the end of this book, but I can't emphasise enough how important it is that you do a bit of digging and aren't afraid to question things when purchasing a product. I've tried to include as much useful information as I can, but unfortunately, I cannot cover everything. Google Scholar is my go-to resource for correct and up-to-date information, and I tend to look for articles that are less than five years old and relate to my country of residence.

NEXT UP

Ultimately, getting to grips with the ABCs of sustainability makes navigating this journey so much easier. You're less likely to be hoodwinked, and more likely to make choices that genuinely align with your values and your budget. So, use your judgement, do your research and utilise this knowledge to increase your awareness. Also, don't be afraid to question your own behaviours and beliefs.

The 'project' of sustainability today needs a rebrand, and that's going to involve re-evaluating what we traditionally consider to be sustainability best practices. I want to help you navigate this changing space and make actual, real-life progress, starting with one of the most urgent sustainability problems: food waste.

2.

Food waste:
stop being
a tosser

Savings scale

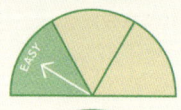

SAVE
UP TO
$75 A MONTH

Level 1
You do your bit,
buy what you need,
and set up your
storage systems.

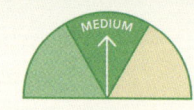

SAVE
UP TO
$150 A MONTH

+ Level 2
You trial having a
no-waste week and
a no-spend week
each month.

SAVE
UP TO
$210 A MONTH

+ Level 3
You don't throw out
anything at all! And
you join a food co-op
(see page 46).

Have you heard?

* Australians throw away one in every five shopping bags.
* The average Australian household throws away between $2000–$2500 worth of food each year.
* If global food waste was a country, it would be the world's third-biggest carbon emitter after China and the US.
* The total global greenhouse gas emissions from food waste are greater than flying, plastic pollution and oil extraction combined.
* One-third of food produced globally goes unsold or uneaten.
* There is enough food produced around the world to feed everyone.
* The US throws away 80 billion kilograms of food each year.

Food waste sucks, both for the planet and for your wallet. I mean, you're paying for a lot of food that's just going to end up in the bin. Sounds pretty silly, doesn't it?

There are lots of reasons why food waste is such a huge problem. Our culture of constant consumerism means we often buy more than we need, don't plan before going shopping, and tend to have quite a disposable attitude to food. But even though something will break down in landfill, it doesn't mean you should waste it. And the environmental impacts of food waste are more dire than you might think.

It's estimated that one-third of all food produced is not consumed. This is a shocking waste of resources, energy and money, especially when you consider everything that goes into growing that food: think water, energy, land management and transport. Food production alone is responsible for 37 per cent of the world's greenhouse gas emissions. So, if one-third of all food produced is wasted, then 12 per cent of all global greenhouse gas emissions have been created producing food that doesn't even get eaten! All of that work – and environmental cost – is literally for nothing.

Before we start pointing the finger at restaurants and supermarkets throwing away rotten, left-over or out-of-date produce, know that a staggering 41 per cent of all food waste is created inside the home.

But, the damage doesn't stop there. Once food arrives in landfill, it sits there and 'cooks', creating a lethal greenhouse gas called methane, which is thirty-two times more potent than carbon dioxide. Think of methane as a thick smog that smothers the globe, trapping heat and causing global temperatures to rise (aka global warming). And it just goes on and on; more food waste means more landfill sites. In fact, it's such a monumental issue that in Australia, the UK and the US, governments have set national targets to halve food waste by 2030.

Food waste has a huge impact at a personal level, too, starting with a loss of between $2000–$2500 per household each year. That's your hard-earned money that you're quite literally tossing in the bin. Spending money on food that you don't eat doesn't make sense. Yes, it's terrible for the planet, but it is also the biggest waste of money there is. Making changes to reduce food waste makes both financial and planetary sense.

Now, I wish I could tell you that the project of reducing food waste was a straightforward one, but unfortunately that's not the case. Saying that, I don't want you to down tools and walk away from the task just yet! There are so many meaningful and actionable steps you can take that, added up, create enormous positive environmental and economic change.

In this chapter, I'm going to walk you through how to plan, how to shop and how to store your food so that you can maximise its lifespan. I've got great recipes that make the most of your produce, and hacks and tips for better meal planning so you can mount a multi-pronged attack on food waste. Really, a lot of what I'm pushing for here is a return to (or adoption of) old-world skills and a simpler attitude to food that we've all become alienated from – basically, the way our grandparents used to do things: buying only what they needed, what was in season, and preserving it to avoid waste.

While researching and writing this book, food waste was a problem that came up over and over again. It's the most pressing sustainability issue we are facing, and it's one that is shared by everyone, which is why it must be a core part of your planet- and money-saving quest.

No matter how vigilant you are about using up the food you buy, I can guarantee there's something lurking in your fridge that you've forgotten about. I just checked my own and I found one sad, wrinkly cucumber and a jar of pasta sauce that's starting to resemble a snow leopard. So, this is on all of us. In fact, Project Drawdown, a science-led resource on climate change, has revealed that individuals reducing their food waste is the third-best way to address climate change. Let me show you how.

I want to start with the most common culprits. According to OzHarvest, one of Australia's largest food-rescue organisations who work with industries and the government to drive policy change, the most commonly wasted foods are:

FUN FACT

Did you know that single bananas are thrown out more than any other grocery item? Like singles need to be targeted any more! Shop the singles, buying only what you need, and freeze overripe bananas for smoothies, or bake them into banana bread to save on waste. Yum.

Most commonly wasted foods:
1. Bananas (just think of all the banana bread you're missing out on?!)
2. Bread
3. Meat
4. Spinach and other bagged leaves
5. Dairy

In this chapter, my mission is to move you away from thinking about how you dispose of your food waste and towards stopping food waste in the first place, and the most obvious place to start is with what you buy.

Step one of the plan is to make a plan

One of my biggest hacks when it comes to reducing food waste is pretty simple: I plan my meals ahead of time. I don't just mean making a list of ingredients, I mean performing an audit of what I already have so I can see what I actually need.

Look in your pantry and fridge to see what's still in date and plan meals around those things, or see how you can work them in. You've gotta get into a 'waste not want not' mindset here, like your grandparents had. I promise, you'll be surprised at how much you already have, and the simple act of only buying what's absolutely necessary will save you major bucks.

Start by listing what you've already got in categories: vegetables, meat, pantry items, freezer. Then write down what you need to go with them, and don't forget to note the exact quantities. You might think you're saving money by going in for the two-for-one specials, but who is actually going to use 1 kilogram (2¼ pounds) of polenta?

Shopping

First rule of thumb: never go shopping hungry. It has been proven time and time again that a hungry shop is an expensive, overindulgent shop. Stick to your list and purchase only what you need – no extra-large bags or bundle buys.

And while we're talking bags, don't forget yours! Not just the bags you use at the checkout but a couple of smaller ones for produce, too. You can buy dedicated shopping bags, but I seem to accumulate canvas drawstring bags and totes at a break-neck pace, so I just use these. Once you've got your plan and your bags, you're off to the shops!

'Frozen foods are your friends. Not only do they have a long shelf life, but a lot of the produce has been snap-frozen, which means that it is frozen at extremely low temperatures immediately after harvesting.'

Throwing back to old-school WeightWatchers advice here, I'm going to suggest you stick to the perimeter of the supermarket. It's better for the planet, your wallet – and your waistline. Go big in the fresh produce section, where you'll find the most nutrients and the least plastic packaging. Skip around the processed food aisles (or any others that contain things like sauces or condiments that you can make yourself in under five minutes). Make a complete U-turn at the confectionery. Maybe grab some toilet paper (100 per cent recycled, of course).

Frozen foods are your friends. Not only do they have a long shelf life, but a lot of the produce has been snap-frozen, which means that it is frozen at extremely low temperatures immediately after harvesting. And yes, frozen vegetables usually come in plastic packaging, but some don't and you are much less likely to waste them than fresh vegetables.

On the whole, shopping this way cuts down on unnecessary spending, processed foods and, crucially, packaging. However, I find buying meat minus the plastic more difficult. Plastic-free options do exist, but they're harder to find. The easiest fix is to bring your own reusable containers to the supermarket deli or butcher. You can purchase the exact quantity you need this way too, which helps to cut down on costs and food waste. Keep in mind that this isn't something staff will be used to doing, so make it easy for them by handing over a clean container that's in mint condition.

Dairy is another item that usually comes wrapped in (copious amounts) of plastic. One obvious solution is to make your own dairy items, but if you don't have time to churn your own butter (who does?!), opt for these instead:

- **Butter wrapped in paper** (even if it has a thin plastic lining, it's still a huge plastic saving and you can use the wrapper to grease muffin tins).
- **Dairy milk in glass bottles** (that can then be reused), or if you drink non-dairy milk, opt for making your own (see page 39) over buying difficult-to-recycle Tetra Paks of milk (see page 88).
- **Take your own container** to the cheese shop or deli, or split a larger wheel of cheese with friends (it sounds bizarre, but the savings value checks out).
- **Find yoghurt in glass containers** or make your own. It's a nice weekend project, and home-made yoghurt is much tastier and healthier than any commercial variety!

Support small and local

Where possible, I always try to shop from small, independently owned stores. This means going old-school and getting to know your local baker, butcher, fishmonger and deli owner. Buying from them will usually mean you're getting higher-quality, locally grown and often healthier produce, too. It might not always be the cheapest option, but this slight drawback is more than made up for by fewer food miles, carefully sourced produce and more aligned sustainability values. Plus, they often prioritise seasonality, which means you're buying produce at its most affordable, nutritional peak. You may also find that a smaller quantity of local, seasonal produce has just as much – if not more – nutritional value as a larger quantity of mass-produced, cold-stored produce.

Save the date

This is your reminder to check the dates on your food – and pay close attention to the words, not just the numbers. It's a little-known fact that there is a big difference between 'best before' and 'use by'. (Or perhaps you've never even noticed this subtle distinction?)

Best before is my favourite of the two because it's more of a *guide*. The brand is saying they recommend consuming this item before a certain date in order for you to have the best experience of it. You can be a bit loosey goosey here and consume something a few days after the best-before date, but obviously not if it's covered in mould or smells a little funky – use your judgement!

Use by, on the other hand, is pretty much a hard-and-fast rule. You'll find it on dairy, meat and poultry and it really does need to be adhered to for safety. If you are looking at a ticking time bomb, don't be afraid to throw the item in the freezer to extend its lifespan.

To bulk food shop or not

This might sound controversial, but shopping in bulk isn't as cost-effective as it seems. Bulk food supply stores are optimised for over-consumption, with aisles upon aisles of scoopable goodies. I head to the bulk food store when I need something specific for a recipe, but I don't recommend making it a permanent pitstop on your shopping circuit.

Tips

Did you think trail mix was missing from this section? I love it, but I never buy it premade on principle; it is just too expensive. And there's no need!

I can make my own trail mix for a fraction of the price (about $9.56 per kilogram rather than buying it for $23.53 per kilogram at the bulk food store). And it's the perfect low-waste snack; you can tailor it to your tastes, it keeps for about a month in a sealed jar, and it's so portable!

Even though bulk food stores allow you to buy the exact quantity you need, which helps to reduce food waste, many don't include scales throughout their stores, meaning you are scooping blind before being presented with an eye-watering bill at the checkout. The price per kilogram of some of these items can also be five times greater than the same item in a regular supermarket. So, use your calculator, ask the staff to weigh your items if you need to and make sure you're actually getting a good deal. And my hottest tip? Avoid the snack/treat aisle at all costs! There are so many delicious morsels that resistance is futile, and you are guaranteed to break the bank.

In saying that, I always like to buy direct for a few things:

- **Bakery:** You'll get a fresher loaf that lasts you longer, and nothing beats fresh bread. In most cases, bakeries are fine with you bringing your own bag to cut down on waste.
- **Deli:** If you're purchasing more than one or two things, going to your local deli will be a more affordable option than buying from the supermarket, and is more likely to stock locally made produce.
- **Meat:** Full disclosure, I am not a meat eater, but my housemates are. When purchasing meat, go straight to the butcher, and don't be afraid to explain how you're trying to cut down costs. They will be able to recommend cheaper cuts and ways to cook your meat to make it go further. Remember to BYO your own (clean) container to bring it home in.

Produce

Mindfully selecting produce is one of the simplest ways you can reduce your food waste and make tangible savings. Buying only what you need, what's in season and opting for imperfect vegetables will keep produce from ending up in landfill and ensure you're eating the healthiest, most affordable way.

Shop seasonally

Eating seasonal produce is not only the best thing you can do for your health and budget, it's also better for the environment. It also means that you are buying produce at its peak. It's usually plentiful, which makes it affordable, and grown locally, which cuts down on food miles.

Food miles refers to the distance your food travels from farm to plate. The shorter the distance the better it is for the planet. It's estimated that transport accounts for 6 per cent of your food's climate footprint, which is a pretty convincing reason to shop for what's locally available to you.

The seasonal shopping guide on page 34 shows you what fruits and vegetables are in for each season, but rather than memorising the list, just look out for what's on special at your local supermarket or grocer. Lower prices indicate an abundance of produce, or what's highly seasonal at any given time.

Pick imperfect produce

Did you know that perfectly good fruit and vegetables often go to waste purely because of aesthetics? Wonky carrot? Knobbly apple? If it doesn't pass the prettiness test, you probably won't find it at the supermarket. Up to 25 per cent of apples and 20 per cent of onions grown in the UK are lost along the agricultural food chain because they don't meet beauty standards.

Thankfully, more supermarkets (and consumers) are embracing these previously rejected vegetables through branding and campaigns that endear us to their ugliness. Many supermarkets also offer special packs and subscription boxes of wonky veg, so shop for these as it will save you money and keep them out of landfill.

Is organic worth the $$?

Surely, organic produce is better for the environment, right? Grown without nasty fertilisers and pesticides it should be the easy win, but, in fact, organic farms often require more land and water to grow their produce than conventional farms. This is because organic farming generally produces 40 per cent fewer crops than traditional farming, so more land is needed for less output. Plus, organic produce typically comes with more packaging, because to be truly organic it cannot have come in contact with anything that is not organic. If you're buying directly from a farmer, then great, but be wary of the premium you pay for organic products in a supermarket.

SEASONAL SHOPPING GUIDE

☀ SUMMER	🍃 AUTUMN	❄ WINTER	✿ SPRING

Avocado
Capsicum
  (pepper)
Celery
Cucumber
Eggplant
  (aubergine)
Green beans
Leek
Lettuce
Pumpkin (squash)
Tomato
Zucchini
  (courgette)
	Asian greens
	  (leafy)
	Avocado
	Beetroot (beet)
	Broccoli
	Brussels sprouts
	Cabbage
	Cauliflower
	Peas
	Pumpkin (squash)
	Spinach
	Sweet potato
		Asian greens
		  (leafy)
		Avocado
		Beetroot (beet)
		Broccoli
		Brussels sprouts
		Cabbage
		Carrot
		Fennel
		Onion
		Silverbeet
		  (Swiss chard)
		Potato
			Asparagus
			Avocado
			Broccoli
			Carrot
			Cauliflower
			Corn
			Green Beans
			Peas
			Spinach
			Tomato
			Zucchini
			  (courgette)

Apricot Banana Blackberry Blueberry Cherry Kiwifruit Mango Nectarine Pineapple Raspberry Strawberry	Apple Banana Fig Grape Kiwifruit Lime Mandarin Passionfruit Pear Orange	Apple Blood orange Grapefruit Kiwifruit Lemon Orange Pear Pineapple Rhubarb Quince	Banana Cherries Blood orange Grapefruit Mango Lemon Pineapple Rhubarb Rockmelon (canteloupe) Strawberry Watermelon

Source: My Green Australia

Protein predicament

When it comes to picking the perfect protein, there is more than just taste to consider. Where is the protein from? How much did it cost? What is the environmental cost of producing it? Instead of making recommendations, I am going to outline the key proteins for you with facts and stats so that you can make your own informed decision.

The graph below demonstrates the average greenhouse gas impact (in kilograms of CO_2) per 50 g (1¾ oz) of protein.

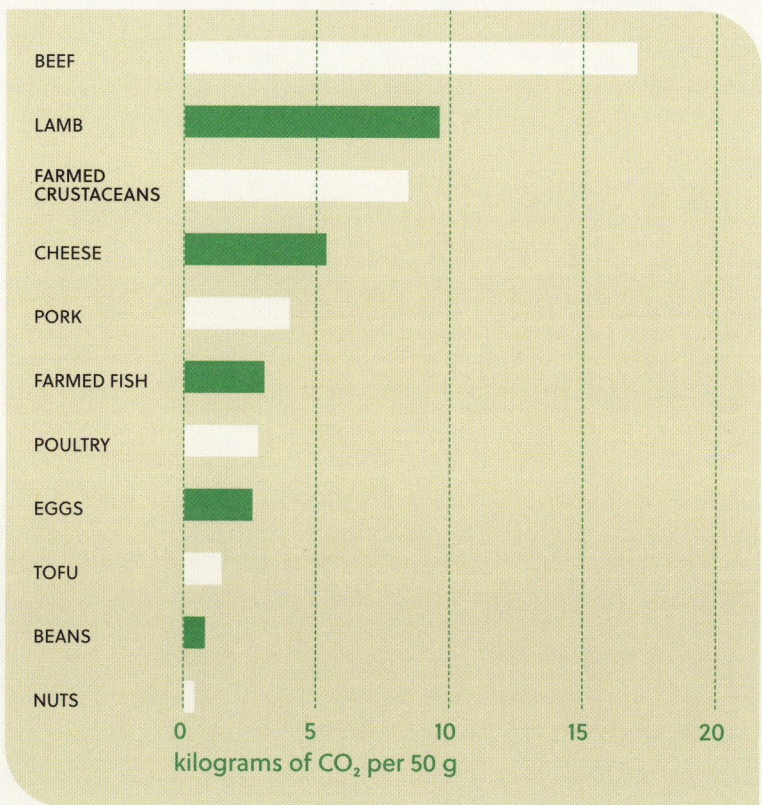

kilograms of CO_2 per 50 g

'I'm not suggesting that you swear off meat for all eternity, rather that you start by making a conscious effort to reduce your consumption.'

A meaty issue

Meat is a controversial issue in the sustainability conversation; the direct impact that consuming meat has on climate change is well researched and documented. Dietary choices (and their knock-on effects on the environment) often spark hot debate, but it's not a fight I'm willing to lose my newfound friends (that's you) over. I will, however, provide you with a couple of facts and allow you to pick your path.

- It can take up to 15,000–20,000 litres (3300–4400 gallons) of water to produce 1 kilogram (2¼ pounds) of beef.
- People who eat meat are responsible for creating an additional 1.5 tonnes of greenhouse gases each year than someone who follows a vegan diet.
- Livestock production accounts for roughly 30 per cent of global biodiversity loss.
- Meat production is also responsible for generating 14.5 per cent of total global greenhouse gas emissions.
- Cows, sheep and goats have the largest environmental impact because they fart the most methane gas.

Now, don't get me wrong; I'm not suggesting that you swear off meat for all eternity, rather that you start by making a conscious effort to reduce your consumption. Try out meat-free Monday, then experiment with having meat every second day. Eventually, you might only eat meat on weekends or special occasions. It's not about giving up, just being more intentional.

A study published in *Scientific Reports* found that if Americans reduced their meat consumption by 25 per cent and switched to plant-based proteins, 82 million metric tons of greenhouse gas emissions would be saved per year.

A 2018 study by Beyond Burgers (so you can take this with a grain of salt, not just fries on the side) found that plant-based burgers have one-tenth of the climate impact of a beef burger. The jury is still out on whether plant-based burgers (made from a combo of oils, plants and beans) are better for your health, though.

Here's a fact to consider: the vegan diet creates the smallest climate footprint of any diet. By eating vegan, you can reduce your food-related carbon emissions by 35–55 per cent, which is pretty staggering. On the other hand, eating a vegetarian diet reduces it by 25–35 per cent.

Here, fishy, fishy

So, what about seafood? When I first started on my sustainability journey, I dropped meat but still ate seafood. It's estimated that if one American meat-eater replaced meat with fish, they would save the equivalent emissions of driving a car 9600 kilometres (6000 miles) per year. Eating fresh, wild-caught fish is less impactful on the environment than eating meat, as it requires no land management and fewer resources to farm, harvest and process. However, the seafood industry still has a lot to answer for and consuming fish is problematic for a number of reasons.

The first is animal welfare. Every year approximately 650,000 whales, dolphins, turtles and sea lions are killed because of the fishing industry, usually when animals get caught in fishing nets or struck by boats.

The fishing industry is often under the spotlight when it comes to sustainability, and for good reason. Overfishing is a global challenge that is causing ecosystem collapse, fish population decline and imbalance to marine biodiversity. In 2022, as much as 37.5 per cent of all seafood (over one-third of all fish stocks) was fished at unsustainable levels. Not to mention that declining fish stocks are driving the price on seafood generally, which is making it a scarcer, less affordable and more 'luxury' resource.

Numerous studies have also reported that fish contain high levels of microplastics, which we know are not as nutritious as those all-important omega-3s. Fish can often come with an expensive price tag, too. To save money, buy frozen varieties and shop the specials because what is seasonal and in abundance will usually also be lighter on your wallet.

Sustainability efforts are being made in the fishing industry, but the problem is complex. You can make a difference by buying exclusively from certified sustainable fisheries. The Marine Stewardship Council (MSC) in the UK and Australia awards accreditations to fisheries that maintain sustainable fishing practices that ensure ongoing healthy fish stocks and minimise by-catch.

The United Nations Food and Agriculture Organization (FAO) reported that 34.2 per cent of fisheries are overfished, so while wild-caught fish are a more sustainable option than intensively farmed fish, fish populations overall are still greatly depleted.

According to the journal *Frontiers in Ecology and the Environment*, the carbon emitted to farm fish and seafood varies wildly depending on the species.

FISH	KG OF CO_2 PER 40 G (1½ OZ) OF PROTEIN
Wild anchovies, sardines and other small fish	0.1
Wild tuna	0.6
Farmed salmon	0.6
Farmed tilapia	3.0
Farmed prawns (shrimp)	4.8

Which milk is better for the planet?

Yes, I am coming for your coffee order. Research shows that the production of cow's milk not only creates up to three times more greenhouse gas emissions than the production of non-dairy milks, but it also requires ten times as much land. So, switching to a plant-based alternative is the best decision you can make for the planet.

Unlike years past where dairy milk reigned supreme, some cafes in the seriously trendy suburbs of Sydney's Inner West are selling more plant-based milks than cow juice! Why? Because alternative milks are not only trendy, they also have environmental benefits, too, using less water, land and greenhouse gases in their creation. Plus, they're easier on the modern millennial's sensitive tummy.

Before you jump ship to almond milk though, consider this. A little while back, almonds got a seriously terrible rap for the amount of water needed to produce a single nut. Almonds are thirsty little devils with a whopping 371 litres (81 gallons) of water needed to create just 1 litre (34 fluid ounces) of milk.

Oat milk and soy milk, on the other hand, require far less water and land to produce, and therefore create fewer emissions in the process. However, despite their impressive sustainability stats, alternative milks do come at a cost (between 50–70 cents more per cup of coffee than one with dairy milk!), so learning to make your own can drastically slash your annual coffee spend.

MILK VS. 'MILK'

Environmental impacts of different milks, per litre/34 fluid ounces.

	EMISSIONS (KG OF CO_2)	LAND USE (SQ M)	WATER USE (L)
COW	3.2	9.0	628
RICE	1.2	0.3	270
SOY	1.0	0.7	28
OAT	0.9	0.8	48
ALMOND	0.7	0.5	371

Source: Science

If you want to go all in on the oaty stuff but don't want to make your own, beware that many alternative milks are shipped from overseas in Tetra Paks, which cannot be recycled in 91 per cent of councils, whereas dairy milk is produced locally and comes in recyclable plastic bottles. Just saying.

Have I given you a straight answer? No. But have I armed you with enough information to make your own decision? Hopefully, yes.

Remember, as with everything else in this book, it isn't about leading a perfectly sustainable life. It's about setting realistic goals and taking small steps to achieve them.

Here are a few ways to reduce your meat and dairy consumption without proclaiming that you will never eat a slice of cheese again:

· **Swap** dairy milk for an alternative milk in one of your daily coffees.
· **Try** out meat-free Monday.
· **Experiment** with eating mainly vegetarian food at home and save meat and fish for eating out.
· **Swap** dairy yoghurt for coconut yoghurt, or make your own.
· **Eat** less meat and buy from smaller, local and organic producers.
· **Save** the cheese for a special occasion!

Tip

Here's my oat milk recipe that you can whip up in less than 10 minutes:

Simply blend 1 cup (95 g) rolled oats, a pinch of salt and 1 litre (34 fluid ounces) water in a food processor or high-speed blender for just under 1 minute. Strain through a piece of muslin (cheesecloth) or cotton cloth (even a clean, old cotton t-shirt will do), bottle it and refrigerate for up to five days. Reserve the pulp for making porridge or cookies.

If you are looking for a home-made milk that froths, add a couple of soaked nuts to the recipe above. The oils in the nuts will add some creaminess, making it perfect for your lattes.

Use it all

I can't tell you how many times I've seen people throwing away perfectly usable (and delicious) parts of a vegetable. You pay for the whole thing – skin, roots and greens – so it's a huge waste for half of it to end up in the bin. Vegetables take a mind-boggling amount of resources to grow, harvest and transport from farm to supermarket, so we have an obligation to the farmer and to the planet to use all edible parts of a plant. Any inedible parts can be added to your compost bin. Plus, these leaves, roots and stalks can really help to bulk out meals, which means you can save some dollar on your weeknight dinners – it's a win win.

There are plenty of under-appreciated and underused bits of veg, but let's look at a few of the most common ones:

- **Broccoli stalks:** Which is crazy because they have so much flavour! Simply chop them up and add them to your dish a minute or two before the florets (because they take a little longer to cook). My favourite way to eat them on their own is lightly roasted in olive oil and sprinkled with chilli flakes and parmesan cheese. That right there is a class-A snack! Raw broccoli stalk also blitzes up well in a pesto and gives it a really sweet edge when stirred through pasta.
- **Celery leaves:** By all means, use the stalks to add some flavour to a soup, but do not throw away the leaves! (I know they're annoying when you're trying to fit everything in the crisper, so this tip should come as welcome news.) Pick the leaves and scatter them on a baking tray lined with baking paper. Cook in a low oven (about 150°C/300°F) for an hour or so until they get nice and crunchy. Leave to cool, then season with salt, finely dice or blitz in a spice grinder and store in an airtight container. You just made your own celery salt! Use it to give things a fresh and salty hit.
- **Beetroot (beet) tops:** These are arguably my favourite part of beetroots. You can use the leaves and stems just like you would silverbeet (Swiss chard) and spinach. Toss them through stir-fries, or sauté and serve warm as a salad.
- **Potato skins:** As someone who doesn't peel vegetables unless they really have to (not only to avoid food waste but out of laziness, too), the amount of potato peels people throw away pains me. You can make tasty potato chips by roasting your peels with some olive oil, pepper and salt. Seriously, try it.

Tip

Don't wash berries until you're ready to eat them. Washing them breaks their natural protective layer and, chances are, if you are buying berries at the supermarket they are sprayed with something to keep them fresher for longer, so lean on that.

Food storage

Okay, so you've taken care when sourcing your produce, but did you know that the way you store your food can drastically prolong or cut short its shelf life? Proper storage means you can get more out of each piece of produce you buy, cut down on food waste and save money all at the same time.

First things first: start by picking produce that's not already on its way out. Choose high-quality, locally grown produce that hasn't been sitting in cold storage for days or bumped around during a long transit from farm to supermarket. That doesn't mean buying perfect-looking veg, just try to avoid any with obvious bruises or damage.

Once you get your food home, don't simply chuck it all in the crisper or fruit bowl. Take a few moments to think about the needs of each piece of produce (see page 42), store it correctly and you'll be rewarded with fresher, longer-lasting fruit and veg.

A damp hug

I love herbs more than I love flowers, but I treat them both the same. As soon as I walk through the door with an armful of fresh herbs, I'm reaching for a vase or glass jar, trimming a bit off the stalks and popping them in water. If the roots are still intact leave them on, as this helps keep them fresh, and you might even be able to replant them if the roots keep growing. Change the water every few days and this bit of TLC will extend their lives for up to ten days.

Herbs are one of the easiest things to grow (see page 208), and they can turn a meal from zero to hero in a matter of seconds. A simple way to save some serious cash is to ditch the store-bought plastic containers and grow your own.

Now, I promised a friend I wouldn't write the 'M' word in this book, but it's hard to get away from the word 'moist' in a section about food storage, so look away now if it bothers you. Moisture – whether removing it or adding it – is usually the answer to keeping your fruit and veg in mint condition for as long as possible.

The inside of your fridge is a cool, dry environment – obvious? Okay, just hear me out – but the downside of this is that it creates a similar microclimate to the inside of a plane: things can quickly dehydrate, turning vegetables limp and dull.

The best cure? Adding a little H2O.

Tip

Eggs certainly do last a fairly long time, but to check the freshness of your eggs simply place them in a glass of cold water. If the egg floats you've got yourself a rotten egg. If you have a recipe that calls for just the yolk or the white, don't throw out the other part! Both can be kept in the fridge for a few days until a recipe calls for them, or you can throw them in the freezer (labelled, so you know how many are in there.) I like to use left-over egg whites for amaretto sours or omelettes, and egg yolks are great for brushing your pastry to help it turn golden brown, or in a hollandaise sauce.

Different produce responds to different levels of moisture (there it is again). Below, I've listed the most common fruit and veg under six different categories, to give you a guide on how to store each one.

SWIMS

Store your vegetables in the fridge inside a large, sealed container filled with water.

- Asparagus (ends only)
- Carrots
- Celery (cut)
- Firm-stemmed herbs (roots only) (thyme, rosemary and sage)
- Ginger
- Lemons and limes
- Oranges

AIRTIGHT CONTAINER

These will last longer when sealed in a container in the fridge.

- Berries
- Brussels sprouts
- Cherries
- Grapes
- Melons
- Mushrooms
- Pineapple
- Pumpkin (squash; once cut)
- Snow peas (mange tout)

HUGS

Keep these items hydrated without drowning them. Wet and wring out a tea towel (dish towel), then use it to wrap your veg.

- Beetroot (beet)
- Broccoli
- Cabbage and kale
- Cauliflower (no leaves)
- Corn (without husks)
- Cucumbers
- Green beans
- Leeks
- Lettuce
- Parsnips
- Rocket (arugula)
- Soft-stemmed herbs (basil, coriander/cilantro, parsley)
- Spinach
- Turnip
- Zucchini (courgette)

ROLLING IN THE CRISPER

These fruits and veg will roll around loose in the crisper quite happily.

- Avocados
- Capsicums (peppers)
- Cauliflower (with leaves)

- Corn (with husks)
- Mangoes
- Pears
- Stone fruit

OUT IN THE OPEN

These items belong in your fruit bowl or in a cool place, like the pantry.

- Bananas
- Eggplant (aubergine)
- Garlic (in a shady spot)
- Onions
- Potatoes (in a shady spot)
- Pumpkin (squash; uncut)
- Tomatoes

OUT UNTIL RIPE

Leave these fruits in your fruit bowl to ripen, then refrigerate.

- Avocados
- Kiwifruit
- Mangoes
- Melons
- Papaya
- Pears
- Pineapple
- Stone fruit

MORE FOOD-SAVING TIPS

1. Store grated cheese in resealable bags in your freezer for up to three months to stop mould forming.

2. If your produce comes with its own protective wrapping (aka cauliflower leaves) leave them on!

3. Throw a bay leaf in with your flour to stop pantry moths (see page 218) from breeding.

4. Keep your onions and potatoes away from each other – onions will cause your potatoes to sprout.

5. Once ripe, cut your melon and pineapple up and store it in an airtight container in the fridge. You'll be less likely to waste it because it's easier to eat.

6. Breaking news: tomatoes belong on your kitchen bench not in the fridge. A cold fridge environment can lead to a powdery texture and loss of flavour, meaning they're less appetising and more likely to be wasted.

7. If you've run out of self-raising flour, don't run to the supermarket for more. Just add 2 teaspoons of baking powder to 1 cup (150 g) of plain (all-purpose) flour to make your own.

8. Freeze chillies whole; you rarely eat them raw, so just slice and dice from frozen and throw them into your curry or stir-fry.

9. If, sadly, you didn't save your herbs before they wilted, channel your inner nonna and hang them upside down in your kitchen to air dry. You can crumble the dried leaves into pasta sauces, or just crush them and use them to refill your spice jars.

10. Use the end pieces of a stale loaf of bread and blitz them into breadcrumbs and freeze. Or, if you haven't cut your bread up, run the loaf under running water (yes, you read that right), avoiding the cut end. The drier the loaf the more water you'll need. Wet the outside, then place the loaf in the oven at 150°C (300°F) for 10 minutes to soften and freshen up. Loaf revived!

Freezer-friendly guide

Did you know that as your vegetables age they actually lose nutrients? (Not like humans, of course – we're more like a fine wine that only improves with time.) So, I like to freeze what I can to lock in that goodness.

I think it's often overlooked, but your freezer acts just like a time capsule, and it's one of the best tools in your arsenal when it comes to minimising food waste. Even if you've audited your cupboards, planned your meals (see page 29) and bought only what you need, there will still sometimes be leftovers or ingredients you didn't end up using.

Your freezer is your food waste bestie; it has got your back when you forget about something or if you accidentally make enough food for a small army. Plus, buying frozen produce allows you to make financial savings even at the checkout, so stock up on your most used items, like frozen peas.

Did you know that you can freeze more than you think? For the life of me, I can never seem to cook the right amount of rice or pasta, but the plus side is that my freezer is now full of perfectly portioned bags of cooked pasta and rice. One of my favourite 'freezer' meals is my Whatever Trevor Fried Rice (page 49) – I just chuck an egg in with the defrosted rice and whatever vegetables are in the crisper that are about to go off. Job done.

But let's take this freezing game to the next level because I want to get you thinking about prepping and planning ahead. I strongly believe that there are two types of people: those who will happily eat the same meal multiple times in a week, and those who get sick of it after two servings. Person A gets an A+ for reducing their food spend and waste, but person B can still get top marks if they plan ahead and get a mixture of meals in the freezer, ready to go.

Always remember to label your frozen meals clearly, because bolognese, chilli con carne and minestrone look very alike once frozen! Freezing in jars isn't as scary as you think, either. Simply fill to just below the bend in the jar with the lid off overnight, then screw on the lid in the morning.

Opposite is a quick guide to how long your produce will survive a deep-freeze.

'... your freezer acts just like a time capsule, and it's one of the best tools in your arsenal when it comes to minimising food waste.'

FOOD	FRIDGE	FREEZER
Raw beef	3–5 days	8 months
Raw pork	3–5 days	6 months
Raw lamb	3–5 days	12 months
Raw chicken	1–2 days	9 months
Deli meat	4 days	Not recommended
Eggs	1 month	2 months (shell removed)
Fruit	7 days	3 months
Vegetables	7 days	12 months
Soups and stews	3–4 days	3 months
Bread	1–2 days	6 months
Cooked meat	3–4 days	2–6 months
Cooked poultry	3–4 days	12 months
Cooked rice and pasta	2–3 days	1 month
Seafood	1–3 days	6–12 months
Fish - Fatty fish (mackerel, salmon, tuna) - Lean fish (pollock, sea trout) - Lean fish (cod, flounder, haddock)	1–3 days	2–3 months 6–8 months 4–8 months

Source: Foodwise

What is freezer burn?

Ever notice those little icicles and crystals forming on some of your frozen food? No, Christmas hasn't come early, this is freezer burn. Freezer burn happens when your food hasn't been sealed properly and has been exposed to air. Generally speaking, it will still be okay to eat something with freezer burn, but it won't taste as nice.

Freezing tips
- Set your freezer to –18˚C (–0.4˚F) for optimal results.
- Store your food properly in airtight containers or reusable food pouches.
- Don't forget to label and date everything. (Honestly, the number of times I have defrosted something thinking that it was something else …)
- Keep an eye on the dates. Most things will survive in the freezer for 2–3 months, so always work from oldest to newest.
- If your freezer starts to fill up, do a grocery-free shop (see opposite) to see what you can use up and create some space.

Veggie co-ops

One of the biggest ways that I have saved money on my grocery bill has been by joining a vegetable co-op. It is another traditional concept that works wonders in today's society, because it plays to the power of buying in bulk, sharing the cost (and grunt work) of grocery shopping, saving money and shopping seasonally – a quadruple whammy!

How to create your own veggie co-op

I've been a part of a veggie co-op on and off for the last couple of years and it has saved me hundreds if not *thousands* of dollars. In my experience, not many people know what it is, so here is exactly how a veggie co-op works and how you can build your own.

Eight to ten families (or, in my case, a friend and I) put in $30 each a fortnight. With that money – roughly $300 – one family heads out to the local wholesale markets and purchases $300 of fresh fruit and vegetables. They return and divide these into large buckets, send a quick message around and everyone scurries over to collect their bucket filled with fresh produce.

Depending on how many are in the co-op, you'll be the one on 'duty' doing the shopping once every 4–6 months.

Here's an example of one box:
- 1 kg (2 lb 4 oz) cucumbers
- 2 kg (4 lb 8 oz) carrots
- 1 kg (2 lb 4 oz) brown onions
- 1 kg (2 lb 4 oz) green beans
- 500 g (1 lb 2 oz) roma tomatoes
- 1 bunch of rainbow chard
- 1 head of cauliflower
- 500 g (1 lb 2 oz) red apples
- 500 g (1 lb 2 oz) pears
- 2 bunches of bananas
- 3 avocados
- 150 g (5½ oz) ginger
- 3 heads of broccoli
- 3 kg (6 lb 12 oz) baby potatoes

Total supermarket price: $89.15
Total paid: $30
Average saved per fortnight: $59.15

Grocery-free shop

Something I like to do once a month is have a grocery-free shop. I have the joy of avoiding the supermarket and, instead, I shop my pantry and freezer. It is so much fun and it forces me to use up and get creative with what I've already got at home, which is a huge money-saver. It also means I use up stored food before it goes off, which means less food waste. #humblebrag

Dive deep into the back of your pantry and to the bottom of your freezer – chances are, you'll find some delicious goodies in there.

Here's some meal inspo:
- **Frittata** (with left-over or frozen veg)
- **Stir-fry** (with dried noodles and frozen veg)
- **Soup** (using frozen stock and frozen veg)
- **Curries** (using curry paste, random veggies and coconut milk)
- **Home-made pizzas** (with jars of olives, sun-dried tomatoes and a creative selection of veg)

One of the underrated benefits of co-ops is you become a better cook! Each fortnight I receive a mixture of produce. This means experimenting with new recipes or, worst case, passing on some produce to my neighbours. (For me, fennel is a taste I cannot stand, whereas it's one of my neighbour's favourites!)

Having a set of idiot-proof rules really helps to govern the process and keeps everyone on the same page. Ours looks like this:

· Only let groups join that are within a 3 kilometre (1.9 mile) radius. This means you won't be driving across town to collect.
· On a Thursday or Friday night everyone drops their bucket (a 42 litre/11 gallon tub that used to be our ice box at house parties) to the families who are shopping that week.
· Wake up early! The earlier the better for the best bargains – 4.30am onwards!
· Do not spend more than $25 per item. This helps people only shop seasonally because that's what will be cheap and abundant.
· Purchase at least three to four fruits per shop.
· Purchase at least one big luscious leafy green per shop (kale, lettuce, cabbage, spring onions/scallions).
· Share with the group a list of what you got and how much you paid for each item. This is a good guide for the next group to use, but it also keeps people accountable.
· If you're going to be away for a shop, find another family to take your bucket. The savings come with the more groups you have.

Don't have eight friends? Don't worry; the co-op I joined had been running for a couple of years and I knew no one.
My link came from one of my friends whose neighbours were in the co-op, so when a space became available, I jumped at it. Often, you'll find groups starting at schools, or you can find people advertising spaces on Facebook.

You could also create a co-op with fewer families, but this just means it will be more expensive and you'll be waking up at the crack of dawn more often.

Recipes

I had a friend show me that you can use ChatGPT to help you find recipes for the random assortment of ingredients in your fridge – genius. But here are a couple of my favourite ways to use up whatever I've got at home without enlisting artificial intelligence.

WHATEVER TREVOR FRIED RICE

This is the perfect recipe for using up all those little baggies of frozen rice that keep being pushed to the back of the freezer drawer. You want to get the rice nice and crispy here, so cold rice is best. Add your own bits and bobs – whatever needs to be used up in the crisper.

It's really important to use cold rice for this recipe, so if you've cooked it fresh, run it under cold water until it's cold. Otherwise, defrost from frozen.

Next, heat a frying pan over medium heat and sauté your vegetables and garlic in half the vegetable oil.

Heat the rest of the oil in a separate pan, tip in your eggs and scramble until cooked to your liking.

Throw in the rice and cook until crispy – the longer the better!

Season with salt and pepper, drizzle with some soy sauce and sesame oil, and finish with some chilli flakes on top.

INGREDIENT SUGGESTIONS (BASED ON SERVING 2)

2 cups (370 g) cold cooked rice

1 tablespoon vegetable oil

2 cups (approx. 300 g) mixed chopped vegetables, like zucchini (courgette), carrot, green or brown onion, celery, capsicum (pepper), peas, fresh or canned corn (if you're feeding fussy eaters, grate your vegetables instead of chopping)

1 garlic clove, minced

4 eggs, beaten

salt and pepper, to taste

soy sauce and sesame oil, to taste

chilli flakes, to season

WINE VINEGAR

Red or white wine vinegar is a great tart addition to salad dressings, casseroles and stews.

To make your own wine vinegar, simply leave a bottle of wine open on your kitchen bench for 2–3 weeks (we've all done this in the past, I'm sure). If it's particularly high in alcohol, dilute with a little water first.

Now you need to create the 'mother', an acidic bacteria that helps the fermentation process. For this, add 4 parts of the 'off' wine to 1 part white vinegar in a large glass jar. Cover with muslin (cheesecloth) and leave in a dark place for 1 week. You'll see the mixture separate, which is when you know it's ready.

The finished vinegar will keep in the jar at room temperature for up to a year.

VEGGIE PULP CRACKERS

1 cup (200 g) left-over juice pulp from your juicer (as dry as possible – leave it on a baking tray somewhere warm for an hour or two)

2 tablespoons olive oil

salt and pepper

½ teaspoon ground turmeric

1 teaspoon chilli flakes

1 tablespoon plain (all-purpose) flour or almond meal, plus extra for dusting

ground linseed (flaxseed; optional)

I am all for a fresh juice. It tastes delicious and is full of nutrients, but the juice is just one small component! Don't forget the best bit: the pulp. Yes, you can compost it, but, even better yet, you can turn it into a delicious and nutritious snack.

Preheat the oven to 160°C (325°F).

In a food processor, combine the fruit juice pulp, olive oil, salt, pepper, turmeric and chilli flakes (or your seasonings of choice).

Once combined, add the flour and stir it through to form a dough-like consistency. If your mixture is too wet add some extra flour or ground linseed. Dust your kitchen bench (or a silicone baking mat) with flour, then tip the dough out and use a rolling pin to roll it into a large sheet about 5 millimetres (¼ inch) thick.

Lightly score the top into a grid, then bake the crackers for 30 minutes, or until nice and golden.

Remove from the oven and leave to cool, then lightly snap the crackers into squares along the scored lines.

Store in an airtight container and eat within 4 days. I love to eat mine with hummus, but anything goes!

CHEAT'S SAUERKRAUT

One of my go-to condiments is sauerkraut. No one has probably mentioned this stringy delicacy since your nan, but it really is a versatile, delicious and highly nutritious addition to so many meals.

Using a box grater, evenly grate the cabbage into a bowl, making sure to use the outside leaves and the central core, not just the inner leaves.

Weigh the cabbage. You'll need to add about 2–3 per cent of the cabbage's weight in salt. Add the salt and massage in well.

Keep massaging until the cabbage's juices start to flow. No water is necessary – you'll start to see it ooze and ooze.

Once the liquid becomes foamy, it's well mixed. Place in a clean, dry jar, ensuring the cabbage is completely covered by the liquid (you can weigh it down if necessary), then seal and leave in a cool dark place for 3 weeks before consuming. I have mine with eggs, in a sandwich for some crunchy tang, or in a salad. The possibilities are endless.

— **TIP** *You can also add carrot to your kraut for more colour and nutrients.*

cabbage (I normally use plain green cabbage, but purple works, too)

non-iodised salt

FOOD-WASTE PICKLES

5 large Lebanese (short) cucumbers, trimmed and cut into 5 mm (¼ in) thick slices or batons

1 tablespoon salt

1½ cups (375 ml) apple cider vinegar

215 g (7¾ oz) caster (superfine) sugar

2 teaspoons mustard seeds

2 teaspoons coriander seeds

1 pinch ground turmeric

Thanks to the veggie co-op (see page 46), one thing I always end up with is kilograms of cucumbers. Not having a tribe of littlies who eat cucumbers for breakfast, lunch and dinner, I always end up with extras. This is where food-waste pickles come in. It's so easy to pickled veg, and I love the flavours that my friend Julie Kirk uses in her recipe, so thank you to her for letting me share it with you all. You can easily swap out the cucumber for carrot, onion or cauliflower, and you will need to start this recipe a couple of days in advance.

Place the cucumber and salt in a bowl and toss to combine. Cover with a plate and refrigerate overnight to soften the cucumber.

Rinse the cucumber in a colander, then pat dry with a tea towel (dish towel).

Combine the remaining ingredients in a saucepan and warm over medium heat, stirring occasionally until the sugar dissolves.

In the meantime, stuff your cucumbers into warm, clean, dry glass jars.

Once the pickling liquid is hot, carefully pour it into the jars over the cucumbers until they are just submerged. Seal the jars, then turn them upside down for 2 minutes to create an airtight seal.

Leave on the kitchen bench for 2–3 days to let the flavours develop. I also like to continue to flip them every few days so that everything mixes well together. After a couple of days on the bench it's ready! Once you've opened the jar, store it in the fridge for up to 6 months. Alternatively, store the sealed jar in a dark, cool place in your pantry for 6 months to 1 year.

FLAVOUR CUBES

Some suggestions are:

Olive oil, garlic and rosemary/thyme

Olive oil and sage

Tomato paste (concentrated purée) and basil

Olive oil, chilli and ginger

Very rarely will I use a whole bunch of herbs in one sitting (unless it's coriander/cilantro). A simple way to store left-over herbs is to make your own herb oil, or to freeze as 'flavour cubes'. Grab a clean ice-cube tray, stuff chopped herbs, oil and other flavourings into each cube and freeze for 24 hours. Once frozen, store in a silicone pouch and date and label them, otherwise you'll find yourself using mystery flavour cubes (which could also be quite fun!).

ACTIONABLE STEPS

- [ ] Organise the 'hug', 'swim' and 'store' sections of your fridge
- [ ] Pickle something!
- [ ] Make Wine Vinegar (page 50)
- [ ] Start using the skin, leaf and peel of your produce
- [ ] Label and date everything in your freezer
- [ ] Plan your meals for a week
- [ ] Have a week off grocery shopping and shop your pantry and freezer instead
- [ ] Join a veggie co-op

NEXT UP

Food waste is such a major issue that tackling it can feel completely overwhelming. However, there are many practical things you can implement right now that will chip away at the problem and help to save both money and the environment in the process.

Closely tied to food waste – and another area where we can really feel empowered to make tangible positive changes – is avoiding plastic food packaging.

But the fight against plastic runs deeper than what goes into your crisper. In fact, plastic is so insidious that it's worked its way into nearly every aspect of our lives, so buckle up and get ready to break up with plastics for good.

3.

Breaking up with plastic:
how to go from lifelong partner to spring fling

Savings scale

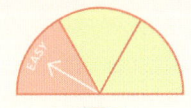

SAVE
UP TO
$75 A MONTH

Level 1
Build your single-use quitter kit + do a dumpster dive to audit your plastic consumption + make two plastic-free switches.

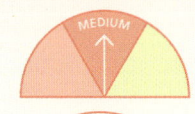

SAVE
UP TO
$150 A MONTH

+ Level 2
Make two more plastic-free switches + have a plastic-free grocery shop.

SAVE
UP TO
$210 A MONTH

+ Level 3
Make another two plastic-free switches + buy something made from recycled plastics.

Have you heard?

* There is 1 tonne of plastic on the planet for every person on earth.

* In 2019, plastic production generated 1.8 million tonnes of greenhouse gas emissions, which makes up about 3.4 per cent of all greenhouse gas emissions.

* 1580 kilograms (3483 pounds) of plastic enters our oceans every hour.

* By 2050 there will be more plastic than fish in the sea.

* Australians eat 1 teaspoon (5 g/⅛ oz) of microplastics every week.

* 50 per cent of the plastic we use is thrown away after one use.

* Microplastics have been found in snow in the arctic and dust in some of the most world's remote deserts.

The plastic problem

Here's something you never thought you'd hear me say: plastic is an amazing material.

It can be moulded into different shapes, made in different colours and thicknesses, and it's easy to clean, making it ideal for use in settings where hygiene is paramount, like hospitals and restaurants.

The biggest design flaw with plastic? Nobody stopped to think about its disposal. We were so caught up in all the wonderful things made possible by plastic that we neglected to plan for what happens once we finish using it. This means that every single piece of plastic that has ever been produced still exists somewhere on our planet today.

It's not that I don't believe plastic has its place. In fact, in some contexts, like a medical setting, plastic is the only material that can be used. But I certainly don't think we need to consume it at the rate that we do.

So, who are the main culprits when it comes to using plastic? It's not like any one industry carries the majority of the responsibility for plastic pollution – unlike, say, the aviation industry does for emissions – because plastic is used everywhere for just about everything. However, there is one kind of plastic that nabs top spot for the spectacular degree of harm it has caused to the environment: single-use plastics. Think single-use straws, food packaging and shopping bags.

There are eighteen to twenty-four shopping bags full of small plastic fragments for every 30 centimetres (1 foot) of coastline on every continent except Antarctica.

In fact, plastic is so stealthy, you might not even know it is lurking in some of your most everyday items, like:

- Tea bags
- Cans lined with plastic
- Napkins
- Sponges
- Chewing gum
- Wet wipes or single-use makeup wipes
- Glitter
- Produce stickers
- Baking paper
- Sheet masks
- Menstrual products
- Band-Aids
- Laundry detergent
- Dishwasher pods
- Receipts
- Cigarette butts

So, let's get to know and understand plastics further so we can really be rid of it for good. Plastic can be cheap and convenient, at the time, but it is costly for our environment in the long run. In this chapter I am going to arm you with facts to quit plastic for good, and empower you with the knowledge and know-how to save money while you're at it.

Microplastics

Here's the macro problem with microplastics: they never break down. Plastic might degrade and get smaller, but it never completely goes away. The result? Microplastics. And they're everywhere, causing harm to the environment and our health.

Plastics take between three and four hundred years to disintegrate, generally speaking. During this time, they disintegrate into smaller and smaller pieces. A good example is plastic clothes pegs. Over time, they dry out in the sun, crack and break, eventually breaking down into small fragments that crumble in your fingertips. These tiny brittle fragments continue to break down into smaller and smaller pieces until they no longer exist (to the naked eye). These are microplastics.

Microplastics are classified as pieces of plastic that are smaller than 5 millimetres (⅛ inch) in size, or the equivalent of a sesame seed. A study by Australia's Newcastle University found that the average Australian consumes 5 grams (⅛ ounce) of microplastics each and every week, which is the equivalent of eating a credit card's worth of plastic as a snack. Every week.

Microplastics have been found in human faeces, hearts, kidneys, lungs, spleens and even in foetuses. The health implications of consuming microplastics aren't yet fully known, but you can imagine that it is not as nutritious as having a garden salad for lunch.

A study completed by the Environment Agency in Austria found up to twenty pieces of microplastics per 10 g (¼ oz) of human faeces.

But how are we ingesting these microscopic plastics, and what are the most common plastic-containing culprits? One study by the Organisation for Economic Co-operation and Development (OECD) revealed that we consume some of these plastics through the air we breathe, but that most come from tiny airborne fibres from clothing – particulate and other plastic pollution that sits in the air.

Scientists believe that we're actually consuming microplastics in the food we eat, from plastic water bottles and even through the use of old plastic food containers.

Several global studies have also found that many of the foods we eat contain microplastics. For example:

1. **Mussels and crustaceans** (that filter the microplastics in the sea)
2. **Canned fish** (contaminants from the canning process)
3. **Fish** (that consume microplastics in our oceans)
4. **Rock and table salt** (93 per cent of salt brands contain microplastics, which are believed to be from ocean plastic pollution)
5. **Honey** (ingested by honey bees through the air, soil, water and plants, and passed on to us through their honey)
6. **Beer colours** (as a result of the production process)
7. **Bottled water** (as the thin plastic bottles degrade over time, contaminating the water)

Sadly, we're at the point where consuming microplastics is unavoidable, although it is possible to reduce your consumption. Researchers are working to determine exactly how these microplastics are consumed, the impact they're having on human health and exactly how we can reduce our exposure to them.

Keen to cut the crunchy stuff from your diet? Me too. Here are five simple ways to cut down on your microplastic consumption.
1. Drink tap water over bottled water, which contains double the amount of microplastics.
2. Don't reheat food in plastic containers in the microwave. One study showed that heating food in a plastic container for three minutes leached 4.22 million microplastics (and some chemicals) into the food. Instead, use glass containers.
3. Avoid farmed seafood.
4. Brew loose-leaf tea or use tea bags without microplastics.
5. Avoid food packaged in plastics.

Garbage patches

According to the United Nations, every year humans produce 300,000 tonnes of plastic, of which 11 million tonnes will eventually end up in our oceans.

When we think about plastics entering our oceans, the first image that might spring to mind is a beach smothered in a sea of plastic bottles, bags and debris but, in actual fact, this isn't the reality. Half of the plastic that gets washed into our seas actually sinks to the ocean floor where it starts to degrade.

Floating plastics, on the other hand, which form in accumulations or 'islands' on the surface of the water, are commonly referred to as garbage patches. There are six large garbage patches around the world in specific locations that have been formed by the ocean's currents. The largest garbage patch is the Great Pacific Garbage Patch, located between Hawaii and California. It is estimated to be three times the size of France and contains approximately 80,000 tonnes of plastic, or the equivalent weight of 740 Boeing 777 passenger jets. There are over 1.8 trillion pieces of plastic in this patch alone, which is the equivalent of 125 pieces of plastic for every single person on earth. These patches are made up of everything from fishing nets to rubber thongs (flip flops) to single-use plastic bottles.

There's an amazing organisation that was founded in the Netherlands called The Ocean Cleanup. It is dedicated to eliminating plastic in our oceans through developing technologies that dismantle these ocean-bound accumulations of plastic.

But it isn't the responsibility of a single organisation to solve the plastics issue. It's how we reduce our individual plastic consumption that will add up to the biggest difference overall.

Recycling plastic

Do you tolerate plastic because 'at least it can be recycled'? I'm sorry to have to burst your bubble, but it's a little-known fact that plastic can only be recycled three or four times before it reaches the end of its life. So, rather than thinking of it as recycling, I prefer to explain it as 'down-cycling', because every time plastic is 'recycled' it decreases in quality.

With this decrease in quality also comes a decrease in market value, meaning that every time an item is recycled it becomes a less and less attractive resource for recyclers.

Here's an example:
A virgin plastic bottle ⟶ recycled plastic bottle ⟶ gym tights ⟶ roads/building materials ⟶ landfill.

Let's look a little more closely. At the top of the chain, we have a virgin plastic bottle made from fresh petrol chemicals. Once this bottle has been recycled, you'll usually see an 'R' in front of it, so polyethylene (PET) becomes recycled polyethylene, or rPET.

Once these are recycled again, the plastic is used to make things like gym tights for which you might see slogans that say things like 'these tights are made from recycled plastic bottles'. This might seem like an ingenious use for plastic, but once these plastics are turned into yarn or material, the fibres become super small, thin and brittle, and microplastic fragments break off and enter our lungs and waterways more easily.

The final-destination use for many of these plastics is in building materials for roads before they reach the bitter end at landfill sites.

Soft plastics

Squishy and soft plastics go straight to the bottom of any recycler's 'Most Wanted' list. I'm talking items like potato chip (crisp) packets, plastic wrap, lettuce bags and plastic e-commerce mailers – basically anything that you can scrunch up into a ball and it will maintain its shape. And they are everywheeeere.

Not only are they flimsy and annoying (how many times have you cut your finger on a plastic wrap box's serrated edge?!), but soft plastics are particularly difficult to recycle. Soft plastics are a low-quality product to begin with. They are often printed with text and pictures, which causes them to turn black or brown when melted down. Even recycling plants struggle to deal with them, and there aren't many people who want the recycled material. In fact, the best solution we've come up with is to turn them back into oil and make plastic fences or carparks, which isn't that valuable.

For these, since they are so prevalent, I would challenge you to focus more on reduction in consumption rather than total elimination.

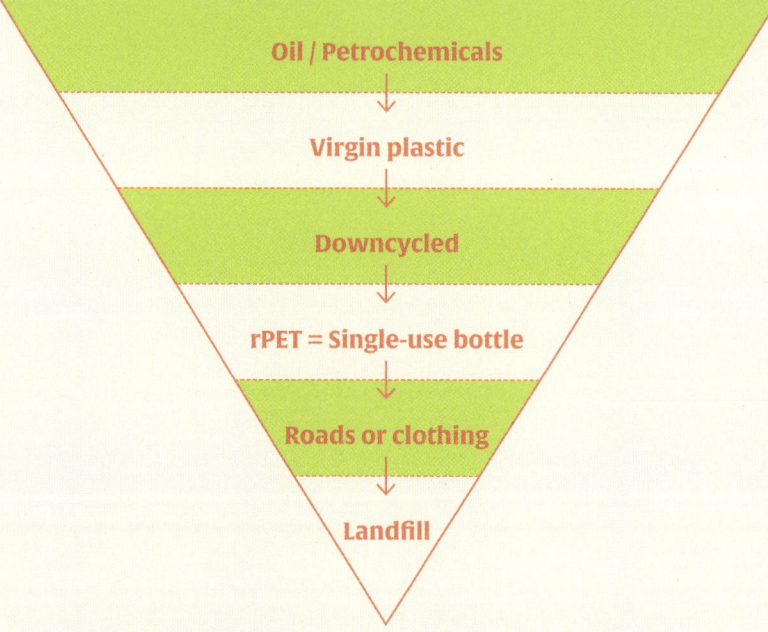

Oil / Petrochemicals

Virgin plastic

Downcycled

rPET = Single-use bottle

Roads or clothing

Landfill

(And this is all predicated on that plastic bottle reaching the correct recycling facility at each stage of its life!)

Rethinking our rubbish

We need to start thinking about our rubbish not as trash but as a resource. Basically, rubbish needs a PR lift! If we started seeing rubbish as something that has value, it would transform the way we deal with it. Here's how that could work ...

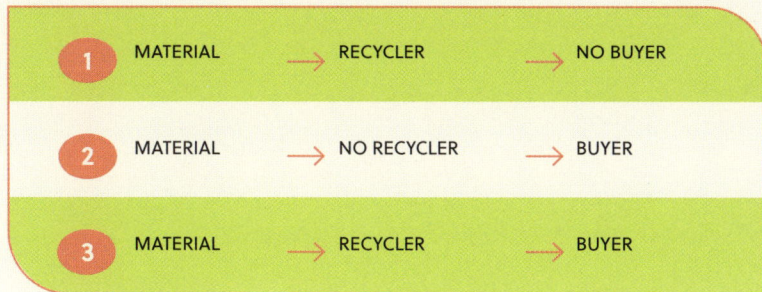

Scenario one is when we have a material, let's say soft plastics, that could be processed and recycled, but the processing is void unless there is a buyer for the end material. With only two of three parties fulfilled, the system doesn't work, and the recycler ultimately ends up hoarding materials waiting for a buyer, or just sends everything to landfill.

Scenario two, on the other hand, is when we have a material, let's say green glass bottles, that are ready to be recycled and a buyer who wants recycled green glass bottles but there's no one in the middle to collect it, transport it, break it down and turn it into green bottles. The buyer is then forced to buy green bottles from overseas or buy virgin material.

Scenario three is the one we're aiming for: a material that has a way of being processed and a buyer at the other end that wants that resource. A good example of this is paper, a paper mill and recycled cardboard.

In comparison to plastic, aluminium and glass can be recycled infinitely and still retain their high quality. This makes them a much better option and worth the slightly higher price tag so we can keep them in circulation over the finite use of our old friend-turned-enemy, plastic.

A circular economy

As much as I love to recycle and find more sustainable solutions to waste disposal, by far the better approach is to consume fewer of these items in the first place.

I'm talking about a whole mindset shift away from a traditional way of thinking about recycling to a more contemporary one, where the emphasis is on how we reduce and reuse instead of just recycle.

This actually keeps products in use, within a circular economy where there is no end point, and not just for longer – but for good.

Our transition to a circular economy is vital. It will not only keep products out of landfill, but will save us money if we are prepared to switch our thinking to return, reduce, repair and reuse instead of, simply, recycle. This means rewiring our attitude to waste, where we no longer see it as 'rubbish', but as a valuable resource.

According to the Ellen Macarthur Foundation, the circular economy is built on three core principles:
1. Eliminate waste and pollution
2. Circulate products and materials (at their highest value)
3. Regenerate nature

> 'I'm talking about a whole mindset shift away from a traditional way of thinking about recycling to a more contemporary one, where the emphasis is on how we reduce and reuse instead of just recycle.'

Cut out hidden plastics

A couple of years ago, when I first started on my journey to live more sustainably, I experimented with going plastic free for one week. I wanted to see if I could measure up to the people on social media proudly showing off their single glass jar containing their entire year's worth of plastic waste (a seemingly impossible task!).

I felt pretty confident going in that it would take me *at least* a month, not a week, to fill the jar. Well, surprise, surprise. Even after I'd made a conscious effort to reduce my plastic use, after just seven days my jar contained a plastic straw (because I forgot to specify no straw at the cafe), a receipt that printed before I had a chance to say no, a tea bag and paper towel.

Truth? I don't think it's realistic to go completely plastic free because, truthfully, plastics have made their way into every part of our lives. Instead, I think we need to change our thinking (and put our energy) into *reducing* our plastic consumption, which is a much more feasible task, and one that will still yield huge environmental and financial savings. Saying that, the glass-jar exercise is a really helpful one to reveal exactly how much plastic you consume over a set period of time, and reveal exactly what those plastics are. Give it a try – the results might shock you!

So, where can we make the easiest cuts to our plastic use?

Simple switches

You're not alone if you feel overwhelmed at the task of cutting down your plastic use. I get it; plastic is everywhere, but this is where small steps and changes add up to big wins in the long run. You will inevitably fail and get caught out by plastics – we all do – but the most important thing is to focus on making 1 per cent improvements every day.

In some cases, products wrapped in plastic are cheaper to buy, but when you look a little more closely at not only the economic cost but the environmental one, the numbers don't usually add up. Take, for example, the single-use coffee cup, which cannot be recycled in your curbside bin because of the heat-resistant plastic lining. They also cost cafe owners $0.30 to $0.70 per cup. Whereas a reusable coffee cup doesn't cost cafe owners anything, and they can be reused over and over before being recycled. It's a win for everybody involved.

Now, I am a big fan of coffee, so I am not going to tell you to stop drinking it each day (that would be unrealistic), but getting in the habit of bringing your own reusable cup to the coffee shop is one simple way to make take meaningful action every day.

A reusable coffee cup might involve an up-front spend of $35, but once you factor in the discount most cafes offer when you BYO (up to $0.50 per coffee), it would only take about 70 days to make back the cost of your cup before you start saving money on each purchase.

Reusable water bottles are similar. They cost about $50 up front – about the same as fourteen single-use plastic bottles. After that, it's all savings, baby.

BYO containers

People seem to have grasped the benefits of reusable coffee cups and water bottles, but why then are we so far behind when it comes to things like takeaway food containers?

I have a simple reusable container that is the same size as a normal single-use takeaway container. I make sure it's washed (just like my coffee cup), and I take it with me to my local takeaway restaurant for them to package up my order. For some reason though, people find this more of a bizarre concept than someone bringing their own coffee cup. But really, how is it any different?

Tip

Call the restaurant ahead of time to let them know that you don't need any disposable napkins or utensils. Napkins are often reinforced with a plastic weave and are just an unnecessary consumption of plastic. Keep a stash of cotton napkins at home to use instead (hint ... you can keep a couple at work, too.)

ACTIVITY: DUMPSTER DIVE

It should come as no surprise that this is one of my favourite activities. Doing a dumpster dive, or, as the professionals would call it, a waste audit, is a simple way to get a grasp on the current state of your household waste. Don't wait until you've made some changes to do it – start now and get an honest look at your trash. The point here is to make a baseline analysis of your current consumption so that in a few months you can assess your progress.

Grab the other members of your household on the night before bin collection day, don some gloves, go through the bags and write down what's inside.

For the sake of example, I had a look in my friend's bins. (Yes, she was just as nervous as you can imagine.) Here's what I found:

Once you've written down the contents of your bin bags, grab three highlighters.

With one colour, highlight two to three items you want to cut back on. With another, highlight two items you could go without. With the third, choose two items where you feel you could pick a better option (e.g. swapping a landfill item for a recyclable alternative or one with no packaging. That might look like buying loose tomatoes instead of tomatoes in a container.)

Now, remember we aren't aiming for perfection but for *progress*. Repeat the exercise in one month's time and see the difference. I'm sure you'll find fewer items and less packaging. Dumpster dive, complete!

LANDFILL

- 1 × Tetra Pak
- 2 × pieces of plastic wrap
- 1 × pasta packet
- 6 × tea bags
- 1 × lotion tube
- 1 × plastic meat wrapper and tray
- 2 × banana peels
- 2 × receipts
- 6 × aluminium coffee pods
- 3 × eggshells
- 5 × paper towels
- 2 × avocado stones and skins

RECYCLING

- 2 × beer bottles
- 1 × yoghurt container
- 1 × pesto sauce jar
- 1 × sun-dried tomato jar
- 1 × cherry tomato container
- 1 × strawberry container
- 1 × egg carton
- 1 × tomato can

Forget tea bags

I was shocked to discover that most tea bags are actually made from, or contain, plastic, especially those fancy silk pyramid-shaped bags. A study by Montreal's McGill University found that, on average, a tea bag brewed in boiling water releases more than 11 billion microplastics and 3 billion nanoparticles.

Switching to loose-leaf tea might seem super luxurious and expensive but, in actual fact, it works out far cheaper in the long run, especially when you buy it from bulk food shops, specialty tea shops and organic food stores for a fraction of the price of fancy packaged teas. You can choose only the amount you know you'll use (how many of us have jars or boxes of unused tea bags sitting around?!) and I find that I get two or three brews out of my tea leaves rather than the one-time dunk of a tea bag. The leaves can just be composted once you're finished with them, too.

The plastic demise

Now that you've got a handle on your household plastic waste, it's time to understand the footprint that you're leaving behind. Once something hits landfill, it is out of sight and out of mind, but an item's lifecycle doesn't simply stop there – it will persist long after you and I have gone.

Even though it's an uncomfortable thought, let's be clear about what landfill actually is: essentially a giant hole in the ground filled with rubbish. Once that hole is filled, it is covered and a new hole is dug – and on the process goes.

In Australia, we're fortunate to have lots of free space, but we definitely don't want to become just an island filled with endless pockets of disintegrating rubbish. Some smaller countries, like the Netherlands and Japan, actually burn their waste instead of burying it, but this doesn't come without consequence, either, as these processes are energy intensive and release fossil fuels into the atmosphere.

Thankfully, we are starting to see regulations come into place in many countries for, as an example, the phasing out of polystyrene and extended producer responsibility, which will see brands ultimately pay for the packaging that they create.

'Let's be clear about what landfill actually is: essentially a giant hole in the ground filled with rubbish.'

Here are the length-of-stays in landfill of some common household items. But don't be fooled; this is no holiday.

ITEM	TIMEFRAME
Cigarette butts	10–12 years
Plastic bags	20 years
Takeaway coffee cups (plastic)	30 years
Takeaway cups (foam)	50 years
Plastic straws	200 years
Aluminium cans	200 years
Plastic can rings	400 years
Plastic bottles	450 years
Plastic cups	450 years
Disposable nappies (diapers)	500 years
Sanitary pads	500–800 years
Plastic coffee capsules	500 years
Plastic toothbrushes	500 years
Fishing lines	600 years
Glass bottles	1 million years

Source: World Wildlife Fund (WWF), Thought Co

Systemic change is coming at a glacial pace, but you have the power to take control of your consumption today. I am a big believer that even the smallest of changes do start to add up. Remember that you might be one person but you're also a role model to so many others. When you remember to take your reusable coffee cup to the shop, you remind everyone in the line that they can bring theirs next time. When you purchase loose carrots over bagged ones, you are showing the supermarket chains that you don't want plastic anymore. The more people who make these changes the more companies – and society at large – will have to adapt.

ACTIVITY: BUILD YOUR SINGLE-USE QUITTER KIT

The saying goes, failing to plan is planning to fail. And this couldn't be truer than when we're talking about living sustainably.

One sure-fire way to reduce your reliance on single-use plastics is to plan exactly what swaps you are going to make and be prepared with replacements. Enter, my single-use quitter kit. (I like to think of it as a first-aid kit, but for curbing unexpected sustainability slip-ups.)

Create it and leave it by your front door to grab on your way out. I promise it will save you time and money (and take the guesswork out of making sustainable choices on the go). You can make an extra one to keep at the office, too, if you're feeling keen. Just bundle it all into a canvas tote bag.

Here's what to include:
- Reusable coffee cup
- Reusable water bottle
- Reusable straw
- Reusable takeaway food container
- Cloth napkin or handkerchief
- Reusable shopping bag
- Set of cutlery (lightweight bamboo or stainless steel, which you can easily find in an op shop/thrift store)

ACTIONABLE STEPS

- [ ] Do a dumpster dive
- [ ] Build your single-use quitter kit
- [ ] Look up the plastic recycling options in your local area
- [ ] Remember to take your reusable coffee cup for a whole week
- [ ] BYO container for your next takeaway meal
- [ ] Make a pot of loose-leaf tea over using a tea bag
- [ ] Purchase loose vegetables over those wrapped in plastic

NEXT UP

It's going to take some serious unlearning to move away from a reliance on plastic towards a more circular economy, where items – especially plastics – can be kept in circulation and out of landfill.

You need to shift your attention away from what to do with plastic items at the end of their lifespan and towards your consumption of them in the first place. As overwhelming as this seems, auditing your own plastic consumption is the first step, followed by some sustainable switches that will positively impact both the environment and your wallet.

One of the easiest places to do this is in your kitchen, where many of the main plastic culprits live. It's one of the most obvious rooms in your house to audit, and it's where you can really start to alleviate the plastic pressure.

4.

Swap 'n' save in your kitchen

Savings scale

SAVE
UP TO
$75 A MONTH

Level 1
Do a cupboard
cleanout and
inventory list.

SAVE
UP TO
$150 A MONTH

+ Level 2
Don't use any plastic
food-storage containers.
Give away/list your
unwanted appliances.

SAVE
UP TO
$210 A MONTH

+ Level 3
Clean out your
'everything else' drawer.
Recycle what you can.
Do an appliance audit.

Have you heard?

* 67 per cent of US consumers would prefer to buy from a sustainable business.

* In 2023, 53 per cent of Australians stated that their biggest obstacle to living sustainably was that sustainable products and services are more expensive.

* 63 per cent of people have already started making sustainable changes in their kitchen.

* Refrigerators often consume the largest amount of energy in the home.

I would argue that the kitchen is probably the area of the home that seems the most overwhelming when it comes to the fight against climate change. It's the site of food waste, plastic storage containers, cleaning products and so many appliances, but I would argue that it is also one of the easiest rooms in the house in which to make some simple sustainable switches.

We've already talked about food waste (see page 24) and plastic (see page 54), which are the two biggest sustainability offenders in the kitchen, but I want to look at other items that might be lurking in drawers or cupboards that you can swap to make savings, both for the planet and your wallet. I'm talking everything from kitchen utensils, cleaning chemicals, cookware, appliances and food storage.

You may not even realise that you have an untapped goldmine of reusable stores just sitting in your kitchen cupboards, so I'm going to show you how you can put those bulk-buy packs, forgotten cans and underused appliances to use.

Tip

If you're pondering moving something in your hardly-ever pile to your monthly musts, give yourself one month to use it. If you don't, then I'd strongly reconsider its place in your pantry.

ACTIVITY: KITCHEN CLEAN

This activity works a little bit like the dumpster dive on page 67. By working out what you've already got, you can make better use of your kitchen equipment, keep items in circulation instead of throwing them away, and buy only what is absolutely necessary going forwards. You'll be surprised what useful things you have lurking in your pantry and kitchen cupboards, so let's start by taking inventory. Pop on an audiobook or podcast, or pump up the tunes, and get stuck in.

As much as everyone loves living minimally these days, it doesn't always 'fit' with living sustainably. Minimalism involves ridding your home of unnecessary clutter – most of which goes straight to landfill. So, before you launch into a crusade to cut down, take a good look at everything you've got, what you can keep and continue using, and how you might rehome the things you don't want. No mindless chucking!

What I like to do is put everything into piles: everyday essentials, monthly musts and hardly-evers. I often find double-ups of things like similar-sized pans, two appliances that do almost the same thing and utensils that I haven't used in the last few years. All of these hardly-evers and double-ups are out! Firstly, I'll try and sell anything I can or see if any friends are in need of them. Then I'll list them for free on my local Buy Nothing group (see page 162) and, poof, they're gone!

Pantry picks

Sitting on a full pantry is like looking at a fat bank balance that has an expiry date. Organise your pantry well and you'll avoid purchasing double-ups and having to chuck perfectly good food that passes its use-by date collecting dust at the back of your cupboard.

Has that box of pasta been open since 2016? Have those lentils gone stale? Are you growing any new household pets? Most of us are guilty of not finding the time (or inclination) to clean and organise our pantries, but doing so means that you can avoid wasting food and unnecessary spends at the supermarket.

A great first step is to reorganise your pantry by putting newer items at the back and bringing older items forward so that you grab those first. Label everything and group them so you can make sense of what's hiding in there. In my experience, browsing a nicely organised pantry makes me much more likely to cook with what's in there, too.

If you come across anything that needs to be used up, set it aside on your kitchen bench and make it your mission to use it up that week. Or, if you've been storing cans of things or bulk-buy packs you know you'll never use, donate them to a food bank instead of throwing them away.

Appliance audit

You've probably noticed by now that one of the main themes of this book is reducing your consumption. The less you consume, the more money you save and the fewer items end up in landfill.

Unused appliances present a golden opportunity to make the most of items you've already got. Firstly, instead of buying new, you can rediscover old appliances that are probably still in fine working order hiding in your kitchen cupboard. Or, if you have something you know you won't ever use, you can sell it on or gift it to someone else. I've made money selling everything from a barely used Mixmaster to a kettle when I moved into a home that already had one.

To start with, I would really recommend looking at any appliances you have two of (such as a blender and a high-speed blender), and then also looking at any you forgot you had – remember that juicing craze?

If you do have any double-ups of appliances or serveware (hello, 7162 mugs!), put them in a box in the laundry or garage and leave them there for a month. If you don't even think about them – let alone have a need for them – in that time, it's safe to say they can go. Clarifying what you have and what you're actually going to use regularly means you're more likely to keep an appliance for the long haul instead of simply storing, then dumping it.

When it comes time to get rid of your unwanted appliances, the best thing that you can do if they're still in working condition is either sell them on Facebook Marketplace or give them away for free (see page 162), otherwise electrical appliances need to go to your local e-waste collection centre, because they cannot be put in a curbside bin.

Energy-sucking appliances

Every time you boil the kettle it costs you money. And the same goes for every appliance in your home, so knowing which ones suck the most energy from the environment and dollars from your bank account is helpful to know from the outset.

Despite being more eco-friendly than a gas oven, an electric oven is far more energy intensive. If you aren't in a position to replace your electric oven, or if you're renting and have no control over what is installed, then the next best thing you can do is make the most of the energy being expended while the oven is on. This might look like roasting vegetables or other ingredients in the oven at the same time as cooking another meal and using the stovetop for cooking whenever possible.

When you cook with gas you're quite literally burning a fossil fuel. Studies have shown that this has a negative impact not only on your health but the health of the planet. Shockingly, researchers from the University of New South Wales have found that these fossil fuels still leach into the air even when you're not using the stove! If you're in the position to make a choice, an induction stovetop is the best option for your wallet, the planet and your health, followed by electric and, at the bottom of the list, gas.

No matter what oven you have, you want to utilise every last bit of energy it puts out, so if you have grimy dishes, fill them with soapy water and put them back in a cooling oven. They will clean themselves and steam-clean the oven at the same time.

When it comes to individual appliances, an obvious way to cut energy use is to opt for appliances with several functions, such as food processors with extra attachments for juicing, or a rice cooker that doubles as a slow-cooker. Fewer appliances means less energy and money expenditure.

Appliance swaps

Here are some easy appliance swaps that are better for both your back pocket and Mother Earth.

Hand washing for dishwasher

You might think that dishwashers gobble up a load of water and energy, but in terms of water usage, they're actually more efficient than running a full sink and washing everything by hand. Who knew? Saying that, dishwashers do still consume quite a bit of energy, so make sure you run yours during off-peak times, only run it when it's full, and utilise the half-wash function to save energy – and your pennies.

Saucepan for kettle

Boiling water with an electric kettle is about 85 per cent more efficient than boiling water on a gas stovetop. If you have an induction stovetop, it's 85 per cent more efficient.

Grill oven (broiler) for toaster

We come back to the gas issue here. Where possible, it's always better to use an electric appliance over gas, and toasting is no exception. Opt for your electric toaster or sandwich press before switching on the gas grill.

Everyday item swaps

It's not just big appliances in your kitchen that you can swap out for more sustainable options. There are plenty of environmental and financial savings to be made with everyday items, too.

Non-stick pans for cast-iron pans

I get it: the ability to cook without leaving half of your meal in the pan is great, but you need to weigh up the health and environmental risks of using non-stick pans.

Per- and poly-fluorinated compounds (PFAS) are the group of chemicals that make things non-stick, and they're nicknamed the 'forever chemicals' because they take so long to break down. The US Food and Drug Administration has also classified them as possible carcinogens.

The most notable in this group is Teflon, which is the name for the non-stick chemical polytetrafluoroethylene (PTFE), and its use in household cookware has been associated with an array of health problems, including increased blood cholesterol levels, liver enzyme changes and Teflon fever, caused by excessive exposure. The US Environmental Protection Agency (EPA) has also warned that exposure to PFAS, even in small amounts, is harmful to the environment. Non-stick pans not only present a host of problems for our health, but, once they're damaged, they release thousands of soft plastic particles into the environment.

Grabbing cheap, non-stick pans from a budget-friendly retailer might be cost effective in the moment, but the expense soon adds up once you've had to replace (and dispose of) them multiple times. Instead, invest in good-quality, durable cookware, like cast iron. Raw cast-iron pots can be quite affordable, sometimes less than $100, while enamel-coated ones are easier to maintain but can be more expensive. Both can last a lifetime. Some of my favourite secondhand cast-iron pans are ones I have picked up from Facebook Marketplace. This is one of many examples where living more sustainably means investing a little more up front to save money – and the planet – in the long run.

Tip
If you do choose to use non-stick pans, cook at low temperatures only and use soft silicone or bamboo utensils to avoid scratching the surface.

Baking paper for reusable baking mats

Despite the name, baking paper is not actually recyclable because of its waxy coating, which is made from paraffins. Paraffins are derived from fossil fuels (read chemicals), which have been proven to cause respiratory infections. Switching to reusable silicone baking mats is simple. Buy them once (they fit perfectly on standard baking trays), then just wash and reuse. Plus, they are non-stick, which makes them ideal for those wanting to cook with less fat.

* **Cost:** $14.95 per mat or $0.08 per use if you're using the mats three times a week

Reusable bags for silicone food pouches

Resealable bags are flimsy and thin, and made from notorious 'soft' plastics (see page 62), and I can't be the only one who finds it difficult to seal them shut?! Enter, silicone food pouches. Not only are these bags super thick and sturdy, the seal is 100 per cent leakproof, so you can store curries and soups without worrying about making a mess in the fridge or freezer.

* **Cost:** $0.35 each vs. $10 for a pouch you will reuse for years

What is silicone and why is it better for the environment?

You'll notice that many of the sustainable swaps I suggest in this book include the use of silicone, which is actually a type of – you guessed it – plastic! I know what you're thinking, but silicone is much more durable than softer, thinner plastics, and therefore more reusable. And even though it takes about the same amount of time to break down as other plastic storage bags (about 500 years), crucially, it doesn't leak microplastics as it degenerates. Also, if you were to use the same silicone spatula for ten years, you would use less carbon than buying a new bamboo one each year. Food for thought.

Plastic wrap for beeswax wrap

It is time to bid adieu to flimsy plastic wrap. It is made from a particularly low-quality plastic, making it very difficult to recycle, as well as being single use; once it's been used to wrap food, it's contaminated and cannot be recycled.

Beeswax wraps (see page 83) are my go-to reusable alternative. They are pieces of fabric covered in a light coating of beeswax, and you can use them everywhere you would normally use plastic wrap (except for meat, fish and pet food). This method of storing food has been used for hundreds of years, and I'm going to show you how to make them yourself. Sigh ... is there anything our buzzy little buddies cannot do?

* **Cost:** $0.10 vs. $0.05

Paper towels for cotton napkins

Another misleading kitchen culprit is paper towel. It's another single-use item that has to go, not to mention paper towel is usually bleached with toxic chemicals, and is often reinforced by a thin plastic weave. Swap it out for fabric tea towels (dish towels) and napkins, which do involve a little more washing, but at approximately thirty wipes per towel are a big improvement on disposable paper towels.

* **Paper towels:** $1.83 per roll of 180, aka $0.01 per towel
* **Tea towels**: $4 each per (equivalent to 400 wipes or three months of use)

Plastic sponges for plant-based cloths

Every time you wring or rinse out a plastic sponge under the tap, it sheds thousands of microplastics into our waterways. Swapping to a plant-based sponge is not only better for the environment, but it also has natural antimicrobial properties – something a plastic sponge can never replicate.

* **Cost:** $4.90 for ten, or approx. one plastic cloth per week
* **Swedish dishcloth:** $19.95 for three (one cloth lasts 300 uses)

Plastic dish brush for bamboo dish brush

Speaking of microplastics, plastic dish brushes have the same impact as plastic sponges. Plus, they're a breeding ground for bacteria. Opt for an untreated bamboo dish brush that has no plastic whatsoever. Once you're done with it, it can be buried in your garden or composted.

But, what about compostable plastic wrap? Several companies have jumped to solve the many problems of plastic wrap, but while their products are compostable, they are still single use. So, I would always recommend opting for reusable items where possible. If you do buy compostable wrap, make sure it's certified home compostable, and that it makes it into your compost bin.

Old plastic bags or paper bags for plastic garbage bags

Once you've banned all plastic bags, knowing what to put your rubbish in can present a challenge. Try repurposing old stored plastic bags, or even sturdy potato chip (crisp) packets or e-commerce satchels. You can also make a bin bag out of newspaper or other scrap pieces. (I'd only recommend this if you're composting at home, because your landfill bin will get soggy and wet.)

* **Cost:** $0.15 per bag (approx. two per week) vs. $0

Dishwashing tablets for dishwashing powder

Bulk-produced dishwashing tablets often contain nasty chemicals and synthetic fragrances, not to mention the plastic casings the pods are sealed in, which don't fully dissolve and fragment into microplastics. Go for dishwashing powder in a recyclable cardboard box. More and more, companies are not including those plastic scoops in their washing powder in a bid to encourage the reuse of older plastic scoops. You can also just use a household spoon.

* **Cost:** $1.60 per wash vs. $0.33 per load

Chemical cleaning products for home-made cleaners

Someone asked me once if I would happily lick a surface after it had been cleaned with a chemical cleaner. It was a lightbulb moment. My answer was immediately 'No', which led me to make my own home-made cleaner from food scraps (see page 99). You can also purchase natural refillable cleaners.

* **Cost:** $7.00 vs. $1.00 per 750 millilitres (26 fluid ounce) bottle

Plastic bottles of soda water (club soda) for a soda machine

Who doesn't love a refreshing drink of bubbly water? Making your own bubbly water with refillable gas canisters means you can have sparkling water on tap, save a boatload of money on bottled sparkling and avoid a heap of plastic waste. It's an all-round win.

* **Cost:** $2.55 per 1 litre (34 fluid ounces) vs. $0.32 per 1 litre (34 fluid ounces)

Plastic bottles of dishwashing liquid for solid dishwashing blocks

Solid dishwashing blocks sound too good to be true, but I promise you they're just amazing. These solid bars work similarly to a bar of soap; just leave them next to your sink, run your wet brush over the top of the bar and, poof! Soapy water to clean your dishes.

BEESWAX WRAPS ARE THE BEE'S KNEES

Beeswax wraps are my favourite reusable alternative to plastic wrap, and they've been created and used by people to store food for hundreds of years.

These pieces of fabric coated in beeswax can be moulded into any shape or size – just use the warmth of your hands to soften the wrap, then use them to package up avocado halves, baguette ends, to cover bowls, and much more.

To keep them clean, simply rinse them under cold water. If there's a tough stain, use a little bit of dish soap or castile soap, but whatever you do don't use warm water as this will cause the wax to melt off and the wrap will lose its grip! If you live in a super-hot climate you can store them in the fridge.

For a good-quality set of three beeswax wraps that are locally made and not filled with palm oil, you are looking at around $35. It's another example of spending a little more on a sustainable option that pays for itself when you consider how much of the disposable alternative you'd normally get through. I find that mine last between 12–18 months of weekly use before I need to refresh them.

It is also relatively easy and fun to make your own! You could purchase new material or, better yet, cut up an old piece of clothing that is made from 100 per cent cotton and use that instead.

What you'll need:
- Old towel or tea towel (dish towel)
- Baking paper
- Fabric (use a lightweight, 100 per cent cotton or hemp cloth)
- Box grater
- Block of beeswax (or, if you're vegan, a plant-based resin)
- Iron
- Scissors

Place an old towel over your ironing board, then a piece of baking paper.

Place your fabric in the middle of the paper. Grate the beeswax over the fabric, leaving a 2 centimetre (¾ inch) border around the edges. Place another piece of baking paper on top of the wax.

Switch your iron to the lowest heat setting. Gently glide the iron over the sheet of baking paper, slowly melting the wax. Once melted, ensure that the wax has spread evenly to the edges of the fabric, then remove the paper.

Hang to dry for a couple of minutes, then it's ready to use!

To care for your wraps simply run them under cold water between uses, then allow to dry. When they are losing their grip, repeat the steps above, or pop them in your compost bin and make some new ones.

It's important to note that as they are made from fabric, beeswax wraps aren't suitable for storing meat, fish or pet food.

Common challenges with recycling in the kitchen

One of the biggest challenges this room presents is recycling. So much waste is created here, from food to plastics, energy to appliances. Here's your mini guide to becoming a better kitchen recycler!

Recycling mix-ups

When it comes to recycling, 83 per cent of Australians don't feel confident that they're putting things in the right bin, causing recycling to become contaminated and even more difficult to deal with at the plant.

According to Planet Ark, these are the biggest recycling contaminants:

1. **Soft plastic bags.** Not only do we have very few places to recycle these, they get tangled up in machinery, wreaking havoc on recycling facilities.
2. **Clothing.** While clothing can technically be recycled, it can't be recycled in your curbside recycling bin. Instead, it needs to go to a specialty textile facility (see page 155).
3. **Disposable nappies (diapers).** These stinky, smelly bundles go straight to landfill, and there's not a chance that they can be turned into something else.
4. **Food scraps.** While your recyclable items don't need to be sparkling clean, they do need to be rinsed.

The economics of recycling

For most people, recycling is a stinky business they don't get too involved in. For others, it's a lucrative industry where rubbish is prized for its valuable components.

Recycling is a right. It is a service – one that you pay for, whether it is in your rates or your rental fees. Councils are paid (by you) to dispose of your rubbish.

Recycling companies make money from providing this service to local councils, but they also make money from the materials they receive, depending on how they sort them and how 'clean' the waste stream is. For example, a mixed bin or what are called 'co-mingled materials' isn't super valuable, but if all of the items are separated, their value increases. They're worth more still once they've been grouped by material, and each material has its own market and commands its own price.

The metal market is crazy! Aluminium, copper, silver and other metals can be infinitely recycled, so companies will pay good money for these. Aluminium alone can fetch up to $2000 per tonne. What this means on the ground is that every time an aluminium can is recycled it can be made into a new aluminium can without losing its quality. Recycling these metals keeps them in a circular economy and reduces the need to mine the land for more virgin materials, which causes more harm to the environment.

Glass, glorious glass. It's another material that can be recycled over and over again without losing its integrity (or value). The main drawback is the weight and fragility of glass; processing and transporting it significantly increases its carbon footprint. But the plus side is that it can be recycled infinitely. Some countries also use glass to help rebuild sandbanks and protect and regenerate environments, directly fighting the effects of climate change.

'Aluminium, copper, silver and other metals can be infinitely recycled, so companies will pay good money for these. Aluminium alone can fetch up to $2000 per tonne.'

glass
bottle

recycling
facility

washed
crushed

Case Study: Two students, Max and Franz, were frustrated at the lack of recycling options available in New Orleans, so they turned their anger into action and built Glass Half Full, a grassroots glass recycling plant in Louisiana where they turn glass into sand and other materials. Their sandbags have been used for flood mitigation along the New Orleans coastline, using up to 49,000 kilograms (108,000 pounds) in burlap bags, and their glassy gravel is being used in potting mix.

In another good-news piece, Australia is one of the best paper recyclers in the world. It's estimated that we recycle 87 per cent of all paper, turning it into things like cardboard packaging and recycled paper. A few things to note: oily paper (aka your greasy pizza box) is a no-go, but a little bit of plastic (aka sticky tape on your Christmas wrapping paper) is A-okay. This is because paper is first reduced to a wet, soupy pulp (like Weet-bix) before any paper is removed using a giant corkscrew – kind of like pulling hair out of a drain (gross!).

Now, most of what we've discussed here focuses on how recycling helps the environment, but following are a couple of ways you can make money from your trash. After all, there is a reason behind the saying 'trash to treasure'.

RETURN-AND-EARN SCHEMES

These schemes are popping up more and more. While they won't make you a millionaire, they are a great way to make a bit of extra cash or get the kids involved so they can make some extra pocket money and get to grips with what recycling is all about.

Return-and-earn schemes work in conjunction with your curbside recycling schemes by providing a place to deposit higher-value materials like glass and some strains of plastic.

You place your item in a vending machine where the materials are automatically separated, which helps to take the pressure off the processing and sorting centres that deal with your curbside bins.

Now, don't be fooled – I wouldn't say you can make money on these schemes. More that you can make some money 'back' on the product you buy. This is because those big single-use bottle producers have slyly hidden this cost in the price you pay at the checkout, a bit like a deposit when you stay at a hotel. If you return the room (or the bottle, in this case) in pristine condition, you get your money back (in this case, around $0.10 per bottle).

Setting up your recycling systems

So, you're ready to become a recycling superhero? You're in the right place.

When it comes to setting up a system for your recycling bins, here's what I would recommend. (Again, each household is different, but for 90 per cent of you, the table below is a great starting point.)

A few things to keep in mind:
- Every council recycles differently, so double check your local council's website for information.
- Make your landfill bin the smallest to encourage everyone in your household to throw away less.

LANDFILL	RECYCLING	COMPOST	SPECIALTY RECYCLING SERVICES
Oily food waste	Plastic bottles	Food scraps	BRAD (see page 8)
Nappies (diapers)	Thick plastic	Loose-leaf tea	Batteries
Soft plastic	Cardboard	Dried flowers	E-waste
Meat (and scraps and bones) and dairy	Aluminium and cans	Newspaper	Chemicals
Cardboard	Glass jars	Coffee grounds	Paint
Cork		Eggshells	Fashion
		Hair	Lightbulbs

Your most common recycling questions answered

I know you've probably still got a lot of questions, so I'll cover off some of my FAQs here.

How small is too small to recycle?

Recycling facilities are huge. The machines they use are huge. This means that anything smaller than a credit card will literally slip through the cracks. To avoid this, group similar materials into larger balls, which can then be recycled. For example, collect the aluminium foil seals from hummus and yoghurt containers and roll them into a big ball. Once it is the size of a tennis ball, you can recycle it as normal!

Do I need to remove the lids from my bottles to recycle them?

If your bottle top is smaller than a credit card, recyclers don't want it. For small items like this, screw the lids back on when you can, but, if not, it needs to go to specialty recycling facilities. This is one of the reasons why I started the recycling program BRAD (see page 8).

Also, recyclers usually package up recyclable materials in mega squares, so it helps to keep similar materials together. But, if your glass jar of pasta sauce comes with a metal lid, then separate that lid.

How clean should my recycling be?

Give your recyclable items a quick rinse to make sure they're clean enough that they won't contaminate everything else in your bin.

If plastic can be recycled, then why is it so bad?

Plastic is an amazing material (see page 57 if you don't believe me!). It can be moulded into different shapes, made into different colours and thicknesses, and it can be used in food-grade products and even medical settings. What is bad is our overreliance on it, and our lack of planning for how to dispose of it. How much 'convenience plastic' do you consume? It helps to consider consuming plastic like you (probably already) think about consuming trees: if you don't need it, don't use it.

Help! I am addicted to alternative milk. Can you recycle long-life milk cartons?

I apologise for the devastation I am about to cause, but you cannot recycle these. Most long-life milk products are housed in Tetra Paks, which are made from not one but six different layers: 75 per cent paper, 20 per cent plastic and 5 per cent aluminium. This mashup of materials makes them next to impossible to recycle, so very few recyclers actually want them. If you can make your own non-dairy milk (see page 39), then this is by far the best approach. Or try to find milks in plastic or glass containers, which are much easier to recycle.

Why is recycling so hard?

Golly, golly gosh, where do I even begin? I could write a whole book on this topic alone! Is it the lack of education? The lack of a standardised system? The lack of knowledge on what happens to our recycling, or the negative press and publicity around this industry? If you answered 'all of the above', you'd be right.

ACTIONABLE STEPS

- [ ] Reorganise your pantry

- [ ] Move away from using Teflon pans

- [ ] Swap to a sustainable sponge or bamboo scrubbing brush

- [ ] Activity: appliance audit

- [ ] Use your dishwasher more

- [ ] Make sustainable switches (e.g. reusable baking mats over baking paper)

- [ ] Build an aluminium foil ball

- [ ] Try to keep similar materials together in your recycling

NEXT UP

So, we've looked at the kitchen's main sustainability culprits, discovered some simple kitchen swaps and gone deep on recycling. However, for many, the number one environmental concern in the kitchen is the use of chemical-laden cleaning supplies.

Unfortunately, the use of toxic chemicals extends right throughout the house. Of course, we need to keep things clean, but there are less environmentally damaging ways to do it – and ones that don't involve dropping your hard-earned dollars on seven different sprays!

5.

Clean 'n' mean:
can the nasty chemicals

Savings scale

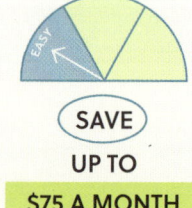

SAVE
UP TO
$75 A MONTH

Level 1
Grab some bicarb (baking soda) and vinegar at the shops. Hang-dry over using the dryer. Do your handwashing.

SAVE
UP TO
$150 A MONTH

+ Level 2
Make your kitchen scrap cleaner (page 99). Switch to sustainable cloths and sponges.

SAVE
UP TO
$210 A MONTH

+ Level 3
Safely dispose of old chemical cleaners. Give your mattresses a deep clean.

Have you heard?

* The average household uses a staggering 30 bottles of cleaning products each year.

* Washing clothes releases, on average, 500,000 microplastics into the ocean each year.

* A 2018 study found that the regular use of cleaning sprays has the same impact on your lungs as smoking a pack of cigarettes every day.

* Your laundry routine is responsible for 30–40 per cent of your household's energy consumption.

Keeping your house clean is obviously necessary, but this chapter will show you how to do it quickly, affordably and in a way that protects the environment.

One of my personal mantras is if you wouldn't drink it or eat it, then don't clean with it. When you think about it, the chemicals that you clean your crockery or wash your clothes with are coming in direct contact with your body. You are ingesting them through your mouth, absorbing them through your skin and breathing them in. And it's destroying your health and the planet.

Cleaners to avoid

The chemicals in your typical household cleaning products are absolutely astounding! Some of them are so toxic it is alarming that they even exist. Here's a list of the ones I have banned from entering my house:

- **Ammonia:** This potent irritant is often used in window and mirror cleaners. Try ye old faithful white vinegar instead.
- **Chlorine:** There's a reason why your hair turns green and your skin dries out when you swim in a chlorinated pool too often. It might whiten and bleach your toilet, but at what cost to your health? Try bicarbonate of soda (baking soda) instead.
- **Phthalates:** These are often found in air fresheners and fragrances, and are toxic and shouldn't be inhaled – the irony.
- **Triclosan:** A petroleum-derived chemical that was classified as a pesticide in 1969 and is banned in Canada and the US as it kills fish and algae and negatively impacts the environment. And yet, we still use it in Australia in mouthwash, dishwashing detergents and aftershave.
- **Sodium hydroxide:** This is the workhorse in your oven cleaners and drain openers. But it is so corrosive that it burns your skin and eyes on contact, and inhalation can cause a sore throat.
- **Sodium lauryl sulfate (SLS):** This is what makes detergent and shampoo foam and, in some cases, has been found to be moderately toxic to marine life. Sodium lauryl sulfate is better for cleaning when derived from coconut oil over palm oil.
- **Phosphates:** The 'p' or 'np' on laundry detergent packaging. It promotes the growth of unwanted algae blooms and harms marine plants.

Beware of microfibre cloths

If you got rid of paper towels as part of your kitchen clean-out (see page 75), chances are you're using a lot more tea towels (dish towels) than you used to, so what about cleaning cloths? Microfibre cloths are probably what you'd reach for, right? Wrong.

As the name suggests, microfibre cloths are made of tiny fragments of two materials: polyester and polyamide (aka nylon, aka plastic). Each microfibre is estimated to be one hundred times finer than a human hair. When you use microfibre cloths, they release microplastics, so they do add to your microplastic tally. Saying that, reusable cloths are a much better option than single-use wipes, so it's not all bad news.

Try to find reusable cloths made from 100 per cent cotton. I cut up my old t-shirts to make rags and purchase flannel wipes (flannel is made from cotton, too).

The mighty four

Less really is more when it comes to your cleaning routine. I am not joking when I say that I use four products – three of which you probably already have at home – for 99 per cent of my cleaning needs: lemon, bicarb (baking soda), vinegar and castile soap.

Think about it like this: everything we spray on our living surfaces or use to clean our household items, we either ingest or inhale, so using simple, natural ingredients adds up to more than just financial savings – it also improves our health.

Don't underestimate these natural cleaning alternatives – they still pack a powerful punch. You can use them to clean:

- Drains
- Pots and pans
- Microwave and kettle
- Clothes
- Carpet
- Bathroom
- Glass and windows
- Stainless steel

Tip

If you go on a rampage disposing of old cleaning products, please do not pour them down the drain or put them in the bin. They are so toxic that they actually need to go to a specialist chemical facility. The Australian government has a free program, so check with your local council when the next chemical clean-out event is.

Lemon

Another key ingredient in your sustainable cleaning toolkit is lemon (lime can be used, too). The naturally occurring citric acid in citrus fruits is not only antibacterial but antiseptic, too – the perfect cleaning combo. Lemon peel is filled with oils that help cut through grease and the scent is the crowning glory.

11 WAYS TO USE LEMON

1. Put half a lemon on the top shelf of your dishwasher and it will act as a rinse aid.
2. Boil lemon slices in your kettle to naturally descale it.
3. Use it to clean your microwave. Simply place a sliced whole lemon in a bowl of water (this could be after you've squeezed it out) and cook on high for three minutes. Leave it to sit for ten minutes, then simply wipe away all of the caked-on stains. This works for ovens too!
4. Ants hate lemon juice, so spray or squeeze fresh lemon juice wherever the ants are coming in (e.g. windowsills, door cracks) and they will stay well clear.
5. Use a cut lemon to clean an oily or cheesy grater. Simply grate the fleshy side of the lemon, which will break down any oily or fatty residue and save your sponges from getting grated!
6. Add a splash of lemon juice to your laundry to brighten your whites.
7. Sprinkle your wooden chopping board with salt, then scrub with a cut lemon and rinse. Pay extra attention to any stains.
8. Polish your wooden furniture with a cloth and a mixture of one-part lemon juice to two-parts olive oil. Do a test patch first on the underside of your furniture, as every piece of wood is different.
9. Remove orange-coloured stains from plastic containers by simply rubbing lemon onto the stains and letting it sit for 15–30 minutes before rinsing.
10. Remove hardwater build-up from your taps with – you guessed it – lemon! Simply rub a cut lemon on the tap, let the juice sit for fifteen minutes, then wipe clean.
11. For baked-on food on a grill, grip half of a lemon with tongs and rub it down a hot grill, working quickly. For extra-stubborn stains dip the lemon in salt first.

Bicarbonate of soda

Bicarb, bicarbonate of soda or baking soda, has been used for hundreds of years in both cooking and cleaning. It is a household staple, but one I don't think people use anywhere near enough, and you might be surprised to hear that it's a potent cleaning agent.

But before you go and buy the biggest box of bicarb you've ever seen, it's important to note that it doesn't last as long as you think. An unopened box can last up to two years, but once you crack the seal you need to use it up within six months. It won't go mouldy, but it will start to absorb moisture and won't work as well. My tip is to always store your bicarb in an airtight container and label it with the date it was opened.

To tell if your bicarb is less 'soda-y', simply add 1 teaspoon to a small bowl with a splash of vinegar. If it starts aggressively hissing, you'll know it's fine, but if the reaction is weaker, then set it aside to use for lighter cleaning jobs, such as points 2, 3 and 4 on the list below.

* **Cost:** $3.95 for 1 kilogram (2¼ pounds)

20 WAYS TO USE BICARB

1. As a smell-sucker – bicarb is a deodoriser and air freshener.
2. Give your mattress a thorough clean. Sprinkle the base with bicarb, leave it to sit for one hour, then vacuum it up. You can do the same with carpets and rugs.
3. Stinky fridge? Place a small open bowl of bicarb on a shelf in the fridge to absorb any funky smells.
4. Pongy bin? Sprinkle a little in the bottom of your rubbish bin before you put in a bin bag.
5. Speaking of smells, sprinkle a small amount of bicarb into your gym shoes to eliminate odours.
6. If your gym or swimming bag is smelling a little ripe, sprinkle some bicarb in the bottom.
7. Remove fishy smells by using a mixture of bicarb and water to clean your pots and pans.
8. Garlicky fingers? Sprinkle a little bicarb into your hands, rub together, rinse and dry – ta-da!
9. Remove any damp smells from your wardrobe by placing a small bowl of bicarb inside.

It's also a potent cleaner:

10. If your stainless steel is lacking its sheen, make a paste of vinegar and bicarb soda and use a sponge to wipe your sink down. Sparkle restored!

11. Got grit and grime? Dust your kitchen bench with bicarb, leave for five minutes, then wipe away.

12. Clean your silver jewellery (see page 110).

13. Refresh your sponges, mop heads and cloths by soaking them in 1 litre (34 fluid ounces) warm water mixed with 3 tablespoons of bicarb and leave overnight.

14. Soak your burnt pots and pans with bicarb and water before using a scouring pad to lift any residue.

15. Remove tea and coffee stains from your mugs by rubbing them with a little bicarb on a damp cloth.

16. Give your blender a good clean by adding 2 tablespoons bicarb to ½ cup (125 ml) cup white vinegar and running it on high speed for 30 seconds. Rinse well and it will be as good as new!

17. Give your stainless-steel water bottle an overdue clean. Add some bicarb and water to the bottle, seal, shake well, then rinse out.

18. Found a damp towel in the bottom of your hamper? Revive it almost instantly by adding ½ cup (135 g) bicarb to the rinse cycle.

19. Clean your drains by pouring ¼ cup (70 g) bicarb and ¼ cup (70 g) salt down the drain. Follow that with 6 cups (1.5 litres) tap water, leave for a few minutes, then run the hot water through the drain afterwards.

20. To clean the barrel of your washing machine, simply add 1 cup (270 g) bicarb to the drum and run a hot cycle, then gently scrub and rinse once it has finished.

Tip

If your kitchen benchtops have a porous surface, like marble, wood or concrete, reduce the amount of vinegar by half and add 1 tablespoon castile soap (see page 100) instead.

Vinegar

Household white vinegar is another cost effective and low-toxic all-rounder. Vinegar is generally made of around five per cent acetic acid, a colourless organic compound that helps it cut through tough stains and films, and kills nasty bacteria. Due to its potency, keep it away from natural stone, waxed wood, iron and aluminium.

10 WAYS TO USE VINEGAR:

1. Fill a small dish with 2–3 tablespoons of white vinegar and place it in a room to help neutralise any funky smells.
2. Vinegar is a potent stain remover. Add ½ cup (125 millilitres) diluted white vinegar to your next laundry load of whites right before the rinse cycle.
3. Combine equal parts white vinegar and water in a spray bottle and use it to clean your mirrors – minus the streaks!
4. Deodorise your rubbish bin by washing it out with a mixture of white vinegar and water.
5. Got stubborn hard-water stains on your shower screen? Use a clean rag with distilled white vinegar to shift built-up mineral deposits.
6. Mix vinegar with bicarb to create a powerful drain unblocker. Combine equal parts vinegar and bicarb in an open container, pour it down the drain and wait 10 minutes, then run the cold tap until the water drains well.
7. Stickers always leaving a tacky residue? Simply soak the sticker first in white vinegar, then carefully peel it off and wipe the surface.
8. Coffee mugs showing a little wear and tear with stains? Half-fill your mugs with white vinegar, top up with hot water and leave to sit for 10 minutes, then pour away and scrub clean.
9. To remove hard limescale deposits from your taps, soak a paper towel in white vinegar and wrap it around the tap head. Leave for 1 hour, then wipe away the caked-on scale.
10. If you're struggling to remove mildew and mould from grout, spray with white vinegar and let it sit for 15 minutes, then scrub with a brush and wipe clean.

POWER PACKED OVEN CLEANER

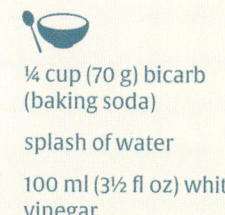

¼ cup (70 g) bicarb (baking soda)

splash of water

100 ml (3½ fl oz) white vinegar

If you can no longer see through your oven window, then it is seriously time to give it a clean. This overnight method is my favourite because it takes barely any elbow grease.

Make a paste by mixing the bicarb (baking soda) and water together.

Rub the paste all over the oven (wear gloves). Leave for twelve hours, then wipe away.

Spritz all surfaces with white vinegar, leave it to react and bubble away for 30 minutes, then wipe away with a cloth dampened with warm water.

MAKE YOUR OWN KITCHEN SCRAP CLEANER

This zesty cleaner, made from citrus scraps, cuts through grease on just about any surface. For stubborn stains, apply a generous dose with a sprinkling of bicarb (baking soda) before wiping away with a cloth.

Fill a clean jar with white vinegar.

As you finish with a lemon, lime or orange slice, place it in the jar and keep going until it's full.

Once full, seal the jar and place it in a dark place for 4–6 weeks.

When it's ready, strain the citrus out (pop them in the compost), then combine the vinegar with equal parts water in a spray bottle. It will last up to one year.

Castile soap

Castile soap is another essential product in your low-cost, low-tox cleaning toolkit. Castile soap is used to describe pretty much any vegetable oil–based soap, but make sure you look for a pure castile soap that doesn't have any additives or blends.

I personally love Dr Bronner's Castile Soap. It's $34.95 for 1 litre (34 fluid ounces), which is a little eye-watering, I know, but it really goes the distance. The recommended quantity for each use is literally drops, not squirts, so one bottle lasts a very long time.

18 WAYS TO USE CASTILE SOAP

1. Washing dishes
2. Rinsing your fruit and vegetables (use an unscented version for this)
3. Shaving cream
4. Toilet cleaner
5. Mopping floors
6. Window cleaner
7. Multi-purpose spray
8. Laundry liquid
9. Dog wash
10. Body wash
11. Face cleanser
12. Shampoo
13. Bubble bath
14. Decongestant steam (peppermint and eucalyptus for this one)
15. Makeup brush cleaner
16. Makeup remover
17. Bug spray on plants (mix with water in a spray bottle)
18. Ant spray

Stubborn grime

Here's where we get serious about cleaning. In the previous section I covered general cleaning, but this is where we call on the big guns so you don't have to use your muscles and instead let the potion do the hard work for you.

Grout

If there's one thing that will tempt you to reach for hard chemicals, it's cleaning grout, but you can get on top of it without the hefty price tag (and dose of toxins) of specialised cleaning products.

For mildly dirty grout, I'd recommend mixing ¼ cup (70 g) bicarb (baking soda) with a squirt or two of castile soap to form a paste. Paint the paste onto your grout, leave it for 30 minutes, then scrub at it with an old toothbrush to remove the grime.

Another tip for lighter-coloured grout is to squeeze lemon juice directly onto it, let it sit for ten minutes, then scrub it with an old toothbrush. All the results, none of the toxic chemicals.

Move over mould

Mould is insidious in the home, as it can grow in unexpected and hidden places, releasing spores that are easily breathed in. Not only are these spores so small that you can't even see them, but surface-level cleaning often doesn't remove them, and they are responsible for attacking your respiratory system, causing fatigue, wheezing and heart palpitations, to name just a few nasty symptoms.

It doesn't just grow around your windows, in damp cupboards or in your linen. It can grow within damp walls, pipes and the ceiling. Start by dealing with the mould you can see by using a 1:1 mixture of vinegar and water. Rub it all over the mould with a damp cloth, then use a clean cloth to remove it. Some people also swear by clove essential oil. Add a couple of drops to the vinegar-water mix to increase its antibacterial properties. This is a great example of the potency of natural products for tackling some of the biggest household cleaning chores.

Remember that balled-up piece of aluminium foil you've been saving until it's big enough to put in the recycling (see page 88)? While you're waiting, add the foil ball to your dishwasher to stop your cutlery from tarnishing. Seriously, it works.

By far the best way to address mould is to prevent it from forming in the first place. So, make sure you're:

· dusting and vacuuming regularly
· using air vents and open windows to allow proper airflow and prevent condensation
· growing plenty of indoor plants, which help to purify the air and absorb moisture
· airing out damp clothes, like soggy winter coats, before hanging them in the cupboard.

Dishwashing detergents

My go-to dishwashing liquid is, you guessed it, castile soap! Just a few drops and you have enough soapy water to get your dishes sparkling in no time. If you'd prefer to use a dishwashing detergent, opt for a loose powder instead of plastic bottled liquid soap. Not only is this more economical, but it will cut down on plastic wrapping or 'biofilm' pod packaging. It's also easier to tailor the quantity to the state of my dishes. As I covered in the kitchen chapter (see page 72), using your dishwasher is actually far more water-efficient than hand washing your dishes, so always opt for using the dishwasher if you have one.

Descaling

Over time you might notice that a thin layer of mineral build-up on things like your kettle, shower head and tap nozzles – pretty much any water-based appliance. Eventually, too much built-up scale will impact its performance, which is why it's important to regularly descale items at home. This process removes the calcium and limescale, and most manufacturers recommend that you descale your appliances every six months to maintain peak performance.

Remove your shower head and soak it in one-part white vinegar to four-parts water for at least one hour. If you can't remove it, I use an old bag and tie it around the nozzle. Give it a light scrub with a brush, rinse and then put it back.

The easiest way to remove scale from your kettle is to simply boil half a lemon in it. Allow it to sit for twenty minutes, then rinse. Repeat the process if the scale doesn't wipe off, then boil a kettle of plain water once, before continuing to use it as normal.

Laundry

In the utilities chapter (see page 170), I talk about how the laundry is the room in the house that uses between 30–40 per cent of your total household energy. Not only that, but it is the room that you'll probably find the most toxic chemicals in ... until now. Making changes in your laundry requires using up everything you've got, reducing the number of products you buy and doing less laundry overall in order to make the biggest savings.

There's no getting away from it: doing laundry is essential to everyday life, but it's also one of the areas where we can make some of the biggest improvements to our consumption of energy and toxic chemicals, and our creation of microplastics.

The microplastic problem with laundry

The yarn in our clothing is made up of tiny fragments all woven together, many of them plastic. When these fragments get wet during washing, they expand, soften and break off – about 10,000 microplastics per wash, to be precise. The friction of washing in a machine, plus the detergents that are added, make these fibres even more unstable.

A 2015 study found that a staggering 250,000 microplastic fibres were released in a single wash of just one 500 g (1 lb 2 oz) fleece jacket! Shockingly scary, I know, but there are some ways that you can reduce the amount of microplastic shedding in your laundry loads:

· Wait until you have as full a load as possible before running a cycle. This cuts down on the total number of loads, and creates less friction in each load, as the clothes are more tightly packed.
· Adjust your spin rate down to reduce the amount of time the clothes get whipped and bashed around.
· Reduce the temperature of your washes to 30˚C (85˚F) or less, which will cause fewer breakages of these fragile fibres and make your clothes last longer. It's also a good money-saver because you won't be paying as much in energy to heat your washing. Plus, your clothes will last you longer – cha-ching!

FUN FACT

The average adult does 208 loads of washing a year, costing $0.42–$0.62 a wash in water and electricity, plus the cost of cleaning products. Reducing your loads by one per week will save 25 per cent on your annual bill!

HOW TO HAVE A GREENER, CHEAPER LOAD
· Wash a full load
· Use natural detergents rather than those with microbeads
· Slow your spin
· Cool it down: wash between 25–30˚C (77–86˚F)
· Shorten your cycle

How often should you wash things?

Overwashing your clothes shrinks, fades and damages them, forcing you to spend your hard-earned dollars replacing them.

Getting savvy about how often to wash each time – or whether you need to wash them at all – is an easy way to make some improvements.

Washing too often also leads to unnecessary microplastic creation, not to mention a waste of energy and water!

ITEM	WASH FREQUENCY
Underwear and socks	After every wear
Bras	2–3 wears
Sports bras and workout gear	After every wear
Hats	Once a month (unless used for sport)
Shirts and blouses	1–2 wears
Dresses	Three wears
Jumpers (sweaters)	Up to six wears if you're wearing something underneath them
Pants	2–3 wears
Jeans	Six wears
Suits/blazers/jackets	Once a season
Sleepwear	2–3 wears
Sheets	Once a week
Bathmats	Once a week
Pillowcases	Every 2–3 days
Towels	Three uses
Doona (duvet) cover (if you're using a top sheet)	Once a month
Pillow and doona (duvet)	Every six months

WASHING TIPS

- **For dark clothes,** like gym tights, turn them inside out before washing. This stops fading and helps get any funky odours out.
- **Separate your darks from your lights** and wash similar materials together, for example, cottons with cottons.
- **Levi's CEO and President Chip Bergh** says that you should never wash your jeans! Instead, spot-clean them with an old toothbrush.
- **Spot-wash wool.** As it is naturally antimicrobial, pure wool shouldn't need cleaning. If you do wash your woollen items, it's a good idea to hand wash and air dry them. Never put them in the dryer, as they will shrink to a fairy's size!

Pillows

This is a bit gross, but the average person sheds 4 kilograms (9 pounds) of skin each year, most of which ends up in your bed or pillows. Using pillow and mattress protectors means this debris can be regularly washed out instead of becoming embedded in the fibres. These protectors are worth the investment, and you don't need to replace them very often. I also wash mine every 4–6 weeks, which furthers its lifespan.

Ideally, you should wash your pillows at least twice a year. Just place two in the washing machine and wash on a delicate cycle, then allow to air dry in direct sunshine.

By looking after your pillows you're extending their lifespan, meaning that you'll need to buy fewer over time, saving both money and the planet.

It's a little-known fact that your pillows actually have an expiry date! Generally speaking, they should only be used for two years before they need to be replaced. Before sending them to landfill, see if you can reuse them. Do you have a pet that could use them, or could you donate them to a local animal shelter? Can you use the stuffing to make couch pillows?

When you make your next pillow purchase do your research and look for a brand that uses organic material. Because your face comes in direct contact with your pillow, you're breathing in all the microfibres it releases.

How to wash your washer

We get so focused on washing our clothes that we often forget to wash the washer itself. Looking after your washer will keep it running longer and provide you with a more efficient clean – it's a win-win.

Place a small scoop of dishwashing powder in the drum and set it on a short hot cycle every few months to give it a deep clean.

Keep your washing machine mould free by leaving the door ajar after every load and wipe the rubber rim clean each time. You can also use a solution of white vinegar and water to give the rubber a deeper clean.

Draining the washing machine is something that we barely think about, too, but this annoying chore plays an integral role in keeping your washing clean and your machine running for longer. It is recommended that you drain your washing machine every four months. Never done it before? You're in for a real treat. Use the instruction manual that came with the machine, or the general guide below:

- Turn off the water and power.
- Shimmy the machine away from the wall.
- Locate the small door at the front of the machine and the drain hose.
- Grab a large bucket or a large shallow dish, undo the drain hose and use the bucket to catch the liquid as it drains out.
- Run it until all the water has come out.
- The more frequently you clean it the easier it is.

A task we often forget about is caring for our appliances. They work tirelessly for us, but in order to have them function like they did when you first purchased them, you need to look after them. This means keeping them clean, rinsing them and getting regular services over dumping them on the curb.

Simple laundry swaps

Just like the kitchen, there are some simple swaps you can make in the laundry to reduce your energy consumption and pinch some pennies.

LAUNDRY DETERGENTS

One of the more 'woo woo' swaps I have made is to use soap nuts, or berries. As the name suggests, these are the berries from the Indian soapberry, or *Sapindus mukorossi*, tree and have been used for centuries as a natural surfactant. When the shell of the berry hits water it releases a natural form of saponin, which cleans your clothes. They are fragrance- and chemical-free, so particularly good for people with sensitive skin and eczema. You use one berry per load, which works out to be about $0.20 a load! Absolute bargain.

Alternatively – but if you don't want to be 'that' alternative – look for a laundry detergent that doesn't contain palm oil, microbeads, synthetic fragrances or sodium lauryl sulfate. Again, opt for something where you can choose your own dose and don't trust the scoop or bottle lid measuring caps, as some companies design these to be too big so that you get through the product faster.

FULL WASH FOR SPOT WASH

Do you have a tiny spot on your favourite jumper (sweater) or pair of jeans? Rather than washing the whole garment, simply do a spot-wash clean of the stain and wear it again and again. This not only saves you time but also the energy required to wash the whole item.

PLASTIC PEGS FOR STAINLESS-STEEL PEGS

One of my favourite sustainable switches has been to stainless-steel pegs. Plastic pegs get brittle and splinter in your hands, eventually creating microplastics. Wooden pegs never seem to go the distance and are prone to leaving rust stains. Stainless-steel pegs, on the other hand, are made from marine-grade stainless steel that doesn't rust or become brittle, meaning they will literally last a lifetime.

'Stainless-steel pegs are made from marine-grade stainless steel that doesn't rust or become brittle, meaning they will literally last a lifetime.'

Tackling common stains

I've shown you some simple ways to reduce grime and stains with bicarb (bicarb soda; see page 96), but there are other tools in your low-tox, low-cost arsenal for dealing with stubborn stains.

The best advice I can give you? Think fast! Stains and grime are far easier to remove if you tackle them straight away.

Couch or carpet

Start by wrapping a pot lid with a cotton cloth. Mix some boiling water with a squirt of dishwashing detergent or castile soap. Dip the cloth-wrapped pot lid in the soapy water and use it to clean the couch or carpet in circular motions.

Grass and blood

Despite the name, hydrogen peroxide is actually a great non-toxic cleaner. Its chemical makeup is simply water and oxygen, and it works well to brighten and whiten grass and blood stains. It adds oxygen to the area, which helps to lift stains. The hydrogen peroxide from the chemist is perfect for laundry and relatively inexpensive.

For blood stains, be sure to use cold water as warm-to-hot water will actually embed the stain further.

Oil

Any natural detergent that gets rid of oil and grime from your pots and pans can also be used on any oily stain. Apply some dishwashing detergent or castile soap directly to the stain, then hand wash or give it a quick rinse.

Red wine

Soda water (club soda) is the best cure for a fresh red wine stain. Blot as much of the wine as possible, then pour soda water over the stain allowing it to bubble and work its magic. Blot again and the stain should be gone, and not a chemical in sight!

Sweat

Starting to notice some yellowing under the arms of your fave white tee? Soak it in white vinegar for three minutes before washing to brighten and revive it.

Cleaning personal items

There are some items, like our beauty tools, jewellery and hairbrush, that we just don't clean enough. I am guilty of forgetting to clean mine, which is not great considering they're things I use and that come in contact with my body on a daily basis. If neglected, personal grooming tools and jewellery can easily become breeding grounds for bacteria and result in poor hygiene. Proper maintenance also means replacing these items less often, which benefits both the planet and your bank account.

To keep me on track I put a calendar reminder in my phone once a month titled 'Deep clean power hour'. I literally schedule in time every month to tackle tasks like cleaning my beauty tools, washing my pillow and mattress protectors, and deep-cleaning the dishwasher and washing machine.

Beauty tools

I know I'm not alone in neglecting to clean my beauty tools, but if you wear makeup regularly it is really important to clean your brushes. Bacteria builds up and breeds over time, causing acne and skin infections, so I try to wash mine at least once a month. Good-quality makeup brushes often involve a bit of up-front investment, so keeping them in good condition will save you money as you won't have to replace them as often.

To clean them, just wet the brushes, add one or two drops of castile soap and rub this into the bristles for a minute or so, then rinse in a small bowl of warm water. Repeat until the water is clean, then allow to air dry.

Hairbrush

Over time your hairbrush will accumulate your natural hair oils, dandruff and dead skin cells – gross. If you never clean it, you're just rubbing these back into your hair.

The hairbrush you already have at home is the most sustainable option for you, but if you do need to buy a new one look for a brush with bamboo bristles and an FSC-certified handle.

If you prefer a plastic hairbrush or comb, you can purchase ones made from recycled plastic. Simply remove all of the hair (you can put this in your compost bin) and place your brush on the top of the rack of your dishwasher for a deep clean.

Here are a few hairbrush tips

Frequently remove hair from the bristles (at least every two weeks) and put it in your compost bin.
I find the easiest way to remove the hair from my brush is by combing it out from top to bottom.

- Once a month swish your hairbrush in a solution of water and castile soap, which will break down any oils. Don't soak it for longer than five minutes, especially if the brush has a wooden handle as the wood could split.
- Remove it from the water and use an old toothbrush to rub the base pad in between the bristles.
- Run under some warm water and leave to dry on a towel, bristles facing down.

Jewellery

If you're someone (like me) who sleeps, swims and sweats in your jewellery, then it is probably long overdue for a clean. The method below is perfect for cleaning rings, necklaces, earrings and anklets, but don't dunk anything like watches with small inner workings.

No need for pricey, toxic shining products, just follow these steps:

For silver:

- Cover a small dish with aluminium foil.
- Place your silver on top and cover with bicarb (baking soda).
- Pour some warm (not boiling) water in and allow to sit for 30 minutes.
- Use stainless-steel cutlery to remove them from the water so you don't contaminate the mixture, rinse and pat dry with a cotton cloth.

For gold:

- In a small dish place warm water and a couple of drops of liquid castile soap.
- Add your gold jewellery and soak for fifteen minutes.
- Gently scrub with an old toothbrush, the softer the better.
- Rinse under warm water and pat dry with a cotton cloth.

You'd wouldn't rest your cheek on your toilet seat but studies have shown that your phone screen has more bacteria than a toilet ... gross.

Give your phone a quick once over by wiping it down with a glasses lens cloth.

For a deep clean use an alcohol-based cleaner (use rubbing alcohol). Do not spray directly onto the phone but onto a cloth first.

Do not use an all-purpose kitchen spray or bleach.

Remove any lint or dust from your charging and headphone ports.

ACTIONABLE STEPS

- [ ] Set a reminder in your phone to wash your doona (duvet) and pillow
- [ ] Give your makeup tools and hairbrush a deep clean
- [ ] Do the handwashing that's been in your laundry pile forever
- [ ] Clean your jewellery
- [ ] Make your own kitchen scrap cleaner (see page 99)
- [ ] Do a chemical cleaner audit and dispose of the nasties responsibly

NEXT UP

Cleaning agents in the home are one of the most insidious culprits when it comes to environmental damage, and they're expensive too! So, replacing chemical-laden products with natural alternatives is a really good grass-roots place to start when embarking on a journey to live more sustainably.

Another area where getting back to basics with simple ingredients and doing things the way our grandparents used to is in our beauty practices. No fuss, no fancy products, just elbow grease and cost-effective ingredients that are better for our health and the health of the environment.

In fact, we can look even further back than our grandparents for inspiration. The Ancient Greeks were pioneers of the earliest 'cosmetics', and we can borrow many of their principles to create a modern-day beauty routine that prioritises sustainability, affordability and health.

6.

Mirror, mirror on the wall, who's the greenest of them all?

Savings scale

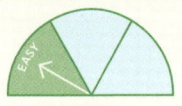

SAVE
UP TO
$75 A MONTH

Level 1
Start dating your beauty products when you open them.
Bring back soap bars.
Use a bamboo toothbrush.

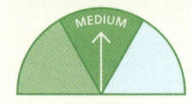

SAVE
UP TO
$150 A MONTH

+ Level 2
Declutter your beauty cupboard.
Have a palm oil-free shop.

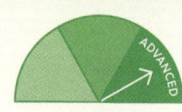

SAVE
UP TO
$210 A MONTH

+ Level 3
Make your own beauty product.
Do a service you'd normally outsource.
Try a plastic-free period product.

Have you heard?

* It is estimated that the beauty industry is responsible for 120 billion units of waste every year.

* 95 per cent of beauty products are thrown out after a single use.

* Only 14 per cent of beauty plastic is recycled.

* In Australia we throw away over 30 million toothbrushes annually, which creates around 1000 tonnes of landfill a year.

* Buying a refillable product reduces carbon emissions by 74 per cent.

* The average person with a vagina uses 12,000 period products in a lifetime.

I would argue that beauty routines and products present one of the trickier sustainability problems to solve. Plastic products are everywhere – lining your shower, filling your sink, beside your basin and deep in your drawers, so reducing them is a marathon, not a sprint.

Like many other things in this book, here I encourage you to use up your current beauty products before making sustainable swaps, because there is no sense in creating even more waste (or spending more money) on new products before you've used up what you've already got.

It might surprise you to hear that my own beauty routine isn't filled with discount-store picks. I have a combination of bougie products and bargain buys and, as I'll explain later, I use my custom criteria when purchasing new products to make sustainable choices that work for me and the planet.

That's the beauty of this chapter (pun intended): it will show you how to make swaps and savings so you can put that budget towards more sustainable products. Because this is the modern challenge of sustainability: how can we best allocate the resources that we already have to live sustainably in a way that's actually affordable.

So many of the affordable and sustainable swaps I suggest in this book are about getting back to basics – a theme you might have already noticed, because it's one of the easiest ways to make sustainable changes.

Our grandparents didn't have cupboards full of plastic-packaged makeup, and didn't indulge in expensive beauty routines. They had a few essential items that were used on heavy repeat until they had to be replaced. I like to channel my own grandmother here: her shower shelf wasn't packed like a Taylor Swift concert. There was a bar of soap, a loofah and not much else, which got me questioning my own 193,821-step beauty routine.

If we look even further back than Grandma to the Ancient Greeks, we can take inspiration from the earliest (and simplest) beauty routine. The very word 'cosmetics' comes from the Greek word *kosmetikos* (to arrange or adorn), and it's been around since the seventeenth century – a lot longer than the brands you see today.

A traditional Greek routine consisted of:

- An antibacterial mask made from honey and olive oil (sounds delicious!)
- An exfoliator made from salts
- A hair mask made from olive oil
- Makeup remover (also made from olive oil – sensing a theme?)
- Moisturiser – you guessed it, olive oil.
- But, before you go and luxuriate in an entire bathtub of the slippery stuff, this chapter looks at some other things you can do to make your bathroom routine both planet and budget friendly.

Target toxic offenders first

Before we get down to business with environment- and money-saving beauty swaps, we have to target the low-hanging (toxic) fruit.

Our beauty and personal care products are right at the top of the hit list when it comes to the overuse of chemicals and plastics, and some ingredients in many of the most common products significantly damage our health as well as our planet.

Palm oil: the great pretender

One substance lurking in a staggering amount of beauty products is palm oil, and it is one of the leading causes of deforestation around the world. In South-East Asia alone, three hundred football fields of land are cleared every hour to make way for palm oil plantations. In the process, vital rainforests that are home to hundreds of thousands of animal species are destroyed. And, with them, biodiversity.

The problem with palm oil is that it's amazingly versatile. It improves the shelf life of ingredients, helps mixtures to set and stops them from melting, among other things.

Palm oil yields are also high in comparison to other vegetable oils, making this crop extremely attractive to producers. It makes up 40 per cent of the demand for vegetable oils, but only needs a fraction of the space to grow compared to other common plants, like rapeseed, sunflower or cottonseed.

To eliminate palm oil from our beauty cabinets, we first have to find it, which is another challenge. You won't often see the words 'palm oil' on an ingredients list. Instead, you'll find one of four hundred other code names, the most common of which are listed opposite. You will also often see these listed as 'palm-oil derived', which is just as bad as palm oil itself.

Palm oil can also be called...

1. Elaeis guineensis
2. Ethyl palmitate
3. Glyceryl
4. Hydrogenated palm glycerides
5. Octyl palmitate
6. Palm fruit oil
7. Palm kernel
8. Palm kernel oil
9. Palm stearine
10. Palmate
11. Palmitate
12. Palmitic acid
13. Palmitoyl oxostearamide
14. Palmitoyl tetrapeptide-3
15. Palmityl alcohol
16. Palmolein
17. Sodium kernelate
18. Sodium lauryl lactylate/sulfate
19. Sodium palm kernelate
20. Stearate
21. Stearic acid
22. Vegetable fat
23. Vegetable oil

> 'Palm oil is everywhere. It is in approximately 70 per cent of all cosmetics, and even up to 50 per cent of all packaged food items on supermarket shelves.'

Palm oil is everywhere. It is in approximately 70 per cent of all cosmetics, and even up to 50 per cent of all packaged food items on supermarket shelves. It's also odourless and flavourless, making it easy to add to products without changing their flavour or smell.

You might be surprised to see the kinds of products it makes its way into:

- **Bread:** As a natural preservative that helps extend bread's shelf life
- **Chips:** Masquerading as vegetable oil (so always look for olive, sunflower or coconut oil instead)
- **Margarine:** Just don't use it
- **Ice cream:** As the additive that stops ice cream from going all icy and getting freezer burn
- **Pizza bases:** Many store-bought ones do, but check the label
- **Instant noodles:** Don't go there
- **Chocolate:** Rare, but it's been known to happen
- **Soap:** Again, palm oil helps the bars to set, so buy from local makers and ask if their products contain the nasty stuff
- **Shampoo:** As with soap, support local makers

The problem with parabens

Parabens are one of the most common chemical preservatives used in cosmetics, cleaning products and foods. You'll find parabens listed as methylparaben, ethylparaben, propylparaben and butylparaben.

Always check the back of the packaging to make sure your chosen product doesn't contain these harmful ingredients. Most brands that have done the hard yards of sourcing superior ingredients will draw attention to the fact that their products are paraben free.

Your skin is a giant sponge

When we start to think of our skin like the porous, thirsty sponge that it is, we start to rethink what we put on it. Everything you put on your skin will be absorbed by your body. It's that simple. The chemicals you apply to your face and body (in skincare products and makeup) will enter your bloodstream and vital organs. If that's not enough to make you rethink your beauty routine, I don't know what is.

Identifying toxins in your beauty products can feel totally overwhelming; sometimes the labels looks like they've been written in a whole other language. So, instead of trying to decipher it yourself, download the Chemical Maze or Think Dirty apps. Both of these apps will help you better understand your products. Simply scan the barcode and you'll be provided with a score on their rating system that explains the naughty and nice ingredients.

Perfumes stink

Something that I no longer buy is perfume. It contains a chemical cocktail of synthetic fragrances and phthalates – none of which I want anywhere near my body, but especially on areas like my neck, behind my ears or the back of my wrists where all my lymph nodes live.

The fragrance industry is self-regulated, which means natural or non-toxic alternatives actually haven't been vetted by anyone but the fragrance producers themselves to meet standards that don't exist. This means you need to proceed with caution (even some natural substances, like essential oils, can cause allergies in some people).

Even the word 'fragrance' should prompt scepticism. It is listed freely on the back of cosmetics labels, but no definition of 'fragrance' is ever given. Why? Usually because it refers to one or more of over 2000 toxic chemicals. For some reason, the term 'fragrance' regularly stands in for a list of actual ingredients. In my opinion, if a brand writes 'natural fragrance', then they should be comfortable to list what that fragrance consists of.

For me, the solution is going without. No one has commented on my lack of signature scent, and my body – and my wallet – is thanking me.

While we're on the subject, here are a few more products that I don't see the point in:
- **Shaving cream** (for me, a foamy block of soap will do)
- **Eye cream** (I just use my richest face moisturiser under my eyes)
- **Toner** (I'm pretty sure the jury's still out on what this even is ...)

Sunscreen

Where do we start with sunscreen? I for one will never tell you not to use it (for obvious reasons), but you do need to look closely at what it contains before you buy.

You've probably seen the words 'reef safe' or 'planet friendly' on sunscreen tubes before. Generally speaking, you can take this to mean the product doesn't contain oxybenzone.

Oxybenzone is an organic compound used as a sunscreen agent. It absorbs UVB and UVA II rays, making it a very effective sunscreen. But with 14,000 tonnes of sunscreen being washed into our oceans each year, chemicals like oxybenzone are doing irreparable damage to marine ecosystems. These substances are absorbed by corals, which can disrupt their reproduction and growth cycles, ultimately leading to coral bleaching. In the US, Hawaiian lawmakers recently passed a bill banning the local sale of sunscreens containing oxybenzone and octinoxate in a bid to protect corals and other marine wildlife.

Another important thing to note with sunscreen is the difference between a physical and chemical sunscreen. Chemical sunscreens (which usually contain oxybenzone) absorb into the bloodstream, whereas physical sunscreens sit on the top of the skin forming a barrier. This means you need to reapply physical sunscreens more often, as this barrier is more frequently breached, for example when drying off with a towel. Fortunately, the increase in supply of natural sunscreens (that use active ingredients from plants) is driving the price down, so now you can pick reef-safe sunscreen without paying a planetary premium.

Tips

Some people struggle when switching from an antiperspirant deodorant to a natural one. They feel like they're sweating more and smelling more! But although you are sweating again (which is the whole point), you shouldn't be smelling. There's an adjustment period for your body of a couple of weeks where you may need to reapply the deodorant twice a day – more for your sanity than anything else, so I recommend switching during the colder months.

If you have sensitive skin, I recommend buying a natural deodorant that doesn't contain bicarb (baking soda), as this can often irritate sensitive skin.

Antiperspirants

Have you thought about exactly what it is in your antiperspirant that stops you sweating? Aluminium salt is used to block your sweat glands, keeping inside all the moisture your body is trying to expel in order to cool and detoxify you (a rather essential process).

A natural deodorant, on the other hand, allows you to sweat like normal but masks your body odour. As everyone's energy and sweat levels are different, it might take two or three goes before you find a natural deodorant that works for you, so be patient.

The good news is that when applying natural deodorants, you only need to use a pea-sized amount. This makes them more affordable than standard deodorants, and they often come in refillable packaging, so you'll save again when you refill over buying new.

Remove unnecessary plastic

It's nearly impossible to avoid plastic when it comes to beauty products, but I have a few golden rules for *reducing* your consumption. Always use things up before replacing them, do your research before buying a new product, and consider swapping some of the main plastic culprits for products that use less or no plastic packaging.

Plastic-free periods

Full disclosure: when I started my journey to reducing my plastic consumption, I never thought I'd be someone who went near menstrual cups and period underwear. I found the idea gross, confronting and too much to handle. I couldn't even say 'menstrual cup' and referred to them only as moon cups. Now I've converted most of my girlfriends to using reusable options, and I feel so strongly about them as a way to drastically cut down plastic waste that I've dedicated a large part of this section to them!

I quickly became one of the biggest advocates for reusable menstrual cups after discovering just how easy and simple they are to use. And don't even get me started on the amount of money you can save by going all in on reusable period products. As with anything in this book, choose your own adventure. Make switches where you can, but no one is going to shame you for what you do or don't do.

> **Food for thought:**
> · **It's estimated** that a person who menstruates will spend approximately $2700 on period products in their lifetime, which works out as roughly 10,000 single-use products!
> · **It takes** a traditional period product, like a tampon or pad, approximately 300–400 years to break down.

Swap tampons for menstrual cups

A menstrual cup will set you back about $55, so it's yet another example of investing a few extra dollars up front to save heaps of money in the long run. One cup costs about as much as three months' worth of tampons, and it will last, on average, 5–10 years. All you need to do is sterilise it between uses. I use a simple cup cleaner, but you can also boil it to sterilise it.

Menstrual cups are made from medical-grade silicone, i.e. they are sterile and built to last. Making the switch means you'll instantly stop putting thousands of tampons into landfill, which take hundreds of years to break down. You'll also reduce your exposure to chemicals, such as the bleach used in cotton tampons.

To use a moon cup, luna cup – or whatever you're going to call it – fold it into a C-shape and place it inside your vagina. It won't sit as high as a tampon, but once it is in you shouldn't feel it or worry about it falling out. The cup suctions to the walls of your vagina, meaning there's no leakage, and even if it does fill up, it won't overflow. This allows you to monitor your period more easily, too, because the blood isn't being immediately absorbed by a tampon.

The exit strategy is what scared me the most. My top tip for beginners is to practise inserting and removing it in the shower, which means that if you have any accidents there won't be a mess to clean up. I also started by wearing my cup for shorter periods or overnight before using it for a whole day. I was most concerned that it was going to fall out or cause a leak when I was at the gym, but neither of those things happened.

It depends on your flow, but you can safely wear a menstrual cup for 10–12 hours before needing to empty and change it, which is handy for when you're at work or while sleeping. For me that means that 90 per cent of the time I am able to change it at home, which makes it easy to empty it, rinse and wash it in the sink before replacing it. If I am out and about, I tip the contents into the toilet bowl and use a piece of toilet paper to give it a quick clean before inserting again.

Swap pads for period underwear

In my experience, if you're a pad wearer, period underwear is a simple and easy swap. Once you've finished with a pair, simply rinse them under the tap, then wash with your darks.

I wear these on my 'It could be today' days, or at the end of my period. On the heavier days, I use a menstrual cup. A pair of period underwear costs approximately the same as three boxes of pads and will last you for years. It will also save hundreds if not thousands of pads ending up in landfill. You can also buy reusable pads that simply clip on and go. I personally just find period underwear easier and more comfortable to wear.

Swap plastic disposable razors for safety razors

Despite the name, I was petrified of safety razors. I mean, they look anything but safe.

Safety razors have been around for yonks, and my research tells me they came to be called 'safety razors' because of the obvious dangers of straight-edge razors. Saying that, they can still do an impressive amount of harm if you don't handle them correctly.

Once I learned the tricks of the blade, however, I was converted. Not only do safety razors offer a closer shave, but you're less likely to get ingrown hairs, and did I mention the cost? A safety razor will set you back about $45 but the blades themselves cost $0.30 a month (depending on how much you're shaving). On the other hand, a plastic razor will last between three to ten shaves before becoming blunt and clogged, plus it takes between 300–400 years to break down in landfill.

My top tips for mastering safety razors:

- Take your time – it's a new experience and you don't want to rush it.
- Turn off the shower or shave in the bath so you don't have lots of steam and can see clearly.
- Lather up using a really foamy soap bar instead of using shaving cream.
- Go with the grain. That's not a typo – go *with* not against.
- Change the blades about every four to five shaves.
- Store in a dry place in between uses to avoid rusting.

Swap plastic-bottled body wash and shampoo for soap and shampoo bars

When did we decide that huge plastic pump bottles were the answer to our personal hygiene issues when all that was ever needed was a bar of soap? Our grandparents knew it, but the message was obviously lost along the way. Going back to basics is one of the key mindset shifts you need to make if you're going to live more sustainably. A bar of soap is cheap, efficient, lasts a long time – and often comes without any plastic packaging.

It's not just soap that comes in a handy bar; shampoo bars work just the same way and are game-changing for reducing plastic and saving money. It normally takes me 6–8 months to get through a single bar, where I used to go through four or five plastic bottles of shampoo in the same amount of time. Cha-ching!

Look out for soap bars that don't contain any palm oil or parabens. If you have dry skin, opt for a bar that contains hydrating ingredients, and if your skin is prone to breakouts, try a bar with a charcoal base.

Tips

If your partner, family member or housemate isn't feeling as enthusiastic about sustainability as you, I find that shampoo bars are a great starting point for piquing their curiosity. Slip one into the shower and let people give it a try for themselves. It won't take them long to see that they are simple, easy and effective!

When I'm travelling, I just cut a little knob off my bars and throw them in an old aluminium can. If I am feeling particularly basic, I'll use my shampoo bar slice as a three-in-one body and shave bar, too. This means I can say no to plastic hotel samples.

'When purchasing reusable makeup wipes my top picks are dark or black fabrics, as they won't show stains over time, so you'll end up using them for longer.'

Swap plastic shower pouffe for a loofah sponge

Here we are again with another heartbreaking example of how microplastics end up in our waterways. As you use plastic shower pouffes, tiny fragments of plastic break off and wash down the drain. And that's before you even get to the mould and bacteria that builds up in your plastic pouffe over time. Yuck.

A loofah sponge, as the name suggests, is made from the fruit of the loofah plant. Once dried you can simply use the loofah fruit as a natural full-body exfoliator and sponge. Rub it in circular motions to promote blood flow and the removal of dry skin cells. It also dries out really well between uses, making it less likely to harbour bacteria.

Loofah sponges also make a great tool for dishwashing, as they will remove grit and grime without harming your pots and pans.

Swap single-use makeup wipes for reusable makeup wipes

If you wear makeup you need to remove it. I wish that a simple cleanser would do the trick, but, as you know, this isn't the case. The problem with single-use makeup wipes is that they are made from plastic fragments, so they break down into smaller pieces of plastic in landfill or, worse, if you flush them, they clog up our drains. They also come with quite a hefty price tag.

We are seeing more and more 'biodegradable' and 'compostable' wipes entering the market, but while they're slightly better than single-use, reusable products will always win out in the sustainability stakes.

When purchasing reusable makeup wipes my top picks are dark or black fabrics, as they won't show stains over time, so you'll end up using them for longer. I have also dedicated one of my oldest wipes for nail-polish remover. This saves masses of tissue, cotton wool balls and toilet paper. P.S. It's a much taller order, I realise, but the same really goes for baby wipes, too – reusable is best.

Microbeads

Microbeads are small, solid, manufactured plastic particles that do not degrade or dissolve in water. They are in cosmetics, personal care and cleaning products, but the biggest issue is that microbeads can't be captured by most wastewater treatment facilities, which means they wash down the drain into rivers, lakes and oceans.

These tiny plastics have a damaging impact on marine life, the environment and human health due to their composition, ability to absorb toxins and potential to transfer up the food chain to humans. Fortunately, microbeads are being phased out in Australia, with 99.3 per cent of products being microbead-free in 2020.

At the basin

Let's take this thinking to the basin, where there are several sustainable swaps you can make.

Plastic cotton tips for bamboo cotton tips

Many states in Australia – and countries around the world – have banned or are phasing out plastic-stemmed cotton tips. Hallelujah!

The plastic stems themselves aren't recyclable as they are too small and thin, so many of them end up on our beaches and in our waterways. I remember doing a beach clean one day and thinking traditional lollipops were making a huge comeback only to discover the little plastic sticks were actually left over from used cotton buds.

You can buy reusable ear scrapers, or simply switch to buds with a bamboo stem instead.

Plastic toothbrushes for bamboo toothbrushes

Plastic toothbrushes are an absolute nightmare. They are made up of so many different materials: the stem, bristles, grip and lots of colours. This makes them really hard to recycle and, on top of that, it is estimated that plastic toothbrushes take approximately three hundred years to break down in landfill. Then, even when they do, it is only into those tiny microplastics, so they never really go away.

Shower time

The recommended duration of a household shower is four minutes, which could be a little shorter than you might be used to. A hack that I love is to play your favourite four-minute song while you shower, then when it ends, you know it's time to wrap it up.

Be conscious of your water consumption, too; it's finite not infinite! Shorter showers also cut serious dollars off your bill, with the average shower using 16 litres (4 gallons) of water per minute – it all adds up!

If you're an extreme water-saver you'll shower over a bucket or save the water in the bottom of the bathtub and use it to water your plants.

So far, I haven't been able to find a completely compostable alternative that is dentist approved. All of the bristles that are made from natural materials get a thumbs down, but a good halfway-house solution is to use a brush where the handle is made from a compostable material like bamboo or wheat straw. This means that when you're finished with it you can snap off the head and throw the base in your compost or the garden and will only need to bin the plastic head.

Toothpaste tubes for toothpaste in a jar

It is super exciting to see that some toothpaste brands are switching to tubes that are just made from one material, meaning that they can be recycled in your curbside bin (check the back of the tube to see if it applies to your brand). Otherwise, these tubes need to go to landfill or to specialty recycling centres.

Have you heard of toothpaste in a jar? These little pots of paste can be curbside-recycled, keeping both the planet and your teeth clean. There are plenty of recipes out there to make your own toothpaste, too, but I can never get it to taste quite right. One jar is the equivalent of three plastic tubes of toothpaste, so you're (almost) making money by switching!

Dental floss for compostable vegan floss

We don't often think about it – or, at least I never did – but dental floss is actually silk lined or coated with PTFEs, which is a type of plastic most commonly known as Teflon.

As much as we'd love to skip flossing, dentists just won't have it, but rather than flossing your teeth with the nasty coated stuff, look for a compostable alternative. Many sustainable flosses will use either beeswax or a vegan alternative ingredient instead of plastic. Additionally, you can buy refillable floss canisters, resulting in even less waste. And the good news? They're not much more expensive than your standard dental floss!

Toilet paper

It's estimated that each year over 1 million trees are cut down just to make toilet paper. Even if you're using one-ply, it adds up! Plus, it's often bleached white with toxic chemicals.

Recycled toilet paper, on the other hand, is made from recycled paper, such as office paper and textbooks, and switching to using recycled uses 50 per cent less energy and 90 per cent less water than bog-standard toilet roll (see what I did there?).

Bamboo toilet paper, on the other hand, uses a resource that grows quickly and doesn't use as much water as traditional toilet paper to produce, but still involves chopping down trees. It's a far better alternative, but is often imported depending on how much bamboo is grown locally. Right now, bamboo toilet paper is, at the very least, cost-competitive, so while you're not saving money, you're getting a much more planet-friendly product for the same price.

Beauty swaps

Curating a more sustainable makeup and beauty routine is easier said than done. We are all working with different budgets, as well as skin types, needs and levels of complexity (are you a wash-and-go person, or one who has a 19,371-step beauty routine?).

If you've already got a stack of products at home, I'd recommend using these first before making any switches. It's tempting to have a massive clean-out of the products you no longer feel aligned with but it's much more environmentally friendly to use up the ones you've already spent money on first.

When you are ready to make your switches, I suggest creating a personal priority list. It's really hard to check absolutely every sustainability box, but having a priority list can help guide your decisions.

As a starting point, list the items to the right in order of importance from one through to ten. This will look different for everyone and there are no wrong answers. To be honest, it will be very, very difficult for any of your purchases to meet all the criteria, but understanding what your personal priorities are can help when it comes to finding new products.

Create your own priority list

- Price
- Vegan
- Cruelty-free certification
- Quality
- Australian made (or equivalent)
- Female founded
- Plastic free
- Packaging free
- Refillable
- Fragrance free

Beauty expiry dates

Yes, you read that correctly: your beauty products actually have expiry dates! They don't have a shelf life like food, but as soon as you open them the clock starts ticking – and they're an open invitation to create waste.

To make sure you get the greatest lifespan out of your products, only open new ones when your current ones are completely finished. This simple trick alone can really cut down on your waste.

My top tip is to use a marker and write on the back or bottom of an item when you open it. If the time bomb has gone off and your product expired back in the nineties, squeeze any remaining product into the bin, not the sink, before disposing of the packaging so as not to pollute waterways any further.

Beauty all-rounders

One of my biggest hacks when overhauling your beauty product stash is having as many multi-purpose products as possible. It cuts down on costs and keeps your routine clutter free. Look for quality all-rounders and let them do the heavy lifting for you.

TEA TREE OIL

I fell for the essential oil pyramid scheme a couple of years ago and I am sure more than a few people reading this book also fell for it, too. These days, I don't use them as frequently, but I do have one or two that I still see the benefit in, and one of these is tea tree oil.

Tea tree oil has been used for hundreds if not thousands of years as a natural antiseptic. Better yet, it is abundantly available in Australia, so it won't cost you an arm and a leg.

Here are some ways to use it:
- **Apply** a drop directly to pimples and acne to reduce redness and irritation.
- **Rub** directly onto athlete's foot or toe fungus.
- **Add** a few drops to your shampoo to help relieve dandruff.
- **Rub** directly onto an itchy spot or bug bite (it's also great for people with eczema).
- **Add** to a body moisturiser or oil and rub into ingrown hairs.

Tip

Always do a spot test on your arm to make sure your skin won't react to a highly concentrated essential oil. If you need to dilute it, simply add one or two drops to a tablespoon or two of warm water.

ALL-PURPOSE BALM

As the name suggests, an all-purpose balm (like Lucas' Pawpaw Ointment) is an absolute must for anyone wanting to get back to basics with their beauty routine. It's the one product that I never leave the house without. I also have some by my bed, in my handbag and in my office drawer. This is one of my favourite beauty hacks, as you get twelve products for the price of one.

Off the top of my head here are a dozen ways that I have used my balm just this week:

1. Moisturised lips
2. Softened cuticles
3. Set eyebrows
4. Highlighted cheeks
5. Tamed flyaway hairs
6. Added gloss to a matte lipstick
7. Soothed insect bites
8. Treated cracked elbows
9. Eased chaffing
10. Removed eye makeup
11. Turned powdered makeup into a cream
12. Soothed a dry, red nose during a cold

HIGHLIGHTER CREAM

Another item in my all-rounder, money-saving beauty kit is a highlighter stick. My highlighter is among my top three most used beauty products. I love the instant glow and lift it provides – I feel like a real-life Golden Globe Award. Okay well, I don't put that much on, but I do use it on my clavicles, under my brows, as an eye shadow and on my cheekbones, so maybe wear your sunnies. Ultimately, the fewer products you use the less waste you create! Keep it simple and save those dollary-doos.

Minimise your makeup brush collection

To be honest, I haven't found a great sustainable solution for makeup brushes, but those made from horsehair (with preferably a wooden handle) definitely trump those made from synthetic (read plastic) bristles with plastic handles. Simplifying your brush collection and using fewer brushes for multiple jobs will also minimise financial and environmental costs.

Keeping your brushes clean will also help them last longer. See page 109 for how to give them a good wash.

Tip

When selecting an all-purpose balm, beware of petroleum-based products. As the name suggests, they use petrol chemicals to create lubrication. Some balms also contain animal products, so if you're vegan, make sure you look closely at the label before buying.

ACTIVITY: BEAUTY DRAWER DECLUTTER

Often, we forget what products we even own because they're lurking at the back of a drawer. So, before you go out and spend more on new products, I recommend you do a bit of a declutter and see what you already have that can be used up.

When I organise my bathroom cupboard, I rearrange the items from most to least used, which for me means skincare at the front and makeup at the back. Everyone's routine is different, but here are some tips for getting the most out of every product:

· **Slice tubes and open bottles** to get out every last drop. You'd be surprised at how much is still in there. Use two bobby pins (hair grips) as a slider on the end of each tube to help get every last bit out.

· **If you have any unopened products** that you don't think you'll use, why not see if a friend or family member would like to have them instead of throwing them away?

You might find it helpful to organise your products by routines, e.g. daytime, night time, makeup, etc. I like to repurpose old jars or containers for storing brushes and grouping items together.

No-tox beauty recipes

Another way to save some serious dollar is to make your own beauty products. (Hint: it also saves on environment- and health-damaging parabens and palm oil.)

Here are a couple of easy recipes that use ingredients you probably already have in your pantry.

Remember, if you're reusing containers (go you, good thing) to store your home-made products, just make sure they are nice and clean. I run mine through the dishwasher or fill them with boiling water to make sure they're sterile before I start.

COFFEE SCRUB

Anyone who knows me knows how much I love coffee, so it comes as no surprise that I will happily bathe in it – and you should too. Give your left-over coffee grounds a second lease of life and use them as a natural exfoliator. Much better than scrubs packed full of toxic chemicals and plastic microbeads! Coffee scrubs have been made and used for centuries, and the caffeine helps to calm inflammation in the skin.

If your oil is solid, gently melt it in quick twenty-second bursts in the microwave, or melt it in a saucepan on the stove.

Slowly add the oil to the coffee grounds, a little at a time. Depending on the ratio of salt to coffee and how dry your coffee is (the drier the better), you may need a little less.

Add the essential oil, then place your scrub in a sealed glass jar or container to store.

Simply wet your body in the shower or bath, turn off the tap and rub the coffee scrub from head to toe in circular motions. Be careful when using it not to get too much water in the jar, as this can cause mould to form.

NOTE

* Some essential oil combinations that I love are citrus, rosemary and tea tree, and lavender and chamomile.

200 g (7 oz) coconut or jojoba oil (not olive oil)

200 g (7 oz) dried coffee grounds (or use salt if you prefer)

10 drops essential oil of your choice (see Note)

DRY SHAMPOO

I love the convenience of dry shampoo, but not the added chemicals, expensive price tags, synthetic fragrances and aerosol cans. The premise is great, and using dry shampoo means shorter showers, which I'm also a big fan of, so ditch the chemical stuff and make your own cheap and effective alternative.

Combine the cornflour and cacao powder in a jar and seal. To use, apply to your roots with a fluffy brush.

Equal parts cornflour (cornstarch) and either cinnamon (for redheads), ground ginger (for blondes) or cacao powder (for brunettes)

Sustainable treatments

Another cost that adds up is your regular beauty appointments and treatments. Not only do they put a dent in your bank account, but many of these treatments use chemicals that are damaging to the environment and produce a lot of waste.

Save these appointments for special occasions and learn how to give yourself the five-star treatment at home instead.

Swap manicures and pedicures for at-home treatments

My feet are so ticklish that I tend to avoid pedicures anyway in order to avoid giving anyone a black eye!

Not only that, but the cost of these treatments really adds up if you get them regularly. Studies are also starting to come out that show the damage that UV lamps wreak on your skin, not to mention the toxic chemicals used in most industry-standard nail polishes and removers. (Not many people know that shellac is made from the secretion of the lac insect, and 100,000 bugs die for every 450 g/1 lb of shellac made.)

You can pay up to $80 for a professional manicure, whereas a pot of non-toxic nail polish costs around $15. If you get a monthly manicure, that's a saving of $780 a year!

Swap waxing for laser hair removal

Not only is waxing one of the most eye-wateringly painful experiences you can pay someone to inflict upon you, but it also produces an astonishing amount of waste with all the used strips.

Laser hair removal, on the other hand, uses a laser beam to remove hair at the root. The up-front cost is similar to waxing, but once you have completed your 'course', you only need to go back a few times a year, which reduces your costs significantly.

Swap waxing for threading

One of the beauty treatments I still head to the salon for is eyebrow threading. It only uses a small piece of cotton and costs about $20 every couple of months. No need for toxic and expensive waxing treatments!

Nail polish remover

There's a reason you can't recycle nail polish remover bottles – it's because the chemicals in the remover make the plastic too toxic to recycle. Instead of putting these chemicals on your skin and nails (where it will be absorbed into your body), use one or two drops of pure lemongrass essential oil on each nail, leave for 1 minute, then rub off using a reusable cotton round. It's cheaper and a lot healthier. You'll hear that acetone-free nail polish removers are better, but be aware that they use ethyl acetate, which is another toxic chemical.

Tip

Be a guinea pig. If you aren't too pedantic about your beauty treatments, have a look to see if your local TAFE or beauty school offers discounted (if not free) treatments for everything from massages to waxes, tinting and haircuts. They get to practise, and you get a free treatment. It also pays to sign up to your hairdresser's mailing list; I often get discount codes sent straight to my inbox.

Hair dye

Colour me pink! You may as well be dyeing your hair with liquid gold considering the cost of hair treatments these days. I understand that for some it might be a necessity, but here are some things to consider.

Firstly, it should go without saying that hair dye is essentially a chemical cocktail designed to permanently change your hair's natural colour – and that's only after it has been bleached first to create a blank canvas. These harsh chemicals can damage and dry out your hair, and even turn it green! Not just that, but they get washed into our waterways, too.

Embracing your natural colour or greying hair is one of the easiest and boldest ways to save money when it comes to hair treatments. It also prevents unnecessary use of toxic hair dye. But if you still insist on covering up with colour, try spreading out your visits a bit. Let's say, for the sake of example, your monthly cut, colour and blow dry sets you back $280 a visit. For those who don't dye their hair, a trim every so often should suffice.

Tip
Hair conditioner masks for the win! I simply use coconut oil on the tips of my hair to nourish the ends, which keeps my hair healthier and stronger and allows for more time between haircuts.

Case study – Sustainable salons: When you think about it, salons produce a lot of waste (and most of it not planet friendly): hair foils, toxic hair dye, plastic shampoo bottles – the list goes on and on! I always feel so overwhelmed by the waste, which is why I prefer sustainable salons.

Sustainable salons are a social enterprise that helps salons better manage their waste. They collect the metal from hair foils and plastic from shampoo bottles to recycle. They even collect hair trimmings, which are used to help soak up oil spills in the ocean.

Sustainable salons have a directory that you can use to find a sustainable salon near you, so give one a try.

Storage

In order to use your products, you need to see them. Out of sight is out of mind, meaning useful products go unused or are replaced unnecessarily. So, I always suggest a beauty declutter (see page 130) followed by a revamp of your storage system. Group items into routines and reuse jars and containers. Make sure all products are well sealed to prevent them drying out, and check the use-by dates to ensure you're using short-date items first.

To rebuy or refill?

I am often asked if it's better to buy a new skincare item in a glass or firm plastic container, or a plastic refill pouch, which is technically harder to recycle? What you need to consider here is not only the recyclability of the product but also the carbon required to make, fill and transport it. On average refillable pouches save 70–80 per cent on carbon emissions. Not to mention that purchasing refills will also save you money. Check to see if the brand offers an incentive for sending back your refillable pouches.

ACTIONABLE STEPS

- [ ] Do a bathroom declutter (see page 130)
- [ ] DIY your next beauty treatment
- [ ] Make at least one old-school swap, such as using a loofah sponge
- [ ] Make your own beauty product
- [ ] Try out a plastic-free period product
- [ ] Have a palm oil–free shop
- [ ] Extend the length of time before your next salon visit

NEXT UP

It's easy to feel overwhelmed once it is pointed out to you all the ways our everyday products and behaviours are harming the environment. However, small changes add up, so think about what feels achievable for you to implement and start there.

Remember, living more sustainably is not a quick fix, it's a journey, and chipping away at the problem adds up to big savings both for your bank account and the environment. You don't need to dump your whole bathroom cabinet in favour of a suite of new products. This is about making gradual, mindful shifts.

Hand in hand with beauty is fashion, and while most people with an environmental conscience are already shunning fast fashion, there is more we can do to make our fashion choices and shopping behaviours friendlier to the environment and to our wallets.

7.

It's fashun, darling: the rise of the slow fashion movement

Savings scale

SAVE
UP TO
$75 A MONTH

Level 1
Do a responsible declutter.
Go shopping at an op-shop (thrift store).
Borrow an item of clothing from a friend.

SAVE
UP TO
$150 A MONTH

+ Level 2
Start mending your own clothes.
Host a clothes swap event.

SAVE
UP TO
$210 A MONTH

+ Level 3
Go on a three, six or twelve-month fashion fast.

Yes, you read that correctly: $3500 a year is what you could save on your clothes spend by doing nothing. That's the beauty of this chapter; one of the biggest action points that will add up to meaningful savings is to simply do nothing. The less you do (consume), the more you save (both planet and money).

But, I get it: saying no to fashion is easy in theory, not so much in practice. Fashion emergencies spring up like real-life ones: out of nowhere. It could be an unexpected invitation to a big event that requires a new outfit, or an emotional late-night browse of an online mega-retailer. Knowing how to respond in these scenarios is just a sustainability muscle you have to learn to flex, and I'm going to show you how.

If you're reading this book, chances are good that you already have an awareness of the myriad ways the fashion industry is negatively impacting the environment. But before you skip over this section, take note, because I'm going to show you exactly how you can turn your fast fashion habit into history. This chapter covers everything, from what's in your clothes and how to repair and rewear them, to how to snag the best op-shop (thrift store) buys.

Here's a fun story for you. While I was working at a magazine in Sydney, I took on a quiet challenge: to have a complete fashion 'fast' and not buy any new clothes for a year. And here's why ...

Have you heard?

* The average person wears just one-third of their wardrobe.

* Each year the average Australian purchases 27 kilograms (59 pounds) of textiles and throws out approximately 23 kilograms (50 pounds)!

* In 2017–19 the secondhand fashion industry grew 21 times faster than traditional retail.

* Globally it is estimated that 35 per cent of microplastics released into the ocean come from synthetic textiles.

* The fashion industry is responsible for producing 92 million tonnes of waste annually.

* Between 80 and 100 billion items of clothing are made globally each year.

* Wearing a garment for an extra 9 months reduces its footprint by 20 per cent.

It's pretty staggering when you look at the real-world effects this single industry is having on our planet.

So many of us are addicted to fashion and jumping on the latest trends that making meaningful changes to how we consume fashion can feel difficult, but it's an essential step towards living more sustainably – and it adds up to huge financial savings, too.

I'll admit that I took a bit of a 'go big or go home' approach to addressing my fashion consumption. I started by unsubscribing and unfollowing as many fashion brands as I could to remove the temptation and pressure to conform to the latest trends. Every time I was invited to a new major event, I browsed the depths of my wardrobe and I steered well clear of shopping malls.

When I looked up ten months later and shared my fashion 'fast' with friends and colleagues, they all admitted they hadn't noticed my lack of 'new' or 'trendy' clothing.

One of my favourite outcomes of the fashion fast was sharing clothes with my girlfriends. When we were teens with little spending money and questionable taste, we operated our wardrobes on an open-closet basis, meaning we all borrowed each other's clothes. It made no sense that as we got older and were able to afford far nicer pieces that the door on our wardrobes suddenly closed. All of my friends were more than happy to share wardrobes again, which made dressing for events and functions in particular so much easier, and helped me not to feel bored by my own stock of clothing.

Another positive outcome was a clothes-swapping night that I hosted. Every guest was tasked with bringing five pieces of clothing, we each then took it in turns to pick an item and walked away with five 'new' pieces. A couple of items that were left over were donated to my local op-shop (thrift store). It was a shopping night without the price tags or overstimulating fluorescent lights!

So much time, money (and tears) were saved as a result of this fashion fast. And the hours I would have spent browsing the racks were put to much better use understanding how I could progress my project of consuming fashion more sustainably. I also found it incredibly empowering, and not having to make endless decisions about what to wear really reduced my mental load.

If you want to consume less fashion, an obvious place to start is giving more thought at the time of purchase instead of wondering what to do with a mountain of cheap clothes you will probably only wear once.

Buying new

One of my favourite fashion mantras is that 'the most sustainable piece of clothing is the one you already own', meaning that the simplest and most sustainable approach to fashion is utilising what you already have – what you've already consumed – before considering buying new, or even secondhand.

    As you learned from the stats on page 139, we actually only wear about 30 per cent of our wardrobe on high rotation. The rest collects dust (hopefully not moths) and is only worn occasionally. In saying that, there will be times when you want – and, more importantly, need – to buy new clothing, and it's how and what you purchase that will make the biggest environmental and financial impact.

> 'So many of us are addicted to fashion and jumping on the latest trends that making meaningful changes to how we consume fashion can feel difficult.'

Purchasing right

Honestly, before I started living consciously, I was that person who loved a bargain (I still do love a bargain, just not the fast fashion kind). I was always on the hunt for the cheapest item with little thought about the environmental impact of my purchase of a garment, or the working conditions of the person who made it. But, on my journey, I've been able to find a balance between the environmental, humanitarian and economic costs.

Now my purchasing process looks a whole lot different and before I buy anything new, I ask myself:
· **Who** made this?
· **What** is it made from?
· **How** often will I wear it?
· **Where** will it end up when I am finished with it?

When it comes to choosing brands and clothing there isn't a 'green tick of approval' to look out for. Instead, look for these:
· External certifications like GOTS and B Corp (see page 148)
· A clear sustainability or impact report, which should be readily available from the brand and include external certifications or reporting metrics
· Transparency about the brand's sustainability journey within their communications, aka what are they aiming for
· Specific types of fabrics that are better for the planet

Fabrics fable

When buying new clothes, there is a lot to consider when it comes to fabrics. Not only will good-quality materials last longer, but fabrics made from plastic break off tiny fragments of microplastic whenever you wash them (see page 103). It's also difficult to understand exactly what blends are going to turn the dial on climate change.

If you do have clothes made from polyester cotton blends (I would be shocked if you didn't – most people do), then keep on wearing them. If they're stained, keep them for wearing around the house, and you'll eventually be able to cut them up and use them as rags.

Garments made from high-quality materials often come with a larger upfront price tag, but if you consider the cost per wear of these items over their lifetime, they usually work out cheaper. I manage this upfront cost by only purchasing one new garment at a time and saving up for it. This also allows me a window to consider if it's actually the right purchase for me and time to check up on a brand's sustainability credentials.

GLOBAL MATERIAL PRODUCTION 2018

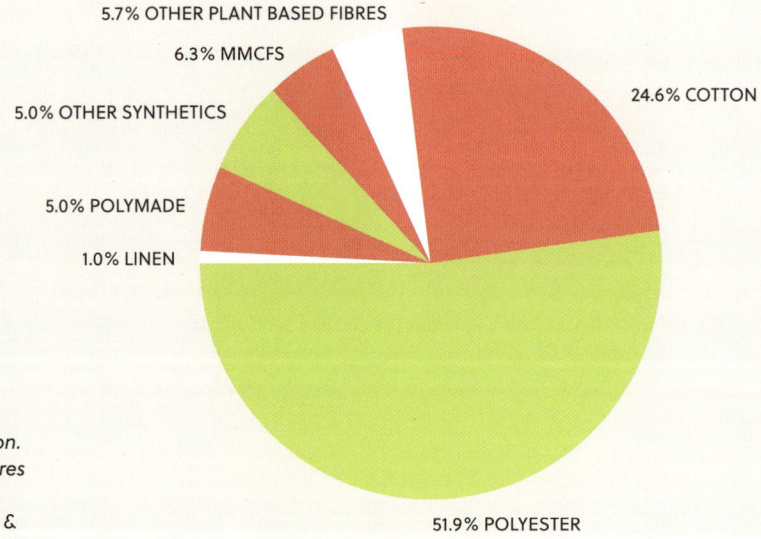

5.7% OTHER PLANT BASED FIBRES

6.3% MMCFS

5.0% OTHER SYNTHETICS

5.0% POLYMADE

1.0% LINEN

24.6% COTTON

51.9% POLYESTER

MMCFs = Man-made cellulose fibres, e.g. viscose, Tencel and rayon. Other planet-based fibres = jute, linen and hemp. Source: Preferred Fiber & Materials Report, 2019

As you can see from the pie chart, plastic and synthetic fibres make up well over half of global material production. These materials are made from fossil fuels, and their production alone contributes millions of tonnes of greenhouse gases each year, causing a lasting impact on the planet. I've divided up fourteen of the most common fabrics into three categories – regenerative, semi-synthetic and synthetic – below to demonstrate and explain the financial and environmental pros and cons of each category.

Right now, we're hugely reliant on polyester. This is the material you'll find in the majority of your clothing, because it bends, breathes easily and is stain-resistant. This might sound like a dream material, but, in reality, polyester is plastic. When you wear it, you're inhaling tiny fragments of microplastics, and when you wash it, even more microplastics drain into our waterways.

Regenerative fashion

Regenerative fashion is a term used to describe fashion that promotes the restoration and regeneration of the environment through farming practices that improve soil health and biodiversity in comparison to other farming methods that leave soils depleted. At the heart of regenerative fashion is the creme de la creme of textiles: natural fabrics, like linen and hemp. They are breathable, lightweight and sustainable, and have so many great properties that it's easy to see why we've been using them for centuries.

Regenerative fashion researcher, Lucianne Tonti, explains that 'we can regenerate landscapes when we make these products if they're farmed correctly'.

Most of the fabrics that fall under 'regenerative fashion' have been used for hundreds if not thousands of years. You see, so much of living more sustainably really just involves a return to traditional methods and practices. And, in this case, materials. Pieces made from natural textiles are durable and affordable if you shop locally. Similar to food miles, the shorter the distance your clothing needs to travel, the more cost effective it is.

Duck, duck, goose

Around the globe, there are increasing concerns about animal welfare when it comes to down. Seventy-five to 90 per cent of down is made from duck feathers, with the remainder coming from geese. The Responsible Down Standard (RDS) and Traceable Down Standard (TDS) are the most commonly recognised certifications that ensure there is:

- No live plucking
- No force feeding
- Adherence to welfare standards

Some of the biggest manufacturers of down have committed to use 100 per cent RDS- or TDS-certified down, for example Patagonia, North Face, Kathmandu, Columbia, Ralph Lauren and HUGO BOSS.

If you are going to purchase clothing made from down, look for these standards. Generally speaking, I find that down comes with a larger price tag so is something I prefer to buy secondhand.

Silky story

Silk is an animal-based fibre that has been used for thousands of years dating back to 6500 BC, and it's a divisive topic in fashion and sustainability circles.

Silk thread is made from silkworm larvae cocoons. However, the harvesting process is rather grim. To obtain the sticky protein to make silk thread, the larvae and cocoons are boiled and sadly die. Workers then brush and remove the silk filament from the boiled-down larvae to unravel the silk strands onto a reel. It is then twisted, rolled and dyed before the yarn can be used to create silk fabric.

Not only do people have issues with the boiling of larvae, but 187 kilograms (412 pounds) of mulberry leaves are needed to feed enough silkworms to produce just 1 kilogram (2 pounds) of silk. There are also human rights concerns, with few silk producers sharing details about the working conditions of silk farmers.

Silk is the strongest fibre and will last forever but, for me personally, the cost to the animal and the consumer just doesn't stack up. If you do purchase silk, I suggest looking for a secondhand option.

Semi-synthetic fabrics

This middle category of fabrics is a bit of a tricky one. These materials are often spruiked as eco friendly, and while they are better than fossil fuel-based materials, they still aren't particularly sustainable. As Tonti explains, 'these will still biodegrade because they're made from cellulose, but because they're derived from trees, they can be problematic.' For example, 200 million trees are logged every year to make viscose, one of the most commonly used semi-synthetic fabrics.

FABRIC	MADE FROM	FEELS LIKE	USED IN
Hemp	Stems of the cannabis plant	Breathable, lightweight	Bedding, suits, pants
Cotton	Fluffy fibre of the cotton plant	Stretchy, soft	T-shirts, underwear
Linen	Stem of the flax plant	Antibacterial, 2–3x stronger than cotton, absorbent, little elasticity	Bedding, tablecloths, shirts, suits, dresses and pants
Wool	Goat or sheep	Warm, breathable, antimicrobial	Jumpers (sweaters), socks and thermals
Cashmere	Cashmere goat silky undercoat	Soft and silky	Jumpers (sweaters)
Down	75–90 per cent from duck feathers	Lightweight, fluffy	Puffer jackets, pillows and doona (duvet) covers
Silk	Silkworms	Super soft, but the strongest protein fibre	Bedding, intimates, dresses

FABRIC	MADE FROM	FEELS LIKE	USED IN
Viscose (a subtype of rayon)	Tree wood pulp (eucalyptus, beech and pine) paired with masses of chemicals	Looks like silk, feels like cotton and is breathable	Dresses, tops and sometimes synthetic velvet
Rayon	Purified cellulose fibres	Takes on properties of cotton and wool, often blended with other fabrics	Dressier clothing
Bamboo	Cellulose extracted from bamboo	Can be used in similar applications to cotton	Bedding, clothing
Tencel	Type of rayon but usually made from sustainable sources of eucalyptus wood pulp and chemicals	Breathable, moisture-wicking	Bedding, clothing
Leather	Animal hide	Soft, durable	Outerwear

Synthetic materials

The bottom of the barrel would have to be synthetic textiles. These are 100 per cent synthetic materials derived from fossil fuels, meaning that for every garment made fossil fuels are burnt. They are also extremely difficult to recycle due to their complex weave, which makes them destined to litter the earth for hundreds of years.

From a practical perspective, they are also prone to holding onto body odours and stains in comparison to natural materials that breathe more easily.

FABRIC	MADE FROM	FEELS LIKE	USED IN
Polyester (polyethylene terephthalate, PET, microfibre)	Polymers derived from fossil fuels (petroleum)	Soft but strong, easy to wash, most commonly blended with cotton	Just about everything
Nylon	Man made from petrol chemicals	Durable, elastic and waterproof materials	Activewear, underwear, carpeting, raincoats, stockings

When plastic degrades

More and more products are being produced using recycled materials, which is a really big step in the right direction. But (yes, there's always a but), as plastics are recycled, their quality degrades. Threads used in clothing are often mixed with other plastic-based materials, meaning that when they're washed, microplastics break off in the process and end up in our waterways and oceans.

Tip

If you have jackets that you love that are made from polyester but are starting to smell, make yourself some underarm patches from a 100 per cent natural-fibre cloth. It will save on washing and halt any odours that might be getting set in to the fabric.

Certifications

To avoid walking headlong into a greenwashing booby trap when purchasing textiles, the most responsible thing that you can do is look for third-party certification. Like anything when it comes to sourcing sustainable products, you need to do some digging beyond the face value of a brand. Keep an eye out for the following:

· **Global Organic Textile Standards (GOTS)** is the global certifying body for textiles. It examines the entire textile supply chain against ecological and social criteria. The label certifies that the item is comprised of at least 70 per cent certified organic fibres. If a brand has obtained GOTS, they will usually want to brag about it, so it should be easy to find.

· **B Corporation** certification examines and scores businesses across a plethora of industries. It doesn't just evaluate environmental impact but also governance, community, customers and workers. Businesses must score above eighty to reach B-Corp status, and legally change their constitution to state that they consider the planet when doing business.

· **Forest Stewardship Council (FSC)** is mostly related to paper, but some textiles as well. Seeing this standard means that you know that the tree used to make your product wasn't slashed from an ancient or endangered forest.

· **Ethical Clothing Australia (ECA)** is Australia's leading accreditation body for businesses. They map and look at a business's supply chain to ensure that all ethical standards are met. Specifically, they look into the conditions of workers or those working from home who are particularly vulnerable to long hours, workplace health and safety issues and unrealistic deadlines.

Returns to ruins

Another thing that I think we're all guilty of at some time or another is something called bracketing. Bracketing is when you're shopping online and you purchase either multiple sizes or colours of the same item. You try them all on and then return what doesn't suit you. On the one hand, returning unwanted items cuts down waste, but on the other, the logistics involved make it an environmental nightmare.

Tip

Download the Good On You app. It is a great resource that allows you to filter brands by values, and gives an overview of each company's environmental and ethical practices at a glance.

The return rate for clothing purchased online is between 30 and 40 per cent. That means for every three pieces of clothing purchased at least one is returned, which means not only carbon emissions for sending the first parcel, but yet more for returning it.

As part of my research for this book, I was devastated to discover that due to the high cost of labour and low production cost of many fast-fashion items, it is often cheaper for brands to dispose of returns rather than paying someone to check, refold, repack and restock the items. I'm talking brand-new items of clothing straight into landfill.

So, what can you do? Purchase wisely, do your best to figure out your size before you buy, and stick to it. Making more critical decisions at the checkout means fewer carbon emissions and cutting the risk that your unwanted items end up in landfill. Rather than buying everything in your cart so you have 'options', buy a few, well-considered items at a time. If you're confused about the size guide, don't hesitate to contact the company for clarification, and keep a tape measure handy for checking your measurements as size guides vary wildly.

Seduced by sales

Another step towards purchasing right is managing your mindset around sales.

Brands will often have a sale if they see their profits slipping, but the majority of them are influenced by a predictable yearly sales calendar (see right). Sales can send people into a frenzy buying more than they need (spoiler: this is the whole point), but holding firm on your sustainability values will see you snag some bargains without causing more harm to the environment.

- **January**
  January sales
- **March**
  End-of-season sale (fashion mostly)
- **April**
  Afterpay
- **May**
  Click Frenzy
- **June**
  EOFY sales
- **July**
  Fourth of July (US)
- **August**
  Click Frenzy
- **September**
  End-of-season sale (fashion mostly)
  Labour Day (US)
- **November**
  Black Friday/ Cyber Monday
- **December**
  Boxing Day sales

What you can do differently

Buying new is one thing, but what if I told you there are numerous ways to upgrade your wardrobe without buying off the shelf?

Forget trends

It's time to unsubscribe from fashion trends. In my 30 years on this earth, I have already experienced low-rise jeans going from the epitome of cool to uncool and back again. The cyclical nature of trends is unsustainable, which is why I'm opting out of them altogether.

When you consider this alongside the money spent on clothes and the cost to the environment to produce them, it's better just to shop for your body shape, skin tone and personal style over jumping on the bandwagon. I've been wearing the same pair of jeans (yes, they are skinny jeans) for the last five years and no one has batted an eyelid.

When I am purchasing something, I avoid prints because I would argue that prints date more than any solid colour ever will. Also, I prefer to buy matching sets over dresses, which means the top and bottom halves can be mixed and matched to create different outfits, giving me three different uses from each set.

One of my good friends Alex once gave me a very wise piece of advice. She said choose whether you're going to be a 'print on the bottom' or 'print on the top' person and stick with it. This means you've got more options to wear your plain bottoms with your printed tops and vice versa. A genius, I tell you!

Clothes mending

My one-year fashion fast actually ended up being two – humble brag, I know! The second year I loosened the constraints a little and allowed myself to op-shop (thrift) for necessities and purchased a couple of pairs of brand new knickers.

Another wholesome outcome was that my mum dusted off her sewing machine and got back on the tools. Her love language is gifting, so spurred on by the fact that she couldn't buy me any new clothes, she got back into making them like she had done for my brother and I when we were kids. While there were no pairs of matching overalls that came out of it (shame), I was gifted two hand-made dresses with matching scrunchies and a set of flannelette pyjamas! Thanks, Mum!

This brings me to mending. (You knew this one was coming.) I'm not saying you need to rush out and buy a sewing machine and learn how to cut and sew complicated patterns. Just that learning how to perform some basic running repairs will keep your items in circulation for longer, saving you money and fashion waste.

Once again, it's about rethinking how we do things and returning to a more traditional approach to making and maintaining our belongings that is, almost by accident, heavily sustainable.

I haven't picked up Mum's knack for creative sewing (yet), but I have taught myself a couple of basic sewing skills that have been a real money-saver.

The three basic stitches below allow me to mend most things with nothing more than a needle and thread (which I picked up in a hotel sanitary kit).

1. **Running stitch** is probably the easiest and most commonly used, and it's best for hemming clothes.

2. **A slip stitch** is an invisible stitch. I like to use it for small holes and when you need to make an item smaller.

3. **Back stitch**, as the name suggests, it means looping back on the stitch so there are no holes or gaps. Back stitching is one of the most secure stitches.

Another handy stitch to learn is how to sew on buttons. When purchasing new clothing, stash that baggie with the spare button. Next time a button falls off an item of clothing, shop your stash of loose spare buttons. You might not find an exact match, but there'll be one similar enough to use (and exactly zero people will notice!).

ACTIVITY: CLOTHES SWAP

Host your own clothes-swapping night! I personally find this works best with five or six people. Put on a platter of nibbles, grab a bottle of wine (or two) and have a catch-up with your friends, then do a clothes swap. It is so much fun; one person's trash really is another one's treasure! If your friends aren't up for the challenge, you can join in on organised clothes-swapping events. Have a google or look on social media for one in your area.

Footwork

Speaking of mending things, one thing that I do recommend finding is a good cobbler to fix your shoes. Shoes are notoriously difficult to recycle because they are made up of so many different materials. For example, a single shoe can be made up of a rubber sole, leather lining, foam cushion and metal eyelets. But a good cobbler will be able to transform your tired, worn shoes into something that's almost brand new. Make sure you buy a good-quality pair to start with and do the maintenance work in between by using a waterproofer and maintaining your leather with a quality shoe polish or beeswax leather conditioner.

Dress-up box

When we were kids we had a dress-up box at home filled with some of Mum's old dresses, odd bits of fabric and different dress-ups we collected over the years. This box is something I miss so much when I have a dress-up party coming up. Now, when I do have a themed party to attend, I firstly shop my own wardrobe and friends' wardrobes before heading to the local op-shop (thrift store) for any complementary items I need to complete the look. And here's a tip: make sure these are things you can use again or team with regular clothes to get the most out of each purchase.

Building a capsule wardrobe

Think of a capsule wardrobe like your pantry staples. It's the everyday essentials you need to function, then you can add some flavour and spice with some extra flair (or flares).

The one downside to having a capsule wardrobe (in my mind) is that we're in danger of looking like every other girl on Pinterest, so be unapologetic about making it your own, and remember that 'capsule' doesn't have to mean basic, everyday clothing.

Devilish denim

It sounds like a bold statement, but I will never buy brand-new denim again. Denim is one of the thirstiest, most environmentally intensive fabrics out there. It takes around 3870 litres (1022 gallons) of water to produce a single pair of jeans. Don't get me wrong; I love a good pair of jeans, but their impact on the planet is monstrous. Not only are they made from cotton, (a crop that requires enormous amounts of water and pesticides to grow), but the dyeing process uses toxic chemicals. And even though jeans are predominantly made of cotton, many pairs include some of kind of elastic (plastic) thread to make them stretchy.

The best thing about denim is its longevity. My dad still proudly wears his denim jeans, which have come in and out of fashion more times than I care to think about, and have now almost faded to white.

If we all just kept our denim in circulation, I don't think we'd need to make any more. Surely skinny jeans will come back in soon, so pass yours on to an op-shop (thrift store) for when the low-rise skinnies hit the trend circuit (again). This is an example of where we can see the principles of a circular economy at play, keeping an item in circulation for many moons to come.

How to cull correctly

My golly, do we love a good cleanse and declutter! While I am all for people sorting out their possessions to understand exactly what they have (and use them up!), clean-outs do produce a lot of waste. Think hard about what you can reuse, rewear, repurpose or regift to someone else before throwing it away.

If you've already spent your hard-earned dime on something, make doubly sure you're not going to need or want it in the future before getting rid of it (and having to buy it all over again). I don't mean become a hoarder, just think ahead – and maybe invest in some more storage options.

Once you've tidied up your wardrobe, keep it organised so you can see what you've got, which will make it much more likely that

Capsule wardrobe ideas

Feminine
- 2 pairs everyday jeans or pants
- 1 warm coat
- 1–2 simple unbranded T-shirts
- 1 long-sleeved collared shirt
- 1 jumper (sweater)
- 1 blazer or jacket
- 1 pair plain sneakers
- 1 pair boots
- 1 pair sandals
- 3 dresses

Masculine
- 2 pairs everyday jeans or pants
- 1 pair of shorts
- 1 warm coat
- 1–2 simple unbranded T-shirts
- 2 long-sleeved collared shirts
- 1 blazer or jacket
- 1 pair plain sneakers
- 1 pair boots or dress shoes
- 1 pair sandals or thongs (flip flops)

you'll actually wear the clothes. This really refreshes your clothes selection without you even having to hit the shops!

Here are some questions I ask myself when I'm decluttering:
1. **When** was the last time I wore this? (Hint: If you haven't worn it in years, you're very unlikely to in the future.)
2. **What** is the quality of the item? Is the reason I haven't worn it because it has stains or is broken? Can I fix these? If not, will I actually wear it or do I need to rehome it?
3. **When** will I wear it again? Is there a specific occasion in mind? What items in my wardrobe does it work with? If there are multiple and I can see a future for it, then I'll hold on to it.
4. Do I have something **similar**? I found when I did my first few wardrobe clean-outs I had so many similar items – in particular, blue printed mini dresses. These were too short for work and I had too many to wear them all, so I gave some to a friend.

I personally love decluttering; it's almost like shopping in your own wardrobe as you rediscover and fall back in love with different pieces. Remember, once you've decluttered, don't fall back into old habits. Keep it clean and keep items visible so you can get maximum wear out of them.

Where should it go?
So, you've had a good clear-out, but what should you do with your unwanted items? You have four options:

This brings us back to a more contemporary definition of recycling, where reusing and repurposing are prioritised over simply recycling.

If you're tempted to give it all to an op-shop (thrift store), consider this first: 'If you wouldn't give it to a mate don't donate.' It's one of my favourite mottos, and one I stand by when dealing with unwanted clothing. If something has yellowing, stains, a broken zip or missing buttons, you will need to send it to a scrap recycler. It is important that you do not pass the responsibility of disposing of your unwanted clothes on to an op-shop or charity store. It's as good as dumping rubbish on their doorstep for them to use their volunteers' time sorting and putting it in the tip. Also, make sure your item is clean and estimate the rough price that an organisation could resell it for. If it only cost you a few dollars to purchase it secondhand, the value is going to be negligible.

Scrap recyclers take the various materials in clothing and utilise them for other purposes. Cotton is repurposed as an agricultural fertiliser, and scraps are turned into insulation for homes.

Give to an op-shop or charity something that:
· You'd give to a friend
· That is clean
· That's in good condition with no stains or buttons missing
· That has a good resale value (i.e. you bought it for more than $50)
Give textile recyclers something that is:
· In poor condition
· Old, has stains, holes or missing buttons
· Is fading or threadbare

How are textiles recycled?

The Ellen MacArthur Foundation estimates that less than 1 per cent of all clothing is recycled back into clothing, which is a frankly frightening statistic considering the amount of clothes that are disposed of each year.

Why? Because it's really hard to recycle clothing. You learned on page 85 that a recycling centre splits all the materials it receives into glass, paper, plastic, etc. But the problem with textiles is that it can be difficult to identify exactly what they're made of (often a mixture of materials), and buttons and zippers make it difficult to properly separate items into different materials.

How your clothes are recycled depends on the recycler themselves, but, generally speaking, garments are separated into fibre categories. Depending on the fibre, they could be broken down and respun into yarn, or made into a foam that can be used as insulation or another building material. These fibres probably won't be used to create new garments, but recycling them is better than filling our landfills or exporting them to be disposed of.

Bagging the best op-shop (thrift store) buy

As someone who loves a bargain but disagrees (on the whole) with buying new, thrifting is my in-between. Buying from charity shops is affordable, and you can pick up some really unique and quality pieces if you know where to look. The downside is that there's often so much choice it can feel overwhelming.

With items being quite cheap at op-shops, it is easy to go overboard, so I always take a list of specific things I'm looking for, and this helps to keep me on the straight and narrow.

A couple of pointers when it comes to thrifting:

· **Op-shops (thrift stores):** Are often sorted by colours, so shop the colours you love and that you know work for you.
· **Look for brands:** If the size label has been cut off (which it sometimes is, as big brands don't want their clothes in op-shops/thrift stores) you can often find the brand's name on the care instructions tag.
· **Touch and feel:** If we go back to the types of materials, let your fingers walk the rack. You'll be able to tell the quality of a piece by touch over sight. Soft fabrics that float through your fingers are optimal, but remember that you can always double check what material something is made for on the care instructions tag.
· **Don't buy a garment:** Just for its 'potential'. If you don't know exactly what you'd wear it with or what use it has in your wardrobe, leave it on the rack.
· **One in, one out:** For every purchase you make, be sure to donate one (quality) item in return.

ACTIVITY: OUTFIT REPEAT

Challenge your colleagues to wear a different outfit from their wardrobe every day for one month. They can add accessories and raid their roommate's closet, but they can't buy anything new. You might be surprised how many people enjoy the challenge, and it's often experiments like this that lead people to rethink their shopping patterns.

ACTIONABLE STEPS

- [ ] **Responsibly declutter your wardrobe**
- [ ] **Get a cobbler to revive your old pair of your shoes**
- [ ] **Unsubscribe and unfollow fashion brands on social media**
- [ ] **Look at your clothes to see what they're made from**
- [ ] **Stop washing your denim**
- [ ] **Organise your wardrobe so you can see what you've got**
- [ ] **Borrow something from a friend's wardrobe or organise a clothes swap**
- [ ] **Make your next purchase a sustainable one**
- [ ] **Buy secondhand jeans over new**
- [ ] **Wash your clothes less**

NEXT UP

I'm on a mission to flip the sustainability script and get you thinking about how you *create* rather than *dispose* of waste. It's what you do at the beginning of the cycle that matters more than the end.

I want you to consider how you can keep items in a circular economy, where they are repaired, reused, reworn and regifted instead of sending them straight to landfill. Rehoming and buying secondhand is key to making this work, and it doesn't just apply to apparel, but many household items, too.

You see, sustainability doesn't have to be complicated. In fact, true sustainability – where we get back to basics and make common-sense decisions – is inherently simple. Buying an item secondhand is a great example of a practice that used to be second nature for our grandparents, and that we can and should return to if we want to avert climate disaster (and save a few pennies in the process).

8.

How to
shop and sell
secondhand

Savings scale

SAVE
UP TO
$75 A MONTH

Level 1
List something for
sale online, bonus
points for taking
great pics.
Join your local library.

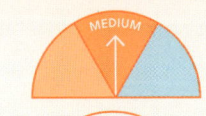

SAVE
UP TO
$150 A MONTH

+ Level 2
Buy something
secondhand over new.
Do an e-waste
secondhand sale.

SAVE
UP TO
$210 A MONTH

+ Level 3
Upcycle a piece
of furniture.
Join your local tool
or toy library.

Have you heard?

* In 2021, the global market value of secondhand and resale apparel was estimated to be worth $96 billion USD.

* Since 2017, there has been a 31 per cent increase in the number of pre-loved fashion items listed on eBay.

* By 2029, the total secondhand market is expected to grow to $80 billion USD – double the size of the $43 billion fashion industry.

* In the UK, 22 million pieces of furniture are discarded each year.

* Over 85 per cent of Aussies have unwanted or unused items.

* The average household could make $7000 selling 21 items in their home.

I couldn't possibly write a book about saving the planet while saving money without talking in detail about buying and selling secondhand. If we go back to those nine Rs of recycling that I mentioned earlier (see page 18), reuse, repair and regift are right at the top, and they are leading the pack when it comes to a modern definition of sustainable living.

Purchasing secondhand is one of those things that used to be standard practice and was literally second nature (pun intended) for our grandparents. During the early 2000s, 'secondhand' became a dirty word. No longer 'vintage', it was looked down upon as something second rate, grimy and smelly. This just so happened to coincide with the rise of flat-pack furniture for the cost of a song around that time, which created stiff competition for secondhand sellers.

I'm really excited to see that secondhand is making a comeback, and there couldn't be a more urgent time to embrace it. Buying and selling secondhand items is key to keeping products within a circular economy where they can be reused and rehomed instead of ending up in landfill. It's a practice we all need to return to if we're going to halt the damage being wrought on the environment.

Prior to now, your closest encounter to buying secondhand might have been op-shopping (thrifting) for vintage fashion finds (see page 156), but there is so much more to be found in these goldmine shops besides apparel. Furniture, décor and appliances can all be bought and sold secondhand, and it's a really obvious way to save money as well as the planet.

In this chapter, we're going to look at all the ways you can buy and sell secondhand, and I'll also be diving deep into the concept of borrowing, which is pretty much the same thing, and another practice our grandparents did on the daily that we need to bring back.

'Buying and selling secondhand items is key to keeping products within a circular economy where they can be reused and rehomed instead of ending up in landfill.'

Buying secondhand

You can certainly source plenty of amazing secondhand items for free (from Facebook Marketplace, roadside clean-ups or hard-rubbish collections), but if you're keen to take it a step further to purchasing secondhand, there are some things you need to consider before you start.

I probably sound like a broken record by now, but when it comes to making sustainable choices, you need to think about waste *creation* rather than waste *disposal*, and this applies whether you are buying a brand new item or secondhand.

Join a Buy Nothing group. These Facebook groups rose in popularity during the COVID-19 pandemic as a platform for people to give away and swap different items. You won't believe the quality pieces that people give away, and you can pay it forward by adding some of your own secondhand items into the mix.

So, before you get your wallet out, think about these things:

1. Do you actually need this item? Secondhand or not, if you don't have a clear use for it, you don't need it. It's easy to get caught up in the excitement of an auction or in a warehouse full of secondhand bargains, but you still need to exercise self-control and think about whether you really need an item or not, otherwise you're just creating more waste.
2. Shop with a list. Decide what you actually need, then go out and look for it secondhand. Searching for specific items will keep you from getting distracted or convincing yourself you will 'find a use' for something.
3. Make the most of your budget. If you do find a unique, one-off piece that is exactly what you're looking for, spend on that, then opt for lower-priced items for your other purchases.
4. Don't be afraid to haggle. Generally speaking, when buying secondhand there is a tolerance for bargaining 10–15 per cent off the sale price. The longer an item has been for sale, the stronger your bargaining power.

By buying secondhand, you'll not only be supporting an industry whose main mission is to keep things out of landfill, but you're also more likely to pick something up that is much better quality than anything you could buy new today.

Making money

As well as buying secondhand, there are huge benefits to selling your secondhand items, too.

An average household could make $7000 selling twenty-one secondhand items in their home. We are all literally sitting on unwanted or unused items that could be making us money, and selling them on also means we can keep them in circulation for others to benefit from, too.

Despite what you might think, it's not just antique furniture and one-of-a-kind artworks that are in demand.

Here are ten of the most sought-after secondhand items:

1. Smartphones
2. Gaming consoles
3. Cars
4. Books (textbooks in particular)
5. Furniture
6. Sporting goods
7. Watches
8. TVs
9. Clothes
10. Lego

If you choose to sell secondhand, I have a few tips for maximising your profits.

Set the stage

Instead of just taking a picture of a plain set of drawers against a blank wall, dress it up with a lamp, some photos and some coffee-table books to create some ambience around your product and help potential buyers to visualise it in their homes. It might sound trivial, but taking a moment to style your products before you snap a (good-quality) photo of them can be the difference between selling them and not.

Honesty is key

How many times have you looked at an ad for something and been disappointed by the product in the flesh? Be transparent about the condition of the product and take photos of any imperfections or damage so that you don't end up wasting a buyer's (or your own) time. Also, explain how it comes – will an item of furniture be flat-pack? Are you missing any of the loose parts? Will it need two people to lift it? Give as much honest, helpful information as possible.

Tip
I have greater success on Facebook Marketplace than some other platforms, but you do need to be mindful of scammers. If you want to list anything for more than $100, Gumtree, Poshmark, Vinted or eBay are better for avoiding scammers, whereas Facebook Marketplace is great for smaller, faster deals.

Bundle items together

If you want to sell a few things quickly, consider bundling like things together, e.g. a few artworks or a pair of bedside lamps, and selling for a slightly higher price. This means fewer transactions and a greater likelihood that your secondhand wares will find a new home.

Give yourself breathing room

It's Murphy's Law that the items you think will sell quickly don't, and the ones you suspect might flop will go off with a bang. So, I recommend giving yourself more time than you think you might need to sell your items – don't rush to move them the a week before you are moving house, for example.

Upcycling

A term you won't find in the nine Rs of the waste hierarchy is upcycling. Upcycling is more fun than recycling and involves taking a used item and improving it. For example, giving a vintage table a makeover with a fresh lick of paint, or turning an old colander into a hanging plant basket. The best part is that upcycling improves the value of an item and – crucially – keeps it out of landfill.

The saying 'one man's trash is another man's treasure' is one that I hold dear. Looking around my living room I can see at least five different pieces that I found for free on the side of the road. At first, the thought of picking through someone's hard rubbish might seem a little demeaning, but it's such a positive intervention to prevent items going to landfill and save yourself some money.

With these secondhand finds comes a golden opportunity to make them your own by repairing and upcycling. You don't even need to be that handy in order to flip a piece of furniture. I am completely self-taught and have proudly sanded, painted and repaired things to really make them my own.

Here are a few cosmetic updates that I have made to make the most of my secondhand pieces:
- Painted black outdoor pots a trendy white
- Removed the backing from a mirror that was mounted on a cupboard door to create a standalone mirror
- Sanded and painted a wooden storage box
- Removed and replaced handles on a coffee table in order to make it look more modern
- Spray-painted rusting plant stands

FUN FACT
Rub a raw walnut on wooden tabletops to remove scratches, similar to how you would scratch a scratchy and watch as it repairs those tiny little faults. Like anything, looking after items is going to help them go the distance, so it is worthwhile using a protectant on the top of different woods in order to make sure that they don't worn and get stained. The same goes with coasters. Yes, your parents might have been a nag about them but they do really help.

Before you contemplate any repair jobs, make sure that the item is in basically sound condition. They don't make furniture like they used to, and most pieces are only built to withstand a few moves. Usually, the tell-tale signs of a good-quality piece are in the finer details, like well-fitting joints that don't use glue or additional nails. Make sure to check for any tiny fractures and chips in glass or ceramic, which can be harder to fix.

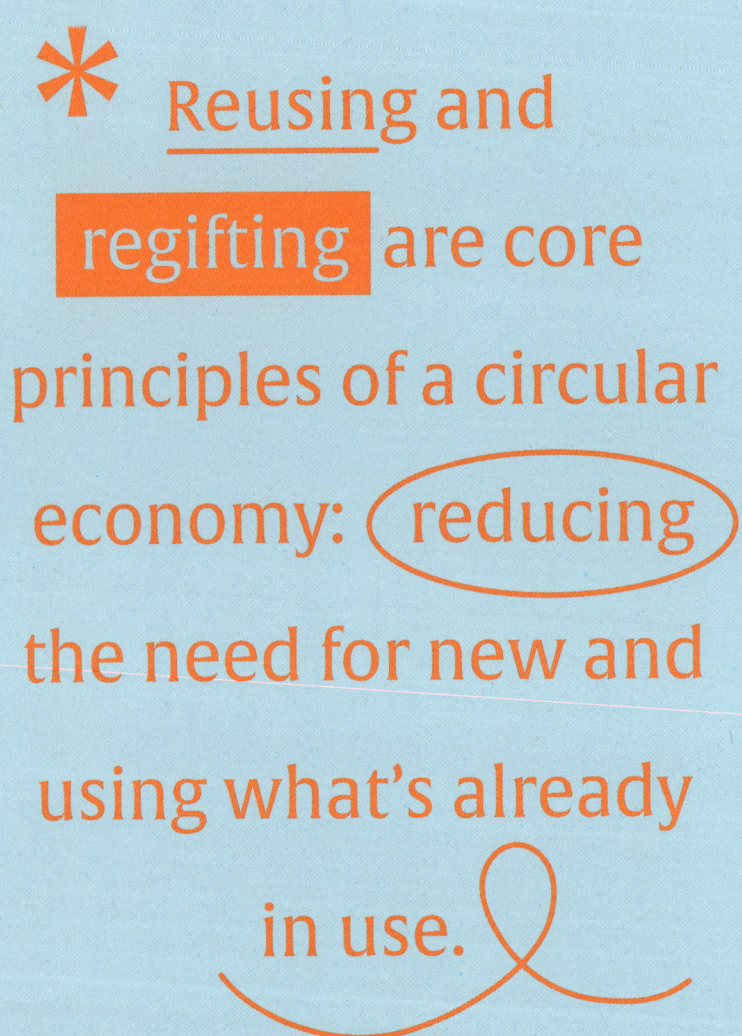

* <u>Reusing and</u> regifting are core principles of a circular economy: reducing the need for new and using what's already in use.

Share economy

Hand in hand with buying and selling secondhand goods is sharing and borrowing them. The 'share economy', where people swap and borrow items without spending a dime, is growing exponentially as more and more people embrace the principles of reusing and regifting.

These two practices are core principles of a circular economy: reducing the need for new and using what's already in use. These ideas are nothing new – it's about going back to our community roots, similar to how people used to borrow a tool from a neighbour or swap produce.

Libraries

One of the easiest and simplest things you can do is join your local library. It is not only a great place to connect and learn about what's going on in your community, but you have hundreds of thousands of books at your disposal to read for education and leisure.

It's a little-known fact that many libraries also have an e-book library as well, so you don't even have to borrow a physical book. You can download it onto your e-reader device instead. This is something that I find particularly handy, because in my book club we read books that are more current and trending.

TOOL LIBRARY

As someone who doesn't call themselves handy or live near a parent with a fully stocked toolshed, tool libraries have been game-changing for me when it comes to upcycling furniture and doing general repairs around the house.

I don't want to head out to my local hardware store to purchase tools that I will inevitably only use once or twice before eventually disposing of them just so I can sand back a dresser. Tool libraries are run by community groups as a way for people to borrow and share equipment, from electric drills, to leaf blowers, camping gear to outdoor lights. It really depends on your community, but these local hubs are growing in number. Sometimes there will be a very small fee involved, but it's still a more cost effective and environmentally friendly approach to obtaining tools.

TOY LIBRARY

Growing up, I have vivid memories of heading to our local toy library. Saying goodbye to the toys I had played with for the last few weeks and hello to a new suite of friends was such a fun and exciting experience. It meant as a family we were able to pay a small membership fee and my brother and I would get to play with different toys each month – genius! Again, toy libraries are nothing revolutionary, but they are a simple way to reduce our consumption (of plastic, especially) and spending, and also share resources to cut down a community's environmental footprint.

E-waste

E-waste presents a bit of a recycling nightmare. Your old computers, phones and electronics are filled with so many different materials, including rare metals like nickel and copper, that can be recovered and recycled. This makes them extremely valuable, with many recyclers paying for your old electronics, as they can repair them or pull them apart and easily sell or reuse the different elements.

Many also contain lithium-ion batteries, which are extremely flammable and the leading cause of fires in rubbish trucks and recycling facilities. This is why e-waste items cannot be put in your curbside recycling bin. Instead, they must go to specialty recyclers. Once at these plants, the items are assessed to see if it's possible to repair and restore them to working order for resale. This presents a golden opportunity for people to buy a secondhand or reconditioned item for a fraction of the price of a new one. It's especially helpful for people who need additional electronic devices that don't necessarily require all the bells and whistles of the latest technologies.

Be mindful if you are planning to purchase secondhand or reconditioned white goods or other large electronics. Because they are likely to be older technology, these appliances won't carry the same energy rating as their newer counterparts. Before purchasing, it's a good idea to check the exact model number and do a quick search online to check its energy and/or water rating. In saying that, I picked up a perfectly good and relatively efficient fridge from Facebook Marketplace for completely zero dollars.

ACTIONABLE STEPS

- [ ] **List something for sale online, bonus points for taking great pics**
- [ ] **Join your local library, tool or toy library**
- [ ] **Do an e-waste secondhand sale**
- [ ] **Upcycle a piece of furniture**
- [ ] **Buy something secondhand over new**

NEXT UP

Why, when and how we buy things matters, and the choices we make directly impact the health of our planet. We also know that thinking about waste creation is more important than waste disposal, both for the environment and for our wallets.

Choosing to purchase something secondhand gives you more choice, agency and creative opportunities. But it's also freeing to realise that you don't have to spend your hard-earned money constantly consuming new things, and that keeping products within a circular economy by regifting and reusing them benefits everyone.

Another way to rethink your spending is looking at what comes out of your bank account every month. Sometimes it's so automatic that you barely think about it, but looking closely at your monthly expenses, like utilities, can really help to make each dollar count and go further towards your goal of living sustainably.

9.

Utilise your utilities and vote with your dollar

Savings scale

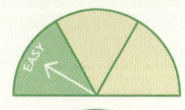

SAVE
UP TO
$75 A MONTH

Level 1
Always use the toilet's
half-flush. Wash the car
on the lawn.
Use cross ventilation to
cool your home.

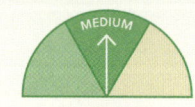

SAVE
UP TO
$150 A MONTH

+ Level 2
Ditch the dryer.
Use a smart meter.
Switch to LED lightbulbs.
Time your outdoor lights.

SAVE
UP TO
$210 A MONTH

+ Level 3
Purchase energy/water-
efficient appliances.
Switch your provider.
Use a water-saving
showerhead.

Have you heard?

* 40 per cent of your household energy bill is responsible for heating and cooling your home.

* Switching your appliances off rather than leaving them on standby could save you 10 per cent on your energy bill.

* The laundry is the room in the house that uses the most energy.

* Washing your clothes at a cooler temperature means you'll use the same amount of energy for two loads in three!

* It's estimated that LED lightbulbs last 25 times longer and use 90 per cent less energy than traditional incandescent bulbs.

As I'm not a homeowner I didn't really think there was much I could do to reduce my environmental footprint when it came to utilities, but I've since realised that there is SO much, and it's all the little tweaks and changes that add up to the biggest difference.

Here's the thing: your energy usage is a whole lot more than switching off a light when you leave a room. Sadly, this isn't something we were taught in school (neither was sustainability for that matter, but I am told that's changing now). So, you're about to be educated. Grab a coffee (make your own at home) and get some energy to tackle your energy consumption.

Honestly, the title of this chapter might not excite you, but the benefits should entice you. Everything that we're about to discuss is extremely practical and you'll walk away with the tools to make some significant changes to your energy consumption at home. From learning when you should run the dishwasher (yes it matters), to reducing your water usage, this chapter demonstrates that the smallest changes really do make the biggest difference.

Understanding the jargon

You hear people throw around words like 'the grid', 'off peak' and 'tariffs', but what does it all mean? One of the biggest roadblocks to improving your energy use is understanding all the jargon and industry 'speak' that utility companies use. If you want to make both financial and environmental savings in this area, you need to take a little time to fully understand the terminology. Here, I've done the hard work for you so let's hop to it.

Peak timing

Firstly, 'the grid' just refers to our energy use per area. Think of your suburb, and every business, organisation or house as one square. Together, it forms a grid. Each square will pull different amounts of energy depending on what kind of building it is and how it's operating. When you use energy you are pulling from the grid so supply and demand principles apply.

If we're all at home cooking dinner (energy), putting the dishwasher on (energy) and watching TV (energy), we are all demanding energy at the same time. It's a high-usage time, and energy companies charge us more during these 'peak times'.

Off-peak timing

'Off-peak times' refer to times of the day/days of the week when not as much energy is being used, so it is cheaper. This means that doing your washing or other non-timely, energy-sucking tasks in off-peak times saves you money.

Shoulder rates

Just to make things more confusing, 'shoulder rates' apply in some areas between peak and off-peak times. The cost of energy use is lower than peak, but not as cheap as off-peak.

Across the world, peak times change depending on your location but, generally speaking, they are:

- **On weekdays** between 3–9 pm (most expensive)
- **During shoulder periods** between 9–10 am (moderately expensive)
- **During off-peak periods** between 10–3 pm (least expensive)

Here are some ideas to make the most of the off-peak times:

- **Electric vehicle owners** listen up: charge your car at home during the off-peak hours of 12–5 am to save big.
- **Use your dishwasher's** delayed-start function to run it during off-peak hours to save up to 30 per cent on your bill.
- **Make the most of** your work-from-home days and run your washing machine during the middle of the day.
- **Turn off your appliances** at the switch when they aren't in use.

Elements

When it comes to looking at our environmental impact, things like energy and water usage are often out of sight and out of mind. But making changes to your consumption can have a significant monetary and planetary impact. As you know by now, I love set-and-forget changes: things like switching to energy-saving lightbulbs or opting for energy-efficient appliances. You make a change once and reap long-term benefits. These simple swaps can be further compounded by changes in your behaviours and habits. Having one short shower won't save you a tonne of money, but a month's worth of faster rinses will.

Lighting

Leaving the lights on when you're not in the room is the equivalent of leaving a tap running. So much energy and resources are wasted!

I don't want to nag you like a parent, but turning off a light when you leave a room is probably the most game-changing thing you can do to save money and energy. Also, consider using more lamps with energy-efficient bulbs and less overhead lighting to cut down on your total use.

For outdoor lights, make sure you're using timers or movement monitors, so your lights only come on when they're absolutely needed. If you live somewhere sunny, swapping to solar-powered lights will make the best use of the sun's natural resources – no paid energy required!

SMART BULBS

Smart bulbs are worth dishing out the extra dosh for. They might involve a little more up-front spend, but once you crunch the numbers around your energy use, they actually work out a whole lot cheaper. One LED bulb generally runs for about 25,000 hours, which is the equivalent of six traditional bulbs. Plus, they don't contain mercury, which is one of the biggest environmental hazards of normal globes.

Water

Water is one of our most precious resources, and one that in first-world countries we often take for granted. One of my core memories from childhood was when our town enforced water restrictions due to widespread droughts. We showered with buckets to catch the water, set timers for bathing, had limits around how many times we could flush the toilet and watering the garden was a big no-no. These water-saving practices have stuck with me for life, and still inform how I approach my water usage.

When you think about it, reducing your hot water consumption not only reduces your water usage but also your energy consumption generally. Hot water requires large amounts of heating, so switching to a water-efficient showerhead (which will set you back between $80–$100) can cut your hot water usage (and energy) by 50 per cent!

Tip
Never ever throw used or broken lightbulbs in the bin. They need to go to a specialty recycler to be recycled responsibly because they contain mercury. This means if you throw them in your regular bin and they end up in landfill they will leach mercury (a toxic chemical) into our waterways and soil.

Following are a couple more ways to reduce your water usage, which will help to save some moolah while also saving Mother Earth. Water isn't just crucial to our survival; it's also the world's largest natural resource. It's finite and irreplaceable, which is why we need to conserve and use it mindfully. To put it simply, without water the earth and its inhabitants (us) wouldn't survive.

FOUR-MINUTE SHOWERS

It's estimated that a typical showerhead uses 15 litres (4 gallons) of water per minute, so knocking a few minutes off your showering time really does make a significant saving.

In fact, cutting down by one minute a day saves over 100 litres (26 gallons) a week.

The best tip I have come across is to aim for four-minute showers (about the length of a song – play your favourite while showering!). I find if it isn't a hair-washing day, this is easy to abide by. On the days I do need to wash my hair, I turn the jets off while lathering up, then back on again for a quick rinse. I kill two birds with one stone by shaving my legs while the water's off, too. No standing under the stream just contemplating life – save that for when you're sitting in your towel afterwards!

REPURPOSING YOUR WATER

So much of living sustainably involves thinking more creatively about how we use the resources we already have. Water is a great example. I repurpose cooled kettle water to water my indoor plants, collect water in a jug while I'm waiting for the hot water to heat up, and wash my fruit and vegetables over a pot to collect excess water, which can be used for cleaning or watering the garden. These things might seem minute, but they add up. It's about forming new habits that gradually become second nature.

More water-saving tips:
- **Turn the tap off** when you brush your teeth or lather up your hands.
- **Soak your dishes** before you hand wash them.
- **Wash your car** on the lawn instead of the driveway.
- **Use a nozzle** to water your outdoor lawn and plants.

Let's gas bag about gas

Remember when gas cooktops were all the rage? At one point I too thought gas was the gold standard in cooking, but the flame that ignites our culinary skills might actually be killing us. It sounds dramatic, but Yannai Simon Kashtan from Stanford University shares a couple of rather alarming statistics. When you're cooking with gas, toxic methane is released into the air, which can wreak havoc on the respiratory system. In fact, up to 12.3 per cent of the total asthma burden in children is estimated to be associated with gas stove use. Plus, a study by the University of New South Wales has shown that the gas from our gas stovetops continues to leak into the air even when it's not switched on. Think about those mini camping butane gas stoves, which are 'only allowed to be used outdoors in a well-ventilated area'. Our gas cooktops present just the same risk to our health and the environment.

Methane is a greenhouse gas that is twenty-three times more potent than carbon dioxide (see page 27), so just having a gas stove contributes significantly to your total methane emissions.

If you're renting, you cannot simply replace your gas oven with an electric one, so I'd recommend focusing on cutting down your total use, for example reheat items in the microwave or oven instead of using the stovetop. And, when you do use it, make sure you open up all doors and windows to allow for maximum airflow.

Phantom power

Phantom power is as scary as it sounds, and it refers to using energy without even realising it! Did you know that so many of your appliances still consume energy even while on stand-by mode? In other words, you might have switched them off on the machine, but they are still plugged into the wall with the switch turned on. Getting into the habit of flicking off the switch at the wall after using your toaster, kettle or blender can add up to huge energy savings.

If you have a swimming pool, be wary of your creepy crawly cleaner. Not only is it annoying to listen to that tick, tick, tick, but the pump in your pool can add a whopping $1500 to your annual bill if you use it for the recommended 4–6 hours a day. And don't even get me started on the cost of heating your pool ...

Tip

Go for an electric barbecue oven over one fired by a gas bottle. It's safer, you don't have the added expense of filling up a gas bottle, and it's far more energy efficient, too.

10 simple ways to cut down your energy use and save money

When you start digging deep into this issue, you'll find there are many ways you can reduce your energy consumption, but here are some everyday ideas you can implement right this second:

1. Utilise the half-flush option on your toilet (an Australian invention in answer to the droughts we often experience here), which uses only 3 litres (¾ gallon) instead of the usual 4.5 litres (1¼ gallons) of a full flush.
2. Plug up gaps under doors, open air vents and window frames to prevent draughts, which can potentially cut your energy bill by 20 per cent!
3. Once your laptop is charged to 100 per cent, unplug it and switch the charger off at the wall.
4. Boil the kettle once and pour straight away instead of forgetting about your tea, then reboiling the kettle later. Kettles are a huge energy sucker.
5. Buy new parts for your existing appliances to extend their lifespan over buying new appliances.
6. Switch regular lightbulbs to LED bulbs.
7. Clean your fridge coils regularly to help your fridge run more efficiently.
8. Unplug your phone once fully charged and switch the charger off at the wall.
9. Cover your saucepans with their lids while you're making dinner to speed up the cooking process and cut down on gas use.
10. Get organised and defrost food in the fridge overnight instead of zapping it in the microwave.

Water efficiency vs. energy efficiency

In a world where we want to have it all, why should we have to compromise and choose between water and energy efficiency? Unfortunately, when making some purchasing decisions, you will need to choose between an energy efficient or a water efficient appliance. Ultimately choosing one that does both is the best, but if you have to choose, a machine that saves you more energy and only a little water will save you more money in the long run than the other way around.

Appliances

I talk a lot about making environmental and monetary savings at the point of purchase instead of trying to fix the problem further down the track. Buying energy-efficient appliances is key to reducing your home's energy consumption.

When purchasing any white good, there is a lot to consider. Look at the appliance's features, size, price and energy rating as a starting point.

Fridge

What people don't realise when purchasing an energy-inefficient fridge and freezer is that it can increase your annual bill by up to $166, meaning it is well worth paying a little more for an energy-efficient model at the outset, as it will add up to huge savings in the long run.

It should be obvious, but buying the right size fridge for your household is an easy place to start making savings. The bigger the fridge, the bigger the bill. Here's a rough guide:

1   1–2 PEOPLE   ⟶   50–380 LITRE (8.8–13 CUBIC FEET)

2   3–4 PEOPLE   ⟶   350–530 LITRE (12–18 CUBIC FEET)

3   4 OR MORE PEOPLE   ⟶   440+ LITRE (15+ CUBIC FEET)

Three out of four households also set their fridges too cold. This increases your monthly bill because it takes more energy to cool your fridge. It can also degrade your food, leading to more food waste. Below are the ideal temperatures for your fridge and freezer:

Fridge ⟶ 3–4°C (37–39°F)   **Freezer** ⟶ –15 to –18°C (5–0.4°F)

Washing machine

Capacity is a massive selling point for so many machines, but it's also the biggest drain on your resources. Unless you're a family of fourteen, you probably only wash between 3–5 kilograms (7–11 pounds) of clothing at a time.

The average Aussie spends 10.4 hours a year just staring into an open fridge. That's 10.4 hours a year your fridge has to use more energy to stay cold! Every time you open the fridge, even if it's just for a second, it adds another 7 per cent of energy use to your bill.

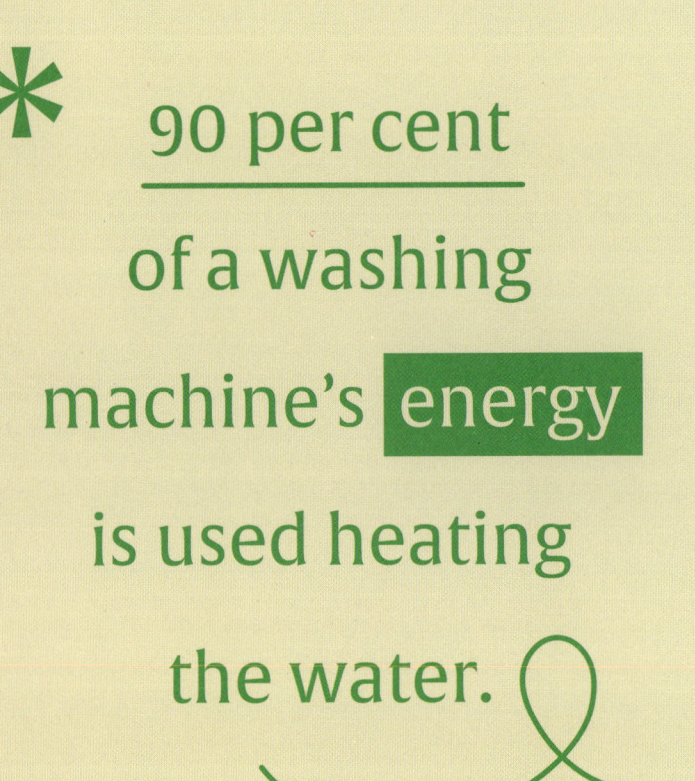

* 90 per cent of a washing machine's energy is used heating the water.

Machines these days come with all of the bells and whistles, but these are the only ones I pay attention to:

- **Auto-sensing water level:** This means your water use will match your load size.
- **Delicates programs:** These are great for extra-special and fragile clothing, helping it last longer.
- **Out-of-balance correction:** If your load is imbalanced it means your machine might be spinning or using more water than it needs to. This feature saves on both.
- **Front loader or top loader:** A front-loading machine saves up to 50 per cent more water compared to a top loader.

TOP WASHING TIPS

- 90 per cent of a washing machine's energy is used heating the water. Cut this in half by switching from hot to warm water, or even more by switching to cold.
- Avoid washer-dryer combos. They are often pricier, prone to breakdowns and their drying mechanism uses even more water.
- Throw a dry towel into the dryer with your washing to soak up moisture from wet clothes, which will speed up the drying process.
- Popping three tennis balls into your dryer will help soften your clothes so they don't go all scratchy. They also create more air and movement in your load, resulting in fluffier towels and pillows.
- If your laundry detergents will only dissolve in hot water but you want to run a cool cycle, dissolve the detergent in warm water first, then add it to the machine.
- Avoid washing in half-loads. Loosely packed loads cause more movement of clothes during a cycle, and more microplastics to break off clothing (see page 103).

Dishwasher

You might think it's the other way around, but using your dishwasher actually uses less energy and water than handwashing-up. But there are still some energy and money-saving things to keep in mind: only run your dishwasher when it's full and use the eco-friendly function. If your dishwasher doesn't have one, work out how to switch the setting from heat dry to air dry, which will save about 15 per cent energy per load.

A full dishwasher load uses around 13 litres (3½ gallons) of water to clean approximately 144 items. On the other hand, the average sink has a capacity of 30 litres (8 gallons) of water. Think about how many sinkfuls you would need to wash 144 dirty dishes and the savings become obvious.

Dry, dry, dry

You know what can dry your clothes for absolutely zero cost? The sun. Dryers get such a bad rap, and rightly so because they are almost entirely unnecessary. Use a washing line in the warmer months and a clothes rack (close to a heat source) in winter. It might add a little more time, but the environmental and monetary savings are worth it!

If you do insist on using a dryer, bear these things in mind:

- **Vented dryers** are the cheapest to buy but the most expensive to run, because they pull the moisture from your clothes and push it out through the vents.
- **Dryers** containing condensers pool the moisture from the clothes into a central condenser, which prevents humidity and condensation in your laundry, but it still expels hot air.
- **Heat pump condensers** work similarly to air-conditioners. They're more expensive to buy, but cheaper to run with good results. The energy is captured and reused during the cycles.

Oven

Of all your household appliances, your oven is the hungriest when it comes to consuming energy. Avoiding long, slow cooking in the oven and using your stovetop to cook as much as possible are two easy ways to cut down on your energy use.

· **Cook** more than one item a time and maximise your oven use. As long as you're not baking a cake, throw everything in together.
· **Turn off** your oven five minutes before the end of the recommended cooking time and let the residual heat finish cooking your food.
· **Stop** opening the oven door! Every time you crack it open you allow heat (and energy) to escape and the oven needs to expend yet more energy reheating again. Plus, it takes your food longer to cook and no one wants that!

Most people haven't heard of their daily gas connection charge. As the name suggests, it's a fee charged by your gas supplier just for the privilege of having gas connected to the house whether or not you use your gas oven.

Buyer's guide

When it comes to making your next appliance purchase, use this handy guide to select one that will not only work better for the planet but for your bank account. Always do your research, ask questions and consider whether secondhand or appliances on sale actually meet your efficiency requirements.

1. **Energy rating:** An energy rating provides a guide on how efficient a product is. Australia uses a star rating system: the more stars the more energy efficient the item. This is a government initiative that allows buyers transparency on the energy use of an item. Similarly, the UK rates appliances from A+++ to G, and the United States has the Energy Star certification.
2. **Water Efficiency Labelling and Standards:** Similarly to the energy efficiency rating, a water efficiency score demonstrates an appliance's water usage. It's known as WELS in Australia and Energy Star in the US, and is a work in progress in the UK.
3. **Reviews:** Rather than listening to the brands, listen to the people who have already purchased the product. Reading reviews is a great way to determine the quality and usability of a product. Make sure you don't just look at the brand's reviews too, but also use a third-party platform like Trust Pilot to dig deeper.

Heating and cooling

Heating and cooling are the biggest expenditures of energy in the home, so it's an area you can make some mega planetary and monetary savings.

Living in Australia, the emphasis has always been on cooling over heating. (I vividly remember Dad teaching me about cross ventilation before I'd even reached the age of ten; see below.) As heating and cooling suck up so much of your household energy, these simple steps can make a world of difference to your energy consumption and save you a ton of money while you're at it.

Here are some top heating and cooling tips:
· **Reduce the thermostat** by 1°C (34°F) in winter and increase it by 1 degree in summer to save 5–10 per cent on your energy bill.
· **Choose the right sized appliance** for your space. If it is too small it will struggle to cool/heat the area and work overtime. Too big, and it's a waste of energy.
· **Close all doors and windows** when heating.
· **Install timers** on your appliances so they turn off automatically after you leave the house or go to bed.

Fans

While fans don't technically reduce the temperature of a room, they do provide air movement, which helps you cool down. They are one of the most energy-efficient cooling methods and my go-to over central air-conditioning or larger air-conditioning units.

What is cross ventilation?

If you're looking for a cheap and effective way to ventilate your home, it could be as simple as opening up the right windows and doors. Cross ventilation uses the breeze from outside your home to create a cross breeze inside your home. By opening doors and windows directly opposite one another air will naturally flow in. See the diagram opposite.

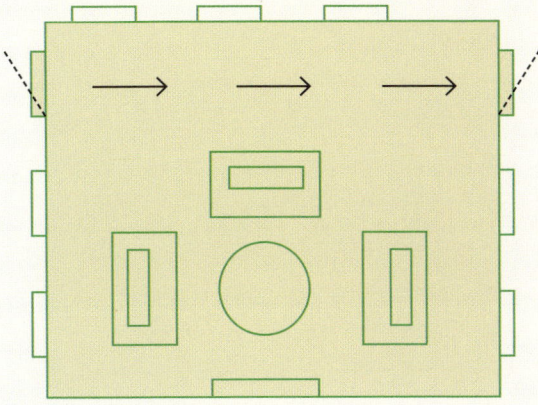

Cross ventilation is an effective and efficient way to cool your home using windows instead of appliances – and it won't bite into your bank account.

Thermostats

Traditionally, it was recommended that you set your thermostat to 22–24°C (71–75°F) year-round, but the latest recommendations suggest you should set your air-conditioning to 25–27°C (77–80°F) in summer and 18–20°C (64–68°F) in winter during the day (note that these temperatures differ for babies). These temperatures are based on average seasonal temperatures in Australia, so be sure to check your local guidelines, which you'll find online. Doing this will significantly reduce your energy consumption and your bill as your thermostat won't be working overtime.

Goal setting

Okay, so how do we bring these improvements together? First things first – grab copies of your most recent utility bills and get a sense for what your current usage is. It doesn't matter what size these bills are because we're going to use them as the top of the scale and, from there, make some savings.

It's a good idea to compare each quarter's consumption to that same quarter from the previous year instead of comparing quarters within the same year. We consume energy differently depending on the season. In Australia, for example, we use more energy in the summer as we crank up the air-conditioners, whereas in cooler climates like Europe, winter sees higher rates. Comparing your usage from the same season the previous year provides a more accurate benchmark to work from.

How to set great goals

This works best when everyone in the household is on board. It is a fun activity (no, really it is), as you race against your past self to make improvements!

- **Download** your previous year's bills to understand your consumption.
- **Reflect** on what you can do to improve your usage and write down some ideas.
- **Set a target** I find a good place to start is a saving of around 10–15 per cent. Remember you're not just saving energy but money too!

From here, you can identify where you need to make swaps or changes. Use this chapter to work out which ones will add up to the biggest savings for your household.

Get a smart meter

Whenever you work towards a goal, it's important to track your progress. A smart meter is a digital device that helps monitor the amount of energy an appliance uses. It will set you back around $30 (some councils in Australia give them out for free), and you can use it to monitor your daily usage, and to test your appliances on different settings, for example when a light is dimmed or your hair dryer is on high versus low.

This takes me back to the science lab. By testing your appliances and usage you can tell what products are guzzling the most energy and also capture phantom power (aka the energy your appliances use while in stand-by mode) in action – spooky stuff.

Monitoring your usage rather than unplugging and waiting for your bill in the mail allows you to make small sustainable changes across the period, and it can also help you weigh up the impact of the swaps you've already made. Tracking your progress helps motivate me to keep going and keeps the household morale high.

ACTIONABLE STEPS

- ☐ Set a timer and have four-minute showers for a week
- ☐ Water your plants with saved water
- ☐ Check the energy ratings of your appliances
- ☐ Utilise cross ventilation to cool your home
- ☐ Use your dryer less
- ☐ Switch showerheads to save water
- ☐ Switch over to LED lightbulbs and recycle your old bulbs properly
- ☐ Change your fridge and freezer temperatures
- ☐ Wash your clothes less

NEXT UP

Reducing utilities will make an enormous positive impact on the health of our planet – and to the health of your bank account – but it's just one piece of the puzzle. You need to think more holistically about how you can vote with your dollar for sustainability.

It's also helpful to take these sustainable principles and thinking and apply them outside your own home, such as in your workplace. In communal spaces like this, the responsibility to carry out sustainable practices falls to everyone and no one, which means they are often not carried out.

10.

Go to work without the waste

Savings scale

SAVE
UP TO
$75 A MONTH

Level 1
Build a work version of your single-use quitter kit (see page 70). Cut down on your printing. Sustainably commute to the office.

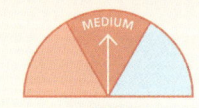

SAVE
UP TO
$150 A MONTH

+ Level 2
Say no to single-use cups. Nail your workplace wardrobe. BYO takeaway container.

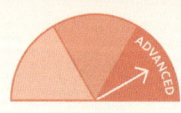

SAVE
UP TO
$210 A MONTH

+ Level 3
Start a workplace dual with your colleagues. Pack plastic-free lunches.

Have you heard?

* We spend 14 per cent of our lives in the office so make an impact while you're there.

* It's estimated that cars are responsible for 50 per cent of Australia's total transport emissions.

* Australians use, on average, a whopping 230 kilograms (507 pounds) of paper per person each year.

* Over 8000 companies worldwide have committed to reach net zero emissions by 2030.

Considering the amount of time that we spend working, I wanted to include a whole chapter on sustainable workplace habits. By now you will have built a safe sustainable cocoon of a home, but it is time to expand that thinking and those behaviours to your workplace. In this chapter, we will cover everything from getting to work, to your habits inside your office and how to level-up your lunch break.

Getting to work

We've gotten really good at working remotely these past few years. So good, in fact, that we have cut down on travelling for meetings and needing to be in a physical office. But there is still work to do when it comes to those times we do have to commute to work.

Transport by emissions

The transport industry is the third largest emitter of carbon in Australia. How you travel from home to work or school and back can make a massive impact on your carbon emissions. By choosing a more sustainable mode of transport, you can make a massive positive difference to your wallet and to the environment before you've even made it into the office.

> **Here are the transport options from best to worst in terms of emissions:**
> - Walking/running
> - Cycling
> - Bus
> - Train
> - Carpooling
> - Driving
> - Flying

Driving vs. public transport

Catching public transport is about four times cheaper than running a car to and from work and, in most cases, will give you a better chance of getting to work on time, too.

Car transport is also responsible for 50 per cent of all transport emissions, so switching to public transport is a simple and easy way to help the planet. Plus, catching public transport will make you more active, so that's three benefits in one!

Tips

When you arrive at the office, take the stairs. Not only will it get your blood pumping and get your steps up, but you will also save energy by avoiding the lift. (I am only talking a couple of flights – don't try to walk up to the thirty-ninth floor, unless you're game!)

Make the most of your commute and catch up on a podcast, speak to a friend, learn a new language, or do some work before you get to work to make your day easier.

Lunch break

So, you've arrived at work, but how do you continue your project of sustainability in the office itself? Believe it or not, there are huge savings to be made even at your desk and on your lunch break.

Plastic-free lunches

Schools around the world are encouraging parents to pack plastic-free lunches for their children, but why stop at the kiddies? Let's make your lunchbox plastic free, too.

Start off with the box itself. I'm all for a pretty stainless-steel bento-style box, but you're not trying to impress anyone, so you can just use an old container from home or, better yet, reuse your takeaway box. Op-shops (thrift stores) are also a great place to find old lunchboxes and food containers, as well as reusable coffee cups for a portion of the price of new.

Bring some cutlery from home, as well as a reusable napkin, and make sure these are stashed away in your desk drawer in your single-use quitter kit (see page 70) ready for the next day.

Takeaway mate

I get it: you're a busy bumble bee and you don't always have time to make a gourmet lunch (or you left it on the kitchen bench). But when buying takeaway, there are a couple of simple ways to reduce your food footprint.

Never be afraid to ask a restaurant if they'll accept your reusable container or plate. In my experience, if it is sparkling clean then very few actually say no. Not quite ready to go that far? BYO cutlery at least. If you're dashing out of the office, make a detour via the kitchen (sorry to anyone in Human Resources reading this right now), pop a knife and fork in your bag or pocket and use these instead of disposable cutlery from cafes. Also, don't forget to decline the disposable napkins that invariably get stuffed in with your order. Just pop a cloth napkin in your single-use quitter kit!

If you're an office slave, sorry I mean worker, here's a quick refresh of what you need in your single-use quitter kit (just stash it in your desk drawer or locker):

· **Reusable coffee cup**
· **Reusable water bottle**
· **Cutlery**
· **Cloth napkin**
· **Reusable shopping bag**
· **Reusable straw for cold drinks**

Good news: most cafes these days will reward you for bringing your own coffee cup with 50 cents off! That's $2.50 a week, or a free coffee once a fortnight!

ACTIVITY: OUTFIT REPEAT

Try wearing the same three outfits to work on repeat and see if anyone notices! You'll save so much time and stress, plus I doubt no one will even bat an eyelid.

The communal challenge

Because offices are communal places, often there is no one single person who thinks to takes the initiative to make sustainable changes. Are there any small and seemingly insignificant changes you could make that would make a difference? (Hint: the best ones are those that don't cost your company money and require very little effort to implement.)

Here are some ideas:

· Make a simple printout of what can actually be recycled and stick it by the bins.
· Use reusable plates and cutlery at your next workplace gathering.
· Go paperless – send an email instead.
· Opt for 100 per cent vegetarian catering for your next work event.
· Lobby for a food waste bin to be installed in your kitchen.
· Add a sign by the exit reminding people to remember their reusable coffee cups.
· Create a collection point for items like batteries or e-waste to be recycled (offices are a top producer of e-waste).
· Ask the powers that be if you can find a tea/coffee supplier that is plastic free.
· Turn your office computer/screen off at the wall every day before you leave to avoid stand-by mode.
· Encourage sustainable transport (public transport, carpooling, walking/riding).
· Get more indoor plants to purify the air (plus, they're known to boost productivity by 15 per cent!).

Tip

Etsy ran a test and removed individual waste bins from next to employees' desks and replaced these with communal bins. The results? At first, everyone was grumpy, but it worked! Removing individual bins in offices decreased waste by 18 per cent and increased recycling by 20 per cent!

ACTIVITY: A WEEK OF REUSE

This is fun to do yourself, but it's even more fun to do as a group. Recruit your coworkers and agree to go one week without using single-use items. This means no single-use coffee cups, cutlery or takeaway containers. Better yet, create a couple of teams and stir up some healthy competition to see who can use the least! Create two team 'collection points' for all the naughty stuff and see who's used the most at the end of the week. This is a fun activity to apply to plastic use, too.

If you're working part-time from home, make sure everyone continues the challenge when you're away by encouraging your colleagues to snap pics of their home brews and make those habits stick.

Working from home

Nowadays, we're working from home more than ever before. For some, this is a dream come true and for others not so much. When you're at home it's arguably a whole lot easier to save money, but it can also be easier to spend it, too. Here are a couple of budget-savvy ways to make the most of your work-from-home days.

- **Put a load of washing on** during a work-from-home day to take advantage of the off-peak time, and hang it out to dry.
- **Take the opportunity** to make a 'Whatever Trevor' lunch (see page 49), making something with whatever you've already got in the fridge. While you're at it, double the batch and use the rest as your meal prep for the next day.
- **Spend the time** you'd normally commute on one of your 'I'll get to this later' tasks like renegotiating your power bill or researching a brand's sustainability credentials.
- **Dress for the weather** and avoid using the air-conditioner or heater. Layer up or off depending on the temperature.

'When you're at home it's arguably a whole lot easier to save money, but it can also be easier to spend it, too.'

The set up

Since the pandemic, the way we work has fundamentally changed, and working from home isn't going anywhere anytime soon, so take some time to set up your home office space.

If you need new office equipment like a desk or office chair, see what you can source and/or upcycle secondhand. A good place to start is Facebook Marketplace, especially for the largest items of furniture.

Secondhand office furniture is available in abundance. Big businesses pay for quality pieces that are built to last and when businesses downsize, redecorate or move offices, these products are up for grabs! Some businesses will list these on Facebook Marketplace, otherwise look up your local re-commerce warehouse.

As amazing as it is to buy a matching set of pens, the likelihood of you needing new pens is slim to none. Pens are the adult equivalent of party bag goodies; they get handed out like candy at dentists, conferences and doctors' surgeries. When I do a big clear-out, I always find an abundance of pens in old handbags, drawers and odd spots. Put them all somewhere central and I highly doubt you'll ever need to buy more.

Keeping a bin next to your desk only increases the likelihood that you'll drop items in there without thinking just out of convenience. Instead, force yourself to walk to the kitchen or laundry and dispose of your rubbish in the right bins. Plus, you'll get in a few more steps for the day!

Use natural light and LED lighting where possible to illuminate your at-home set up. Remember to turn your computer and other devices off at the wall once you're finished with them.

Use the time you would normally spend on a commute going for a morning walk, but try to stick to making coffee at home to save those pennies. And if you've been eyeing off a coffee machine, stop and weigh the costs of a barista-esque machine with a simple stovetop percolator.

Tip

If possible, try not to have your desk set up in your bedroom. Studies show that it is easier to have a work-life balance when you can separate your workspace from your living space. If you can't separate it, then try and have set hours that you're on the clock and off and stick to them.

Studying

If you're studying, then pretty much all of the work-from-home tidbits on page 194 apply to you, too. Here are some more:

· Try and find secondhand books online or, better yet, make friends with someone in the same year or semester and arrange to share books – fewer trees needed!
· Pack a single-use quitter kit (see page 70) and take it with you to uni. You'll often save by bringing your own coffee cup and you can take any leftovers with you.
· Make the most of the library. There are often computers available to use, your tuition will cover the cost of the internet and it will probably have air-conditioning, which will save you running yours at home. Remember to pack enough snacks, too; those vending machines are expensive!

'Pack a single-use quitter kit (see page 70) and take it with you to uni. You'll often save by bringing your own coffee cup and you can take any leftovers with you.'

· Split it! Are you and a friend both struggling with a subject/concept? Split the cost of a tutor and study together.
· Student discounts! I didn't realise how many places I could get student discounts until it was too late. The most popular concession passes are for transport, movies and gyms/exercise facilities. But there are so many more, so have a look at a discount aggregator like Unidays and never miss a deal.
· Catch public transport or walk to university if you can. It's a simple way to do your bit for the planet.

ACTIONABLE STEPS

- [ ] Nail your work uniform

- [ ] Start a workplace sustainability duel with your colleagues

- [ ] Pack plastic-free lunches

- [ ] Make a coffee cup pact with your bestie and don't leave the office

- [ ] without your reusables

- [ ] Sustainably commute to the office

- [ ] Stop printing and start emailing documents to your colleagues

- [ ] Build your work single-use quitter kit (see page 70)

- [ ] BYO takeaway container

NEXT UP

So far, we've talked about a lot of changes we can make inside the home and workplace, so let's take this thinking out to the garden, because there are serious financial and environmental savings to be made in your own backyard.

11.

Build a thriving garden **and a blooming bank account**

Savings scale

SAVE
UP TO
$75 A MONTH

Level 1
Start a compost bin.
Plant one native plant
in your garden.
Propagate something.
Grow something in
water.

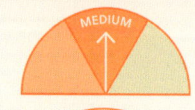

SAVE
UP TO
$150 A MONTH

+ Level 2
Don't overwater your
garden.
Install outdoor solar
lighting.

SAVE
UP TO
$210 A MONTH

+ Level 3
Use a non-petrol
lawn mower.
Build an insect hotel.
Start your veggie garden.

Have you heard?

* 40 per cent of your household waste could be composted.
* Organically active material contributes a whopping 3 per cent of Australia's total greenhouse gas emissions.
* People who enjoy gardening have been intrinsically linked to those who care more about our environment.
* Growing your own fruit and vegetables is healthier! Home 'farmers' generally use fewer chemicals and pesticides, which is better both for your health and the health of the planet.

If you haven't dabbled in the delights of gardening yet, you are missing a major piece of the sustainability puzzle. Not only has gardening been shown to be great for your health (both physical and mental), it presents a myriad of opportunities to proactively improve the health of our planet.

At first glance, you might not associate gardening with saving money, but there are financial gains to be made here. Growing your own veggies, repurposing food waste as fertiliser, better managing your water usage and living simply in a way that's genuinely in tune with Mother Nature all add up to big savings.

It wasn't until I first moved out of home that I embraced gardening for the first time. My dad was always a keen gardener, so the irony of my green thumb only presenting itself once I'd moved 900 kilometres (560 miles) away into my first flat, with a one-metre-square balcony, is not lost on me.

I have had my fair share of gardening failures, and sadly have killed more plants than I care to admit, but now my gardening instincts are blossoming (pun intended), and I'm honoured to share my learnings with you so that you hopefully don't make the same mistakes.

I want to assure you that gardening isn't just for those with rolling hills and a bottomless pit of time and money. No matter how small your space – or your budget – you can make gardening a central component in your sustainability mission.

From the root up

Lots of the tips in this book involve reducing consumption and quitting bad habits, but here I want to focus on building new ones.

Not only does growing your own produce cut down on costs and food miles, it's also an education in the effort and resources it takes to grow food, which will surely lead to wasting less of it!

The agriculture industry has an enormous impact on our planet, and in order to build future food systems, we need to better utilise the land we've already cultivated. Repeatedly planting the same crop laden with pesticides and tilling (or mechanically raking), results in poor soil health. To combat this, more and more farmers and producers are embracing regenerative agriculture practices that renew, improve and restore soil health.

If you look at it like a simple maths equation, traditional farming looks like:

Soil + fertilisers + heavy tilling + single crop
= poor soil quality and health

Soil + cover crop + crop rotation + little to no fertiliser + no tilling
= improved soil quality and health, and better yields

You can have a direct impact by supporting regenerative farmers. It's as simple as starting to grow your own produce at home, planting seasonally, purchasing pesticide-free and locally grown produce.

Tip

Kiss the Ground is a great documentary if you want to dig deeper into the world of regenerative farming.

Planting 101

If you don't have a particularly green thumb, the list below is a good starting point for keeping your plants alive!

- Plants need sunlight to survive. Different plants need more or less, but they all need sunlight for photosynthesis. Before purchasing your plants, study the light in your garden or on your balcony and buy specifically for those areas.
- Next stop – water! As much as possible, reuse water from running the sink, showers and all those little times in the day you can collect water around the house (see page 175).
- Putting down good roots. Your plants are much more likely to survive if you've given the soil a little TLC before planting. Even better if you use your own compost (see page 210) or fertiliser (see page 216).
- If it's dead, chop it off. Save your plants some much-needed energy by trimming dead leaves and flower heads so they can direct that precious growing energy to newer blooms.
- Think about your drainage. All plants need to be able to drain excess water, so make sure all your pots have holes and your garden is planted out with this in mind.
- Never ever throw away a plastic plant pot. Those little black plastic pots you buy your plants from in garden centres are almost impossible to recycle. Plus, you'll need them when it comes time to propagate (see opposite)!

Here's a quick troubleshooting guide for diagnosing the most common plant problems:

· **Brown tips** = too much water
· **Floppy and sad leaves** = need a good drink
· **Roots at the surface of the soil** = needs a bigger pot
· **Very little growth** = needs more sunshine
· **Little holes all in one line** = caterpillars

How to propagate your plants

One thing I was guilty of when I first started gardening was purchasing so many new plants. I didn't think about splitting up my existing plants to use elsewhere. Never heard of propagating? It just involves taking a cutting from one plant to use to grow more. It really is that simple. It might sound cruel, but this actually stimulates new plant growth, not to mention saves you money on buying new plants from the nursery, which in turn cuts down on all those plastic pots!

PROPAGATION TIPS

When it comes to giving your plants the snip, here are a few things to remember:

· Snip below the node, which looks like the elbow joint of your plant. This is where a root will grow from.
· Cut 2–3 centimetres (¾–1¼ inches) towards the main plant.
· Remove any existing leaves that will be submerged in water because they will rot.
· Pop your cutting in some clean water. I just use an old jar and change the water once a week or whenever it looks murky or runs out.

Once 3 centimetres (1¼ inches) of root has grown on your cutting you can plant it in soil, but I have also left mine in water for yonks to get it a bit further along before planting.

My favourite plants to propagate in water are:

· Devil's Ivy (by far the easiest)
· *Syngonium* 'White Butterfly'
· Agave
· Peace lillies
· Aloe vera

Tip
Want to expand your plant collection? Swap cuttings with your friends to up the variety in your garden without increasing your spend.

Growing seedlings from veggies

If you've got fruit and vegetables at home in your fridge or fruit bowl, then you've got what you need to grow your own. So many of your favourite fruits and vegetables are grown from seeds, which are easy to acquire from the produce itself. Yes, this will save you money but also growing your own lightens the load on the agriculture industry, which emits around one-third of all greenhouse gas emissions. You're also more likely to eat something that looks funky, is too small or too big because of the TLC you put into growing it, whereas at the shops it's easy to become picky and choose only perfect-looking produce.

HERE'S A BASIC GUIDE TO GROWING SEEDLINGS FROM SEED:

- Remove the seeds from your fruit or vegetable.
- Place on a cotton towel to dry for 2–3 days.
- Bury in well-drained soil and place in a sunny position.
- Wait until the seed successfully germinates and grows a seedling 3–5 centimetres (1¼–2 inches) tall, then transfer to a larger pot.

VEGGIES TO GROW FROM SEED:

- Cucumber
- Capsicum (pepper)
- Chillies
- Pumpkins (squash)
- Zucchini (courgette)

FRUITS TO GROW FROM SEED:

- Tomato
- Rockmelon (canteloupe)
- Watermelon
- Papaya
- Mangoes
- Avocado
- Strawberry
- Blueberry
- Raspberry
- Blackberry

Easiest fruits and veggies to grow in pots

Even without a garden, you can grow your own delicious vegetables in pots, planter boxes and old tubs and containers. Make the most of your small storage options to save money purchasing new planters.

HERE ARE A FEW REASONS TO POT:

- Pots are great if you are renting because you can pick them up and take them with you when you move.
- Pots contain the spread and size of your plants by keeping them in a confined space.
- You can move pots around depending on the season to get more/less light.
- Pots are the ultimate space saver!

SOME OF MY FAVOURITE FRUITS AND VEGGIES TO GROW IN POTS:

(VEGGIES)

- Spinach
- Silverbeet (Swiss chard)
- Lettuce
- Potato
- Radish
- Beans
- Eggplant (aubergine)
- Chilli
- Carrot
- Zucchini (courgette)

(FRUITS)

- Blueberry
- Strawberry
- Pineapple
- Raspberry
- Figs
- Melon
- Watermelon
- Apple
- Or go big with a citrus tree, like lemon or orange

Tips

With lettuce, the more you pick the more you'll grow! Keep on eating to get the most out of it.

If you're looking to get a head start with your fruit trees, head to your local nursery to pick up a couple of saplings (baby trees). The older they are the more expensive, but they're also harder to kill! Your local nursery will also have lots of great tips and tricks for what to plant and grow in your local area, so don't be afraid to ask lots of questions.

Pesty peeves

Whenever you're growing fruit and veg, you're going to be cultivating something else too: pests. Keeping them at bay without harsh chemicals can be a bit of a head-scratcher, but it is possible with some simple, environmentally friendly (not to mention more cost effective) kitchen formulas.

SLUGS

If you've spotted one slug, chances are there are many more hiding under the leaves. The most effective way to get rid of these creatures is to set an overnight trap. To do this, pour a little bit of your least favourite and cheapest beer into a small dish. Place the dish or container near the place you spotted the slug at the base of the plant and leave overnight. The yeast in the beer attracts the slugs who will come and drink and sadly drown overnight. Doing this for one or two nights should be enough to get rid of an infestation.

INSECTS

If you're dealing with multiple infestations and you don't know where to start or what exactly is eating your veggies, whip up a concoction of garlic spray. Simply combine three to five crushed garlic cloves with 1 litre (34 fluid ounces) boiling water and a dash of castile soup. Allow to cool, then transfer to a spray bottle, give the bottle a good shake and spritz over the leaves of your plants, taking care to also cover the undersides.

SNAILS

The best way to deter snails from eating your plants is to create a barrier that they won't want to cross. To do this, sprinkle a line of coffee grounds or crushed eggshells around the perimeter of the garden bed to keep them at bay.

RATS

If you're dealing with a couple of unwanted rats, you'll know about it. You will see droppings scattered around as well as the ghastly smell of their urine. You'll also probably hear them causing a ruckus. These pesky house guests love parsley and coriander (cilantro), but what they don't love is mint! Plant a fragrant mint shrub next to your veggie patch and sprinkle crushed leaves near where rats normally dine to help deter them.

Tip

Wasps also hate coffee grounds. Place a small amount in a heatproof dish and burn the grounds to keep wasps at bay while you're sitting outside.

MOSQUITOES

Mosquitoes don't only play favourites when it comes to blood (it's been scientifically proven they prefer Type O). Here are a couple of ways I head them off at the pass:

Remove the source. Mosquitoes breed in stagnant water, so make sure you empty all old water vessels around your garden.

If you're sitting outside, you can try burning a citronella candle or putting a few drops of citronella oil on your skin. Or create orange lanterns by cutting oranges in half, removing the flesh and placing a tealight candle inside. Mosquitoes also don't like used coffee grounds. Once dry, leave a bowl of grounds on your outdoor table.

If you're looking for year-round support, go no further than Balm of Gilead or cedronella (*Cedronella triphylla*). Simply rub its lemon-scented leaves on your skin to ward off mozzies. Plus, they are easy to grow.

'Create orange lanterns by cutting oranges in half, removing the flesh and placing a tealight candle inside.'

Weeds

Weeds really love to put their roots down and ruin my weekend. Here are a couple of ways that I deal with them without the harsh and expensive chemicals:

- Singe them with boiling water – just be careful the runoff doesn't hit your lovely plants.
- Use salt on weeds that crop up between the cracks in pavers.
- Use sugar on nut grass (in Australia).
- Smother them with mulch or cardboard and remove their energy.
- Dilute one-part white vinegar and twenty-parts water in a spray bottle and spray onto weeds to dry them out and kill them. This is potent so make sure to only spray the weeds.

Herbs for beginners

When people start thinking about growing their own food, I recommend they begin not with vegetables, but with herbs. Herbs are more forgiving, require less space and will give you year-round love.

An unlimited supply of flavour sensations is great, but this also means you don't need to spend your money on those pesky plastic-wrapped herbs from the supermarket that go limp before they've even made it into your fridge.

Mint is amazing and so difficult to kill that you won't ever be rid of it. Because of this, I always plant mint in pots and always alone as it tends to take over.

Rosemary is one of my favourite herbs to grow, especially in a warm, dry climate like Australia. It works well as a herb but also as a bush to create a lush-looking garden.

If you're looking for something easy that won't grow out of control, chives are good, and they're really versatile to use.

Whenever I buy a pot of basil at the supermarket, I just plant it straight in the ground. Nine times out of ten, it keeps growing and I'll get a couple of months out of it before it goes to seed. Much better than using a few leaves off the top, then throwing the plant away! I reuse the plastic pot for my other seedlings, or return it to a nursery, because if it's made from black plastic, it's really hard to recycle.

Another one on the easy-to-grow list is parsley. Flat-leaf (Italian) or curly, it doesn't matter. They are both simple to grow, and the more you use them the more they'll thrive.

I love coriander (cilantro), but for some reason have no luck growing it. Every time I've tried, no matter how much love I give it I never seem to be able to get coriander to thrive. My friends who manage to grow it live in cooler climates, and say it thrives in shady, partially sunny spots and to grow it in pots.

It's a good idea to plant like herbs together. This is called companion planting – cute, right? Look at the stems to work out which herbs will be the best housemates. Soft-stalked herbs like coriander, parsley and basil get along well, and woody herbs like sage, rosemary and thyme make another great trio.

Grown from packet, seedling or plant, it really doesn't matter. These hardy kitchen companions are the easiest place to start growing your own produce.

Food scrap veggie patch

When it comes to starting your own veggie patch, you might think growing plants from seeds is the easiest way to begin, but I have another method that will save you money and cut down on food waste at the same time – growing from veggie scraps!

The easiest vegetable to regrow from scraps is spring onion (scallion). Just trim 2–3 centimetres (¾–1¼ inches) off the root ends of your bunch and place these in a jar of water, roots facing down (you can use a rubber band to hold them all together). Change the water every two or three days and watch your spring onions grow right before your eyes! When you need to use them, just snip what you need off the top, then keep growing.

Regrowing in water actually works for lots of different vegetables, including:

- Lettuce
- Spring onion (scallion)
- Carrot
- Celery
- Parsnips
- Radishes
- Turnips
- Leek
- Fennel
- Onion
- Beetroot (beet)
- Bok choy
- Ginger
- Garlic
- Pineapple
- Herbs, such as mint, basil and rosemary

If you are planning to grow multiple veggies at once, fill a shallow baking tray with 2–3 centimetres (¾–1¼ inches) of water and place the root ends in.

If you do buy herbs in a container from the supermarket, remove the plant from the tub (store this for propagating other plants!) and separate out the stems to create six or seven smaller plants. From here, you can:

- Remove all the soil gently to expose the root system, then place the herbs in a jar of water to keep them growing.
- Pot them in a planter on your windowsill so you have ready access to snippings whenever you need them. The planter can then be moved in and out to take advantage of the rain and sun.

For woodier herbs like rosemary, take a cutting from a larger bush and place it in a jar of water in a sunny spot. Within a couple of weeks, you will see new roots form, at which point you can plant it in a pot or another spot in your garden.

Composting

Composting dates back to 5000 BC where evidence shows that crops were planted in rotting manure, but it is revolutionary in the quest to live more sustainably. It's estimated that 41 per cent of the average Australian households' waste is organic matter which could be composted. What happens when this organic matter, goes to landfill? It cooks and creates a toxic greenhouse gas called methane, which is twenty-three times more potent than carbon dioxide. By composting, not only are you helping the planet by cutting down on this lethal gas, but you're saving a boatload on pricey fertiliser by making your own!

First things first, let's debunk some common composting myths. It doesn't smell (if you do it correctly), it isn't difficult, and you don't have to do much to maintain it. It is simply the process by which food scraps and other organic materials are broken down naturally. The only thing you need to make sure of is that you have the right ratio of wet and dry 'ingredients'.

I prefer to explain it like baking a cake. You need the right amount of eggs, milk and butter, plus the right amount of flour and sugar to bring it together into a homogenous mixture. Composting is no different: wet ingredients (nitrogen), dry ingredients (carbon), some oxygen, and you have the perfect recipe.

Wet ingredients are things like food scraps, which produce nitrogen, one of life's building blocks that helps elements grow. If there's too much nitrogen, you'll have a sloppy wet mess. Dry ingredients, or carbon, feed your pile and include things like dried leaves, egg cartons and shredded paper. Too much of these and your pile will be too dry and take longer to break down.

Once you have the right ratio your compost won't smell and will resemble a dirt-like powder. If it is smelly or sloppy check below for my troubleshooting guide.

Composting at home has a magnitude of benefits, including:

- The addition of organic matter improves the health and structure of your soil, which gives your plants and veggies the perfect base to grow in.
- Reducing organic waste in landfill directly reduces greenhouse gas emissions.
- Saves you money on chemical-ridden fertilisers (just use your home-made compost).

What to compost

There aren't many rules when it comes to composting, but if you want to keep the microclimate of your compost in check, stick to adding these ingredients:

- · All of your vegetable and fruit scraps
- · Eggshells
- · Tea leaves and coffee grounds
- · Green grass clippings and weeds without seeds
- · Dried leaves and flowers
- · Newspaper and shredded paper
- · Non-glossy cardboard and old toilet rolls
- · Straw and hay
- · Dog hair

What not to compost

Steer clear of adding these to your bin:

- · Meat, bones, dairy and fat
- · Animal manures, including pet poo – let's keep it vegan
- · Magazines and glossy paper
- · Large branches and weeds with seeds
- · Plastic and glass
- · Vacuum dust
- · Tea bags

Composting is like one giant science experiment, but one constant is the need to turn it every week. I like to use an aerator, which looks like a giant corkscrew, but a shovel is fine. This helps to add oxygen to your heap – the final ingredient in your perfect compost cake.

Tips

If you're worried about pests getting into your compost bin, simply line the base with fine wire mesh to keep mice and rats away.

Make sure you remove those pesky plastic fruit stickers before tossing the peels into the compost. They won't break down but will litter your bin like confetti. Remove them first, otherwise you'll be spending your precious weekends sticker fossicking.

Secrets to success

While composting is relatively simple, your bin will require a little TLC. You need to turn it once or twice a week to allow oxygen into the compost, which helps speed up the composting process.

To maintain your compost's delicate ecosystem, you probably won't need to add any water as your food scraps will provide enough moisture.

For every one-part nitrogen (e.g. food scraps), you want to be adding two- to three-parts carbon (e.g. dry leaves). As a general rule, every time I empty my compost caddy I try and add at least two caddies full of dried leaves or paper.

Troubleshooting

Rest assured, your compost bin will let you know when something is not quite right. It's actually one of my favourite things about composting: treating it like a scientific investigation and learning along the way.

- **Funky smell = too many food scraps,** not enough carbon.
- **Worms scrambling to the top of your pile** = too many food scraps, not enough carbon.
- **Soggy, sloppy compost** = add some brown matter and aerate the compost often.
- **A white snow-like mould** = this is just a normal part of the composting process
- **Too lumpy and crunchy** = give your compost a helping hand by chopping up larger items, like corn cobs or eggshells, which will take longer than other food scraps to break down.
- **Large white maggots are in my bin, help!** = you have hit the jackpot! These aren't a pest but black soldier fly larvae. About half the size of your thumbnail, they are the best composters around and will chew through your food like no tomorrow. They also happen to make great chicken feed!

The result? Aside from the fact that you've reduced your household waste by approximately 40 per cent just by composting, you've also created the best organic fertiliser money can't buy! There's no need to purchase expensive, chemical-laden fertiliser, just use handfuls of your own.

How long your compost will take to break down really depends on your climate (the warmer, the faster) and the number of scraps and the size of your bin as well as the types of materials you throw in.

Generally speaking, a compost bin will set you back about $50, but it's a good idea to keep an eye out online for a free secondhand bin, as these are often up for grabs.

You can also build your own using five old wooden pallets (the ones with narrow spaces in between the boards are best for obvious reasons). Make a box using four pallets and secure the joins with some old rope or wire. Use the final pallet to make a lid and lay a piece of tarp over the top to keep out pests and too much rain.

Animal allies

You might not be living on the hobby farm of your dreams just yet, but there are a few animal friends that can help break down your food and provide countless hours of entertainment.

Worm farms

If you don't have a garden or the desire to start a compost bin, a worm farm is just as amazing! They can be kept in a dark cool place, like your laundry or carport, and will create 'worm tea', which is the liquid at the bottom of the farm (called worm leachate) caused by the food being processed by the worms – a liquid gold that makes a delicious natural fertiliser. Just remember to dilute it one-part worm tea to twenty-parts water, as it can pack a punch! You will also be able to collect worm poo, or castings, from your bottom tray, which can go directly on your garden.

You can feed your worms pretty much everything you'd put in your compost bin, but avoid citrus, onion peels and garlic as these are too acidic for their little tummies. Worms love eggshells too, but sometimes have a hard time breaking them down, so help their tiny mouths by crushing them up first.

Tip

If you've got a mate with a farm, ask them for a handful of worms to get your farm started. Otherwise, you'll need to purchase some from your local hardware store. Worm farm worms are a special breed, so don't go digging just any old worm up from your garden.

FUN FACT

Did you know that a happy worm can eat four times its body weight in a day?!

Worm farms will also cost roughly $50, but you can make your own using an old bathtub; the drain makes for a perfect liquid-gold dispenser. Or you can use a couple of old polystyrene boxes.

· Use a pen or a stick to poke some holes in one of the boxes.
· Place one on top of the other and fill the top box with compost and worms.
· Slowly start to feed your worms little by little. Too much waste and it will go mouldy. before they have a chance to eat it.

If you've got a lot of food waste scraps or you don't want to start your own compost bin or worm farm, ask your local community garden if they'd like your food scraps. I doubt they would say no, as your trash will be the perfect addition to their mix.

If you'd love to collect your scraps and composting them but don't want to actually have a bin, then there is a solution for you. For Aussies and New Zealanders, check our Share Waste: it's like Google Maps but for compost bins in your area. Households, called hosts, list their bins on the app and you can donate your scraps to them!

Chickens

Sadly, I was never allowed chickens when I was a kid, and my beachside apartment isn't ideal for a coop, but they will definitely feature on my grand plan.

The benefits of keeping chickens include:
· Great chompers of food scraps
· Provide fresh delicious eggs (hey, big saver)
· Chicken poop is a great natural fertiliser
· Perfect pest control, as chooks will feast on bugs, slugs and other critters

Chickens are the ultimate four-in-one. They will give you the freshest eggs possible, stop food waste from going to landfill, create an amazing toxin-free fertiliser for your garden and fight off bugs, reducing your need for toxic (and expensive) pesticides.

Have a search to see if anyone is moving and giving away their chickens. Also, rescue hens are often in need of a home and lots of space to roam around in, so keep an eye out on local Facebook groups and animal shelters for the call-out.

EGGSHELLS

As you can probably tell, I don't love putting eggshells in my compost or worm farm, but they do have their place. Eggshells contain extremely high levels of potassium, which your plants love, so you can use them to make a tea to feed your veggies.

- Start by boiling a kettle of water.
- Crush a couple of eggshells in a glass.
- Top up with water and leave to sit overnight.
- In the morning, drain out the shells and use the water as a delicious fertiliser.
- The shells can be ground down to a dust and used to deter snails and slugs (see page 206). Or you can crush them up finely and sprinkle them on the garden for the ultimate slow-release fertiliser!

Eggshells also make the perfect seedling containers. Once you've cracked one in half, use your old egg carton as a stand, then fill the shells with soil. Place a seed inside and watch your seedlings grow! When you're ready to plant, simply plant the eggshell containing the seedling directly into the soil and the shell will just rot away.

Bee-lieve it or not

Bees are crucial for any garden. Any ecosystem, in fact. A bee lives for just 40 days, but in that time will visit over 1000 flowers and travel up to 10 kilometres (6 miles).

Bees are responsible for the growth of two-thirds of all the food we eat, and they are called pollinators because they transfer the male part to female plants allowing flowers to blossom and fruit to grow. Protecting and encouraging bees should be on the agenda of anyone who cares about the health of our planet. Here are some ways you can help:

- Plant native trees; the pollen from these trees are strongly preferred by native bees, so it helps them to thrive.
- Bees use water as fuel but also to cool their hive, so on stinking hot days leave a little ramekin of water with a couple of stones in it and a piece of ribbon or natural fabric on it so that they can safely land and exit the pool to get water. On a warm day, the average hive of bees will drink 1 litre (34 fluid ounces) of water!
- Use fewer pesticides. These are toxic to bees and other insects.

How to make an insect hotel

No this isn't another side hustle – an insect hotel is a safe space for pollinators to have a bit of R&R. These hotels mean that if insects, ladybirds or bees are caught out in the heat, wind or rain with not enough oomph to get home, they can take a rest here, let the weather pass and then be on their way. While you can purchase these online, making them yourself is relatively easy and cheap. Plus, it's a great school holiday activity.

Instead of purchasing a new hotel online, go on a scavenger hunt around your shed and garden and use up what you've got lying around. Your hotel will need to cater to lots of different guests, so it is important to include a combination of big rooms, little rooms, slits and hidey holes.

Make sure you start with a roof, which can be made from a piece of timber or corrugated iron. Use hardwood or ply to form the main walls before stuffing the inside with smaller pieces of bamboo and twigs. Drill some small holes into some plywood so there are little spots for spiders.

Hang your hotel in a tree or place it in a warm spot, like on a balcony that is slightly protected from the elements. Check every few days to make sure your tenants are happy and enjoying themselves!

Food waste fertilisers

One thing that I never spend money on is fertiliser. Firstly, if you've got a compost bin (see page 210), then you'll never have to buy fertiliser again! Secondly, you can easily turn so many food scraps into fertiliser for your garden.

Banana peels

Banana peels contain high levels of calcium, potassium, phosphorus and magnesium – pretty much every nutrient your indoor and outdoor plants know and love.

How to make banana peel tea:
- Boil a kettle of water.
- Place a couple of banana peels in a mug or glass jug and cover with boiling water.
- Leave to steep overnight.
- In the morning, drain out the peels and use the water as a delicious fertiliser.
- The peels can be diced and also spread on plants, or added to your compost bin.

Coffee grounds

Hello, latte lovers! You're not the only one who loves a good dose of coffee – your garden craves it too.

Coffee grounds scattered on the garden work to improve drainage and water retention in your soil. They can be somewhat acidic though, so only apply a tablespoon per pot every month or so. The rest needs to go into your compost bin or worm farm.

Seaweed spray

Algae is one of the best fertilisers for your garden. But liquid seaweed is something I can never bring myself to buy because it's in such abundance (especially if you live close to the beach).

Bundle up some seaweed and take it home. Give it a really thorough rinse to remove as much sea salt as possible. I like to hang it on the clothesline, then leave it to soak in a bucket for a few days. When it gets dark and murky that's when the magic happens.

Fill an old spray bottle with the oozing juice and spray onto the base of your plants. With the remaining seaweed, give it a rough chop and sprinkle it on your garden for an extra dose of goodness.

Indoor pests

Living in Australia, dealing with pests is something we are faced with daily. Deadly spiders and rattlesnakes don't scare me, but some of the critters below get to me. Pests create chaos, they are dirty and require energy, effort and money to remove them. Here's my toxin-free cheap-as-chips guide to bidding adieu to unwanted pests.

Pantry moths

I feel unbridled anger towards very few things in life, but pantry moths and weevils are some of them. They seem to weasel their way into high-security items even if they're tucked away in the pantry. Sadly, there is a very high chance that if you see one pantry moth, there will be more.

First things first, you need to remove absolutely everything from your pantry. If you leave just one infested item they will be back with a vengeance. Check to make sure each pantry staple is secure and has no new protein sources; you can often see moths hanging from the top of packets. Wipe down the entire pantry with a concoction of white vinegar and eucalyptus oil, which will act as a repellent and kill any that have been left behind. Moving forward, they hate bay leaves, so add a single leaf to all of your pantry items (just remove it before cooking). You can also store some items like flour in the freezer to prevent the moths from finding a new home!

Ants

Ants love sugar as much as me, but luckily for you they hate swimming. If you have something that ants seem to love, guard it by placing the jar or container in a dish of water. If you're dealing with a larger outbreak, sprinkle talcum powder, ground cinnamon or borax at their entrance, which will stop them from walking over it.

Cockroaches

If you have one or two unwanted friends and need to deter them, try using the following essential oils: peppermint, eucalyptus, lemon. Put a couple of drops on a cotton wool bud or, if you're fancy enough, diffuse them to ward off cockroaches and help your home smell fresh. Win-win!

Fruit flies

Accidentally left something in the fruit bowl too long and now you're dealing with an outbreak of fruit flies? While they're seemingly harmless, fruit flies breed faster than rabbits, so putting a stop them it is important!

In a small ramekin, combine ¼–1½ cups (60–125 millilitres) apple cider vinegar and a small squirt of dish soap and leave it next to their breeding ground. Every couple of days replace the vinegar as it lures and drowns your newfound roomies.

Household flies

If swatting household flies was an Olympic sport I have no doubt that Australians would win gold. If you're sick of competing or would prefer to not even have the need to participate, then here's how to keep them away.

All you need to do is simply cut a lemon in half, pierce the cut lemon with ten cloves and leave it in the flies' home ground and they'll fly away forever more.

If you're looking for a spray, simply mix equal parts water and vinegar with a squirt of dish soap and keep it handy in a spray bottle.

Water wise

Gardening is a fabulous pastime and a great way to get back in touch with nature, but one environmental impact it has is on water consumption. Fresh water is a finite resource, making up just 3 per cent of all water on earth, which is why we should use it sparingly. Here are a couple of ways to use less water and cut down on your water bills.

Cut down water use

We have already looked in depth at reducing your water consumption inside your home back on page 175, but what about outside? There are plenty of savings to be made here too:

· Use mulch to lock in moisture, which will allow you to cut down on watering and also protect your plants' roots from frost.
· Adding compost to your soil helps it retain water while adding nutrients.

- Cut right back on your watering through autumn and winter and let nature take its course.
- The best time to water your garden is early in the morning or late in the afternoon. You want to give your garden the chance to absorb the runoff into the soil before it warms up and evaporates.
- If you have a big garden, use soaker and dripper hoses to water the base and roots of the plants over the leaves.
- Avoid overwatering. If you see water pooling on the surface of your garden bed, or running across footpaths and gutters, this is a sure sign that you're overwatering.

Watering on holiday

Not everyone has an amazing neighbour who is willing to water your plants while you're away, so to keep your thirstiest plants healthy in your absence:

- **Create a drip system:** Fill old soft drink or wine bottles with water. Dig a small hole about the size of the neck of the bottle near the base of your plant and bury the filled bottle upside down. In theory, your plant will only drink when it's thirsty, so this allows it to take what it needs.
- **Create a wicking station for indoor plants:** Group your indoor plants together, then fill a large vase, bowl or your blender with water. Cut lengths of cotton twine or string and place one end of each piece in the water and the other end in the soil of the plant. You can use a chopstick or spoon to bury it 2–3 centimetres (¾–1¼ inches) deep. This creates a giant straw for your plants, which should continue to drink slowly while you're away.

ACTIONABLE STEPS

- [ ] **Start a compost bin**
- [ ] **Install outdoor solar lighting**
- [ ] **Start a herb garden**
- [ ] **Build an insect hotel**
- [ ] **Plant one native plant in your garden**
- [ ] **Grow something in water**
- [ ] **Use a non-petrol mower**
- [ ] **Use mulch and don't overwater your garden**
- [ ] **Propagate something**
- [ ] **Start your veggie garden**

NEXT UP

So, what about when you want to leave the comforts of your nest and go and explore the big wide world? Air travel is a bit of a fraught subject when it comes to the sustainability conversation, because it's easily one of the worst things you can do for the environment. However, I want to make living sustainably something that actually fits into your everyday life, so I'd prefer to focus on what you can do at an individual level to lessen, not necessarily eliminate, your environmental footprint while travelling. It's not about avoiding travel completely, but making the most informed choices when you do.

12.

Travel the world
but leave no footprint

Savings scale

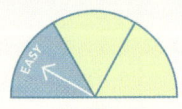

SAVE

UP TO

$75 A MONTH

Level 1
BYO reusables.
Skip room service.
YOHO: You're Only
Here Once.

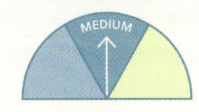

SAVE

UP TO

$150 A MONTH

+ Level 2
Pack light.
Support local businesses.
Stay in one place longer.

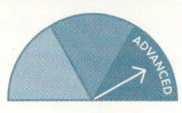

SAVE

UP TO

$210 A MONTH

+ Level 3
Choose home stays.
Avoid meat.
Try housesitting.

Have you heard?

* Air travel alone makes up 20 per cent of the tourist industry's carbon emissions.

* Australians spend more than $900 million a year on travel.

* Three-quarters of British people want to travel more sustainably.

* Flying business class consumes four times more carbon than economy seats because all of that extra room means fewer people on planes and more emissions per person.

Air travel is the elephant in the room when it comes to sustainable living. It's widely known to be one of the worst things you can do for the environment, but it's also a necessary part of life.

I'm not going to tell you not to fly at all; instead, I want to look at what you can do to lessen your environmental footprint when you do travel. Just because you're on a money- and planet-saving crusade, doesn't mean you shouldn't be able to enjoy exploring the world.

I spent the majority of my gap year napping in airports and finding the cheapest supermarket wine I could, so being on a shoestring budget and backpacking for nine months straight did teach me a thing or two – mostly, what 'not' to do.

A lot of financial and environmental savings can be made before you even leave the tarmac by doing a bit of forward planning. Being mindful of how much you pack, how you get to and from the airport and what you can do to lessen your footprint in the air is a great place to start.

Once you've arrived at your destination, reframing how you approach a holiday is essential to making it more sustainable. Using a local laundromat, housesitting instead of hotel-ing and staying longer in one place can all add up to huge savings that don't just look good in your bank account – the planet will thank you too.

Making conscious and careful decisions about how you conduct yourself as a tourist and how you impact a local landscape and support local people and culture are other ways you can ensure that when you do travel you are doing it in as environmentally conscious a way as possible.

Planning

People with Type A personalities will be cheering for this next bit; planning really is the key to saving money and reducing your environmental footprint while travelling. It all comes down to research – and budgeting! For some this comes naturally. For others it can be more difficult, especially when you're organising a much-anticipated getaway.

If you follow me on Instagram, you will know that I love to travel. If I'm not working (which is 99.9 per cent of the time), I will be travelling. I love exploring and discovering new places and cultures. But with all of my travels come a lot of conversations and questions about how I do it sustainably.

The first thing is to acknowledge that, with travel, you are going to consume more energy and create more waste and emissions than you would at home. That is just a fact. After accepting that, the best thing you can do is plan to reduce your impact as much as possible by being prepared. Be realistic about what's possible while travelling, and know that every little saving counts.

Carbon offsetting

The aviation sector currently accounts for about 2 per cent of global carbon emissions, and is one of the fastest-growing polluters. Whenever I book flights, I make sure I carbon offset them. Carbon offsets are used to pay back the negative environmental impact that a company – in this case, an airline – has. It's kind of like a swear jar: you say a naughty word and you put money in the jar. It doesn't completely solve the problem, but it mitigates some of its effects.

There is not a lot of transparency around carbon offsetting in general; you normally have to dig a little deeper to find out exactly how a company is offsetting its emissions, and it won't always be with causes that align with your values. So, when carbon offsetting your flight, make sure you use a third party, such as Gold Standard, so that you are able to track exactly how you are carbon offsetting the flight.

Budget is best

When it comes to making sustainable travel choices, budget options often save more than money; they can be the most environmentally friendly options, too.

'The first thing is to acknowledge that, with travel, you are going to consume more energy and create more waste and emissions than you would at home. That is just a fact. After accepting that, the best thing you can do is plan to reduce your impact as much as possible by being prepared.'

Feel like a sardine in a can when flying a low-cost airline? Not only are budget airlines cheap but their carbon footprint is also lower, as you have more people in a smaller plane rather than multiple aircraft with fewer people.

Need another reason to be proud of your economy seat? It is estimated that flying business class creates up to five and a half times the amount of carbon emissions than flying economy.

And before you go adding stops to your journey, keep in mind that taking a direct flight is also better for the planet, because landing and taking off is when planes use most of their energy.

Of course, one of the easiest ways to save both planet and money when travelling is to avoid flying altogether and find an alternative mode of transport. If it's only a short trip, look into a train journey instead, which is by far the most sustainable of all transport options aside from walking or cycling. Trains emit 66–75 per cent less carbon than other forms of transport, even if they're electric. So, if you have time, opt for an overnight train over a pesky flight.

There's only one form of transport that is worse than flying: boating. Cruise ships emit three to four times more carbon dioxide per kilometre than airlines.

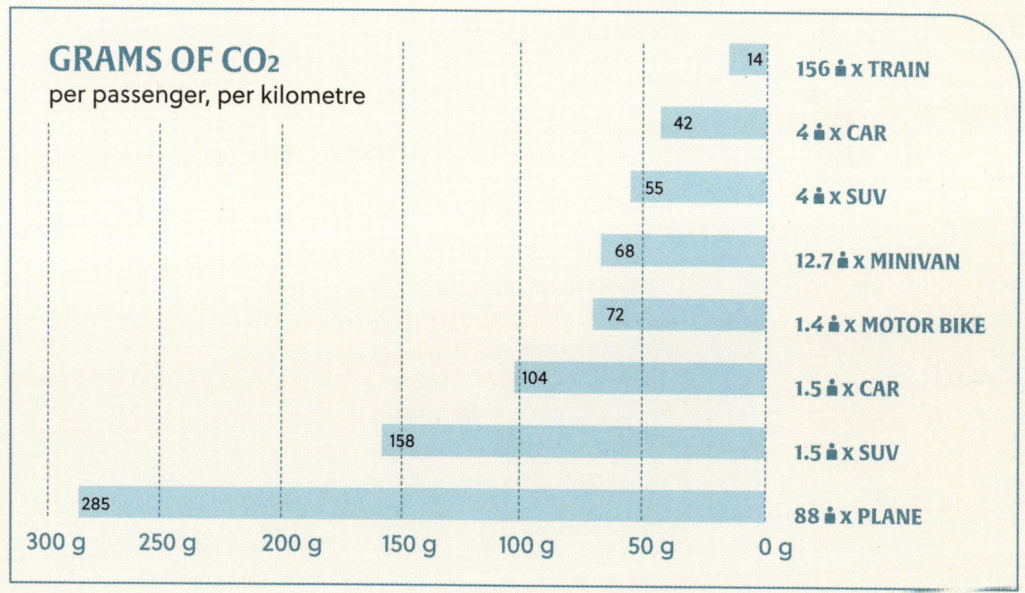

GRAMS OF CO$_2$
per passenger, per kilometre

14	156 x TRAIN
42	4 x CAR
55	4 x SUV
68	12.7 x MINIVAN
72	1.4 x MOTOR BIKE
104	1.5 x CAR
158	1.5 x SUV
285	88 x PLANE

300 g   250 g   200 g   150 g   100 g   50 g   0 g

Booking sustainably

When booking a hotel, I try to make sure that the accommodation follows sustainable practices. Look on the hotel website to check out their sustainability credentials, which usually involve things like third-party certification from platforms like Ecostars or Travalyst. These organisations look at everything from the lightbulbs a hotel uses in its rooms, to drought-tolerant landscaping. Many hotels will have a sustainability page explaining exactly what they are doing to reduce their environmental impact.

If you head to booking.com you will find, along with your usual star rating for each hotel, a 'green leaf' approval that will tell you how sustainable a hotel or hostel is. And, speaking of hostels, while they may bring back memories of travelling in your twenties, they are often more planet-friendly because they're usually closely connected to the community and use fewer resources by offering dorm or shared-room accommodation.

If you're looking for something out of the box, take a look at bookdifferent.com where all sustainability credentials are checked by third parties. Also keep an eye out for hotels and services that operate to a global sustainability standard, which is managed and operated by the Global Sustainable Tourism Council (GSTC). These standards not only look at buildings, but at social and environmental standards, too.

Timing is key

One of the simplest things you can do to make huge savings, both environmental and financial, is being selective about when you travel.

If you can, avoid travelling at peak periods when there is an enormous strain on resources. Greater demand for lighting, heating and water means that, in particular, smaller, less developed destinations will be the most heavily impacted as they don't have the infrastructure to handle these surges. Not only is travelling in off-peak periods arguably more relaxing, quieter and more enjoyable, but without the throngs of tourists you'll be able to connect more directly with local people and businesses.

If you do need to travel during peak times, book early to take advantage of any early bird specials.

Packing

Packing light will not only you save money, but the lighter your baggage the lighter the plane, which means it uses less carbon. If you can stick carry-on only, even better! Plus, if you have lighter and more mobile luggage, you're more likely to walk or catch public transport to the airport over getting a private cab.

Despite my best efforts, I don't think I have ever been on a trip and worn absolutely everything in my bag. Be savvy with your packing list and pack only what you need. Be mindful of any 'just in case' packing; do you really need three different hats? If you're travelling in a group, it can be useful to share common items, which will also cut down on the total amount of luggage.

Just because you're on holiday, it doesn't mean your sustainability habits should go out the window, starting with what you pack. To make life easier (and more environmentally friendly) at the other end, it's a good idea to bring some essential items from home.

Packing essentials:
· Bamboo toothbrush
· Castile soap mini
· Shampoo bar
· Reusable silicone pouches
· Reusable coffee cup and water bottle
· Single-use quitter kit (see page 70)

One of the most powerful tools in my sustainable living arsenal is my single-use quitter kit, and it really comes into its own when travelling and leaning on those convenience items becomes all the more tempting. It can be as simple as remembering to pack a tote bag (for carrying snacks and personal items to and from the beach), a spork (a cross between a spoon and fork), a reusable water bottle (you can always find places to fill it up, or ask a local cafe to do it for you), and a reusable napkin. As you're travelling – and eating – your way through a new place, it's too easy to turn to single-use plastics, so be prepared with your own sustainable options. You could even ask the hotel where you're staying if you could borrow a knife and fork for the duration of your stay.

Transport

The way you choose to travel to and from the airport, and once you arrive at your destination, can greatly reduce the environmental footprint of your trip.

If you can, and if you haven't packed too heavily (see page 229), see if you can get the train or a bus to the airport over booking a private taxi.

Once you land and have dumped your luggage at your hotel, your options open up a bit. Personally, I love cycling around a new city. It's a great way to really experience a place, and you never have to worry about finding a place to park when you want to stop and look at something interesting. Some of my favourite countries to cycle in are the Netherlands and Germany, and most major cities around the world have bikes you can hire.

Even more than cycling though, the best way to really take in a new place is on foot. It's great exercise, you can immerse yourself in the experience of being somewhere new, and there are zero costs to both your wallet and the environment. If you're on holiday, you'll usually have more time up your sleeve too, so I find it forces me to slow down, relax and really take everything in. If you are hiking, adventuring or just walking around a new place, stick to the footpaths and don't damage any local fauna.

Up for a history lesson? Have a look to see if your next holiday destination offers a City Walking Tour. You gain so much cultural and historical knowledge, meet other travellers and the guides will often be able to give you tips for the best places to eat and visit that you won't find on Google.

Want to feel like you have your own personal guide when exploring a city? TripIt is a free app that is just like having a travel agent in your pocket. Upload your booking documents to your unique TripIt email address and it will create an itinerary for you. You can share it with your travel companions or even family at home so they know what you're up to.

Not sure where to start with public transport? Rather than downloading every local city transport app, simply download Rome2Rio – an all-in-one app with all the local public transport information in one place. It also allows you to download maps onto your device so you can get around when you're off the Wi-Fi network.

At the airport

It's not until you arrive at the airport that you finally feel like you're going on a holiday. You might feel like there's not much you can control about the airport setting, but there are a few things you can do while there, and, once you take off, that will help to reduce your environmental and financial spend.

Go ticket free

Unless you are a scrapbooker, most airplane tickets cannot be reused or recycled because they're made from a plastic-coated paper that makes them hard to process. Get your ticket on your phone instead and, if you're somewhere without Wi-Fi, make sure you screenshot it ahead of time.

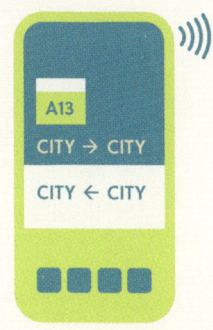

In departures

The departure lounge of most international airports is engineered for over-consumption; there are countless food outlets serving almost exclusively takeaway food, as well as gift shops and duty-free stores that will tempt you to part with your money (and sustainability values) faster than a kid in a candy shop. Here are a few tips for keeping a handle on both:

- Eat before you arrive at the airport so you can avoid the over-priced and heavily packaged takeaway options.
- If the timing doesn't work out and you do need to eat at the airport, bring your own clean reusable container and ask for your food to be packaged in that. You can take the container to the bathroom and wash it up there before boarding. Obviously, a knife and fork won't make it through security, so make sure you're hunting down wooden cutlery, too.
- Do a double check of all those essential travel toiletries before you leave the house to avoid spending big on forgotten items at the most expensive shops in the world.

On the plane

You're on the plane, burning those fossil fuels and eating up that carbon, but there are still things you can do to reduce the environmental impact of your flight. Start by opting for a vegetarian meal, which lowers your carbon footprint – and your chances of getting sick. Bring your reusable coffee cup (I take mine on planes and have never had a problem) and drink your gin and tonic straight from the can – no need for a plastic cup.

Bring your own cord headphones. These days, you don't need a special set of headphones to connect to the plane's in-flight entertainment (and they invariably come in soft plastic bags for hygiene purposes). Plus, the ones that airlines hand out are cheap and often only get used once before being sent to landfill.

Flying budget? Bring your own snacks and don't spend the price of a premium ticket on (usually awful) airline food.

I always pack a small set of toiletries in my carry-on luggage. Even if my big bag is delayed at the other end, I don't want to have to delay brushing my teeth. Plus, using my own means I don't have to consume the plastic-laden airline freebies.

Dress it up! I can tell you right now there's a good chance you'll get cold on your next flight, so pack enough layers to avoid asking for extra plastic-wrapped blankets!

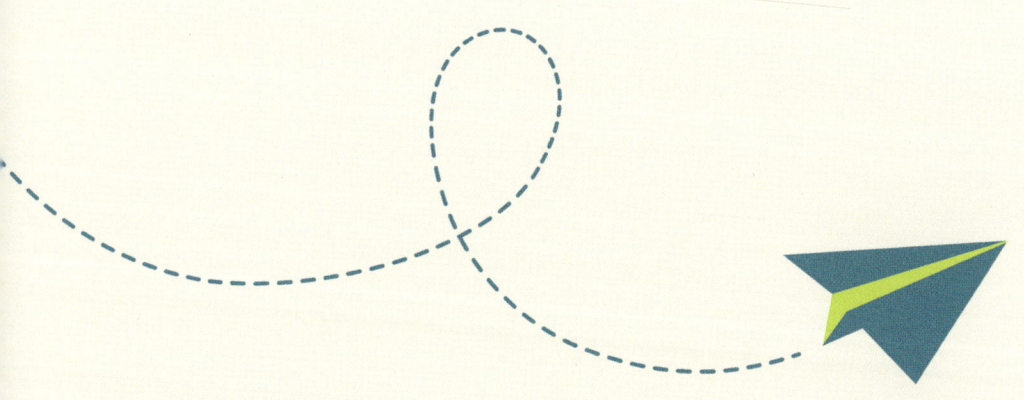

At your destination

You've made it! You stuck to your budget and did so much research on the sustainability credentials of hotels that you're going cross-eyed. Take in that fresh air, give yourself a pat on the back and let the real fun begin. Here are a few small things that I do when I arrive in a new place so that I've got more money to spend on the things that count (aka once-in-a-lifetime experiences) and give the planet a helping hand at the same time.

'More and more people are looking for someone to look after their home and furry friend when they're out of town, and you can often negotiate your stay for free ...'

Washing

If you're on a long trip, especially if you've made those carbon savings by only bringing carry-on luggage, there will come a time when you need to do some washing. Not only are hotel laundry services expensive, but they also often wash your clothes individually and use dryers – hello, energy! Instead, look for a local laundromat for larger items and wash your underwear yourself in the hotel bathroom. I always bring a mini castile soap with me for this (and lots of other purposes!). Once washed, hang your clothes over the towel rail and leave to dry while you go out exploring.

Housesitting

Housesitting is a fun way to feel at home in a new place. More and more people are looking for someone to look after their home and furry friend while they're out of town, and you can often negotiate your stay for free, or even get paid! There are so many different platforms to do this, so look for the one with lots of options for your desired destination.

Do a house swap! Do you live somewhere that someone would love to visit? List your property on a home exchange website and arrange to do a house swap instead of paying to stay in a hotel. I also find Facebook groups are a great place to swap and trade, but you need to be a little more careful as you won't have the back-up research that a verified platform would have done. You pay for what you get!

If you aren't super keen on having complete strangers in your home, why not ask friends who live in overseas if they would like to do a swap (that is if you're not there to visit them!).

'Rather than flying through more destinations than you can remember (and leaving a slew of carbon emissions in your wake), slow it right down and have longer, more enjoyable stays in fewer places.'

Support local

One of the simplest and easiest things that you can do both for your wallet and the planet when travelling is support local businesses. Although they might be the familiar option, try to avoid big global chains like Starbucks and McDonald's and seek out local restaurants and vendors instead. Supporting these smaller businesses means that you're contributing to the local economy, reducing air miles and, generally speaking, having a far more authentic, delicious and amazing experience. Plus, this often means you'll be eating local ingredients that haven't been imported internationally.

Keep any brochures you pick up in good condition and leave them in your hotel room for the next person – it cuts down on waste and helps direct the next international visitor to local haunts.

Long-lasting stays

Take longer holidays. Yes, you read that right: another way to cut down on both your spending and your ecological footprint is to stay longer in each destination. Rather than flying through more destinations than you can remember (and leaving a slew of carbon emissions in your wake), slow it right down and have longer, more enjoyable stays in fewer places. This will also cut down on costs, as it means fewer airport transfers, and you can usually take advantage of a hotel's cheaper rates.

If I am staying somewhere for more than three nights I try and find accommodation that has a little kitchenette. I love cooking, but also, when travelling, sometimes I just want a simple and light meal. It might sound odd, but one of my favourite things to do in a new city is visit a local grocery store or market. I think you learn a lot about a place by its food and food culture. Venture down to the local market and snag yourself some fresh, seasonal – and affordable – local produce, then bring it back and cook it up.

Sans meat

Eating less (or no) meat when you're travelling can significantly reduce your environmental footprint. As mentioned in the food waste chapter, meat has a far higher carbon footprint than vegetables (see page 36). Depending on your destination, embracing a vegetarian or vegan diet can mean you're eating more authentically, too, particularly in countries like India and some parts of Asia. Plus, in most cases, eating authentically and meat free leads to the cheapest meals! You won't see locals lining up for an expensive pepperoni pizza in a South-East Asian country, so eat like a local to get the best experience (and savings).

Water

Depending on where you're travelling, it might not be safe to drink the tap water. If that's the case, or you're unsure, buy a large 5-litre (quart) bottle of water to keep at your accommodation, then fill up your reusable bottle from there. Yes, you are still consuming some plastic, but one large bottle uses much less than multiple individual plastic bottles of water.

Check out the Refill app, which is another great travel companion that shows you where you can find places around the world with free drinking water!

Room service

It might be tempting to indulge in the luxury of room service when staying in a hotel, but to avoid the energy and electricity spent on cleaning your linens, laundering your towels and vacuuming your hotel room, just hang the 'Do Not Disturb' sign on the door. Some chains are even starting to incentivise travellers to say no to the daily clean by providing financial rewards.

The universal sign for 'I don't need new towels', no matter where you are or what language is spoken, is simply hanging your towels nicely back on the rack.

Ethical activities

Sadly, there are so many unethical animal attractions and experiences around the world that it can be difficult to find legitimately sustainable and cruelty free activities. The terms used to describe many of these attractions are a good example of how greenwashing works in marketing. Look out for some of the common culprits below:

- **Sanctuary:** the use of this term isn't policed, so before you visit make sure you ask them for any accreditations.
- **Zoos and aquariums:** Double-check the Association of Zoos & Aquariums to make sure you're visiting an organisation that well and truly looks after its animals.

Closer to home

Of course, there are plenty of amazing holidays that you can take in your own backyard! So many of us associate going on a holiday with leaving the country, but opting to stay on home soil is the most obvious way you can make significant financial and environmental savings.

The most sustainable – and most often cheapest – way to travel is by train, and even in large countries like Australia, you'll be surprised at how far you can go by rail. If you choose to drive, try carpooling with your travel companions over driving four separate vehicles, and split the coast of fuel (and emissions!) along the way.

One of my favourite cost-effective holiday activities is hiking and camping. Most hikes in Australia are free and a campsite is far cheaper than a hotel. If you don't have all of the gear (but you do have the right ideas), then borrow it from a friend! It's better to put it to use than have it collect dust in their garage.

Something I don't think enough people use enough is 'Friendship B&B'! To all my friends reading this, take this as your invitation to come for a sleepover. For the cost of a bottle of wine or a home-cooked meal, you can crash in a friend's spare room or on their couch. If they've offered, it isn't an imposition. When you're travelling, you spend very little time at your accommodation anyway, so chances are you won't be there much anyway. Plus, you can return the favour when they are next in town and before you know it you've both saved a bomb on both money and environmental costs!

'The most sustainable – and most often cheapest – way to travel is by train ...'

ACTIONABLE STEPS

- [ ] **Pick homestays over hotel chains**
- [ ] **Travel light**
- [ ] **Walk more**
- [ ] **Support local businesses**
- [ ] **Say no to room service**
- [ ] **Pack your single-use quitter kit (see page 70)**
- [ ] **Carbon offset your flights**
- [ ] **Go paper ticket free**

NEXT UP

Taking personal responsibility for living more sustainably goes a long way, but let's not forget that the biggest changes that need to be made are systemic, and one way to support these changes is by rallying behind the people and businesses leading us to an eco-friendlier future.

On your individual journey towards sustainability, not everyone in your life will understand your choices or want to participate, but having support from those closest to you will mean it is much easier to implement the changes you want to make.

13.

Relationships: with you, the planet and your loved ones

'Having a support network is so important as you navigate the change to living more sustainably, and your network of support people will ultimately make the process a whole lot easier – or a whole lot harder.'

This chapter was a late addition to the book. I felt like so much of what I'd written was about the simple steps and actions you can take to make savings for the planet and your budget. However, I think it is also important to acknowledge the journey and the impact that it will probably have on those around you.

Having a support network is so important as you navigate the change to living more sustainably, and your network of support people will ultimately make the process a whole lot easier – or a whole lot harder. This chapter is probably one of the most important; it's the glue. These principles and ideas covered in this chapter really are the keys to your success, but it has the least actionable steps.

Come back to this section throughout your journey, and let it reassure you that the path to a more sustainable future is not one you have to tackle alone.

The individual

I am constantly asked how I remain positive about the state of the planet, or if working in the sustainability sphere day in day out weighs on my mental health. You might be surprised to hear that I actually feel energised, inspired and empowered more than I feel a sense of defeat.

I choose to feel fortunate that I can spend each and every day doing as much as I can to help save this planet. I feel privileged to be able to say that no matter what, I am trying my very best. I also acknowledge that this isn't possible for everyone.

The Oxford Dictionary defines eco-anxiety as 'extreme worry about current and future harm to the environment caused by human activity and climate change'. And it is a very real, valid feeling.

The role of the individual in healing and, ultimately, restoring our planet to health cannot be understated. Everyone keeps insisting that it's 'up to the younger generations to fix the damage that previous generations have wrought', but this removes the responsibility of every living person – no matter what their age – to make tangible contributions to solving the problem.

I don't fundamentally believe that the planet is beyond repair. Right now, our future does not look like rolling luscious green hills, butterflies and everyone riding bikes and singing in harmony, but it can look like everyone pulling together to do their bit to make incremental changes that will halt the devastation. This is a much more hopeful picture than the media often depicts.

This is why it is crucial that you aim for progress, not perfection. Making small, manageable changes is of more value to the health of our planet – and our bank accounts – than grandiose gestures. You won't be able to 'do it all', which is why I always talk about 'doing what you can'.

Living more sustainably can feel like a futile task, especially if those around you don't understand or agree with your efforts. This is why I'd encourage you to check in with yourself regularly, and, if you're feeling defeated or a little bit wobbly, there are a few things I suggest you do:

- **Reflect:** It's so easy to get caught up in how far you have to go that you forget how far you've come.
- **Celebrate the small wins:** Have a look back at what actionable steps you've taken. You've probably been able to implement more than you think. Step by step you're making a difference.
- **Get outdoors:** Whenever it feels overwhelming, get outside and breathe. Not only will the sunshine brighten your mood, but feeling grounded on the earth you are fighting hard to save will always bring you back to your purpose.

This book isn't about who 'wins' at sustainability. It's about breaking down the overwhelming task of sustainability into manageable, small and affordable tasks that feel possible for you.

The key to achieving these tasks is the support – or at the very least, acknowledgement – of the people closest to you.

The people around you

Whether you're living with friends, family or randoms, the people in your immediate vicinity are the ones who will see and feel the impact of the changes you're making firsthand. When I made my New Year's resolution to live more sustainably all of those years ago, I was living with two roommates. They didn't jump on the bandwagon, but they were supportive in their own way.

The way I approached it with them is one I would suggest you try, too. Present your co-inhabitants with the changes you're making as 'optional extras' – easy swaps they can make that will help save both the environment and money. I'll give you a few examples.

'Making small, manageable changes is of more value to the health of our planet – and our bank accounts – than grandiose gestures.'

When I first started composting, I was living with roommates in a townhouse with no backyard and therefore no room for a compost bin. Instead, I used a bokashi bin, which I dropped off at one of our neighbour's. I explained to them how it worked and why I was doing it. I managed everything, from purchasing the countertop bin, to taking the fermented goodness every couple of months around the corner. I didn't force anyone to participate, but if they did, then great. They certainly all observed it.

When we moved to a freestanding home, I bought a standard bin and continued to do all of the maintenance and turning. To my delight, when I moved out everyone agreed that they would keep the compost bin and continue composting their scraps.

The same thing happened when I made sustainable household swaps. I didn't remove others' plastic products, just my own. Very quickly some of these changes were adopted by my housemates, and they found themselves switching to more sustainable products.

Even if others aren't ready to join you on your journey yet, they are still able to observe and learn from the changes you are making, which is incredibly valuable.

Living with parents

I am often asked how to make sustainable changes when living at home with my parents. They've been living the same way for the last twenty or so years and aren't looking to change anytime soon. I think it is firstly important to focus on what you can control, not what you can't. For example, there's a very slim chance that you will convince your parents to install solar panels, but you might get them to try one meat-free meal a week.

Previous generations might well be stuck in their unsustainable ways (whether they realise it or not), but before you go on a tirade over the amount of plastic packaging they consume or how many disposable shopping bags they use, consider that – by virtue of their age – they've probably been carrying out other sustainable practices for years. Things like eating leftovers, having a more basic skincare routine, hanging washing on a clothesline or travelling less.

The easiest way to introduce older generations to more sustainable ways is to do it yourself and allow them to observe the positive effects. You never know, they might adopt a thing or two.

Friends

I haven't lived my entire life like this but since I have started living more sustainably, I've still had the same group of friends. Bottom line? You are not going to lose friends over wanting to save money and the planet. The most important thing about your journey to saving money and the planet is that you want it to be sustainable. Sustainable in the fact that you can keep on living life, just simply with less, and more consciously.

This doesn't mean never leaving the house again and becoming a recluse. Or being wary of your friends with 'expensive tastes' and avoiding them like the plague. Frugal can be fun, and true friends will support you in your endeavours. Here are a couple of ways that I catch up with my friends without dropping lots of dosh.

For me, and so many people I meet, we aren't in a group of friends that practises sustainability, but we are the sustainable person within that group. This usually means that we are the go-to point for answering recycling questions, helping people figure out if a brand is greenwashing or not and, most importantly, being a role model. Even within your small circle of friends you can lead by example and have an impact.

Simple swaps with friends

I find that one of the easiest ways to make sustainable swaps is to do it with friends. Bring them along for the ride and they might end up adopting some of these habits, too.

The temptation to meet friends for food is strong. Now, don't get me wrong, I will still have breakfast out every now and again, but more often than not I'll just join my friends for a coffee instead. It saves money, but also means I get to eat the plethora of food in my fridge, so nothing goes to waste.

Likewise, while I do love going out for dinner, it's equally fun to get a group of friends round and cook that recipe you've been meaning to try. Make it a group affair by getting everyone to cook and contribute a dish. Light the candles, put the music on and break out the fancy dinnerware. Cooking at home means fewer transport emissions, less energy used and it's a great way to save money – and have lunch ready for the following day. Win-win!

Nothing makes me happier than a walking date with a friend. I get my steps in, get outside and get to catch up with a friend. Time flies and I always feel so energised afterwards. Plus, I would argue that walking uses zero environmental energy while reminding you of what you are working so hard to protect.

Splitting the bill It can be hard to keep a tally amongst friends of who's paid for what. Splitwise is an amazing free app (there is a paid option, but it isn't worth it for the average punter) that calculates who owes who what. Each person simply puts in what they've paid for and who they'd like to split the bill with, and the app takes the calculation – and the ickiness – out of it for you.

Sharing is caring

I spoke about sharing in the fashion chapter on page 136, but sharing can extend beyond swapping clothes. Why not try out each other's hobbies? Or alternate hosting a barbecue or board game night? Embracing such simple pleasures once so treasured by our grandparents and parents are fundamental to living more sustainably.

Here are some more ideas:
· Walks and runs
· Dinners at home
· Picnics
· Indoor and outdoor games
· Beach day
· Hikes
· Go op-shopping (thrifting)
· Volunteer together
· Go to the gym (most gyms will offer you a free friend pass every so often)
· Trivia nights

Dating

When it comes to starting a new relationship, don't let your newfound affinity for saving money and the planet hold you back. In a term coined by Mintel, the creators of Barbie, the 'eco gender gap' describes the statistical likelihood that women are more likely to live sustainably than men. In my own life I've seen this as an opportunity to subtly start singing my YMCA (see page 247) and educating more people on their behaviours. Not preachy or naggy, just informatively.

As much as I might wish I'd bump into a young David Attenborough, statistically (and realistically), that isn't likely to happen. For me, personally, when dating I found the best approach was looking for someone who was open to learning and making sustainable choices. Activate the YMCA method and bring your spare reusable coffee cup to your next date – if they turn their nose up, it's definitely a red flag!

Roses are dead

Cut flowers are terribly harmful to the planet. Not only do they have a short shelf life, but they are often grown in huge, heated greenhouses and sprayed with pesticides, herbicides and insecticides, which creates a toxic runoff that is dangerous to local wildlife, especially pollinators like bees. They are also often exported (and sometimes imported) internationally by plane, giving them an extremely high carbon footprint. Next time you want to make a romantic gesture, offer a beautiful locally grown plant instead.

'For me, personally, when dating I found the best approach was looking for someone who was open to learning and making sustainable choices.'

ACTIVITY: PICK YOUR OWN ADVENTURE

Grab two pieces of paper, your partner and two jars or envelopes. Now set a timer for five minutes and both of you write down as many sustainable date ideas as you can (not showing the other person). Once you're done, cut them up (one idea per piece of paper) and add them to the 'less than $50' jar or 'over $50' jar. Next time you're prepping for date night, discuss your budget and pull from the different jars.

Tip
Coupons are cute. No seriously, it's the thought, not the money, that counts. Have a look at your local discount or coupon guide to see if you can get an experience for a portion of the price. This could mean going to the dress rehearsal of a musical, filling an extra spot at a restaurant or booking a last-minute trip away for the weekend.

Here are a couple of budget-friendly, sustainable date ideas:

- Go on a day trip to the beach
- Take a hike
- Hire bikes for a day
- Go to happy hour at your local pub
- Visit an art gallery or museum
- Pub trivia night
- Walk through the botanical gardens
- Boardgame night at home
- Movie night
- Picnic
- Explore weekend markets
- DIY at home (pottery or paint)
- Go fruit picking
- Bake something together

Boujee dates:

- Natural spring spa
- Bowling
- Sporting match
- Weekend getaway somewhere local (preferably by train)
- Comedy nights
- Mini golf/driving range
- Winery tour
- Listen to live music

Gift giving

When it comes to giving and receiving gifts, I like to start with a really honest conversation with my loved ones. I set expectations from the get-go about what I am prepared to spend and what sort of gift I am happy to buy. It can feel uncomfortable, but it's a simple way to hold your boundaries and ask the people closest to you to respect your values. Likewise, I tell them exactly what I want (if anything), to make sure what I receive is something I will actually use and that won't simply create more waste. Often, that's an experience of a physical present.

Here are some of my favourite sustainable gifts:

- Plant cuttings
- Something you've baked or cooked at home
- Clothing they've always admired
- Well-loved book with a note on the inside cover
- Time to help them out with something
- Food waste pickles (see page 52)
- A hand-drawn card, even if you're a terrible artist like me
- Sew them something
- Hand-made beeswax wraps (see page 83)

Conversation tools

Once you've drunk the Kool-Aid and fallen in love with your new budget- and planet-friendly ways, it might be hard to understand why more people don't embrace this way of life. Instead of shouting it from the rooftops or dominating your next social catch-up talking non-stop about climate change, here is a useful conversation tool I like to use that I have aptly coined the YMCA method ™ Lottie Dalziel 2024.

Y

(Why) Bring their attention to the issue

↓

M

Message

↓

C

Care/Consider

↓

A

Action

HERE'S AN EXAMPLE:

Why: Insert fun environmental fact or stat.
Message: Tell them how you are doing it differently.
Care: Nurture them through the consideration phase and explain why they should care and how this change will affect them.
Action: Tell them something you're doing that would be easy for them to join you in actioning and implementing.

WHEN TALKING TO A FRIEND:

Why: Did you know that food waste in landfills equates to more emissions than the entire aviation industry?
Message: I am guilty of throwing away mouldy bread, but I am really trying to make a conscious effort to waste less.
Care: I know you are also trying to save money. Have you thought about the hard-earned money you throw away each week? For the average household, it's one in five shopping bags' worth of food.
Action: I'm going to try out a shop-free week where I eat through our pantry and freezer to reduce waste. You can do it with me, if you like?

WHEN TALKING TO YOUR PARENTS:

Why: I am reading this amazing book at the moment about saving money and the planet.
Message: I recently learned that we eat a credit card's worth of plastic each and every week, so I am going to commit to reducing my plastic use as much as possible.
Care: It's really got me thinking about how we need to make a more conscious effort to stop relying on single-use plastic so much.
Action: I am going to stop buying single-use plastic bottles and get a reusable water bottle instead. Christmas is coming up, do you think you would use one if I bought you one?

Conclusion

You've made it to the end of this book – congratulations! But, honestly, your journey is just beginning. Living sustainably and saving money isn't a destination you will one day arrive at; it's a continuous journey with different seasons, ebbs and flows. Some months you'll nail it and some you won't, but what will really make this work is showing up as consistently as possible to compound daily actions into meaningful change. I hope that everyone who reads this book gets something out of it and that it will positively influence and impact the way that you live.

In my own journey towards living more sustainably, I have quite literally turned my life upside down. It has led to a career change and a lifestyle change, and I wouldn't have it any other way.

To be able to be a source of information, inspiration and motivation to so many people each and every day keeps the fire in my belly and my passion growing. All I've ever wanted to do is help people. I never knew exactly how until I really made living sustainably my mission. I saw a problem and I saw a solution.

Banish is anything but an overnight success, it's taken more hard work and determination than I knew I had. I believe that people want to do the right thing when it comes to the planet and their finances, but they simply don't have the tools or information to do it.

My hopes and dreams for this book are to empower readers to take action in their own lives to be more sustainable, while saving money at the same time, so I hope that it has enabled you to do just that. I was never taught this at school and very little of it by my parents. I've fumbled my way through it and dropped the ball on many occasions when it comes to setting up a financially and environmentally sustainable lifestyle.

I hope I've made it easier for you. From starting to compost at home, to making your own food scrap cleaner and selling things online, every small action counts and compounds. I believe that the collective actions of individuals are what will have the biggest impact on halting – perhaps even reversing – climate change.

If this book has had even the slightest impact on you, please help by giving your copy (or a new one) to someone else. In order for people to make sustainable environmental and economic changes, it needs to be as simple as possible, and passing on the suggestions in this book is an easy way to spread the word.

Acknowledgements

I'm so excited to release my very first book. Writing a book was always a goal of mine, but honestly one that I thought wouldn't happen for a very long time. Thank you, firstly, dear reader, for listening to and learning from all of the information I have to share. You are the reason I wrote this, and you are the reason I continue to do the work that I do every day.

To my family, the biggest 'yes' people I know. I still remember the day that I 'pitched' Banish to you, Mum and Dad. You shared my enthusiasm for it from day one and I know you'll always be there for me no matter how far away you are. You give me the confidence to chase after my dreams.

To Lee, who never takes no for an answer and sees my future more clearly than I do. You're the reason this book turned from a dream to a reality and, one day, I hope to be as bold and brave as you are.

To Josh, thank you for being there for me as I added writing a book to running a start-up and working 60+ hours a week. From our sunset walks on the beach to your home-cooked meals, your support means more than you'll ever know.

To my friends, who have watched me turn my life upside down. You don't realise just how grateful I am to have you. From answering the phone at odd hours of the day for a random chat, to connecting me with someone else just in case we have something in common, and to those who shared my story I appreciate you all so much.

To the team at Murdoch, thank you for helping to bring my words to life. I am anything but conventional and have the imagination of a 9-year-old, so thank you for letting me be myself as I embark on this new chapter.

And, of course, a huge thank you to my community. To the people who have followed my sustainability journey from day dot, and for the ones who have joined in along the way. It has been a wild ride and one that I don't think anyone realised would turn out quite like this.

I don't know what my future holds. I don't think I ever have and I don't think I ever will. What is clear is that I will continue to help people. To make it easier for people to be kinder to themselves, to one another and the planet.

Resources

Chapter 1: Sustainability essentials
Stat pack

Page 16: *Recycling 1 tonne of paper or cardboard* ... Recycling Near You, 2024, Recycling benefits <https://recyclingnearyou.com.au/documents/doc-1740-benefits-paper.pdf>

Page 16: *90 per cent of Australians* ... Nijssen-Smith, L. and L'Huillier, M., Sustainability isn't what it used to be, EY, 2021 <ey.com/en_au/future-consumer-index/sustainability-isn-t-what-it-used-to-be>

Page 16: *75 per cent of UK residents* ... D. Tighe., Sustainable shopping behaviors according to UK shoppers 2022–2023, 2023 <statista.com/statistics/1056522/sustainable-shopping-behavior-of-uk-shoppers/>

Page 16: *77 per cent of global citizens* ... Ellsmoor, J., 77% Of People Want To Learn How To Live More Sustainably, 2022 <forbes.com/sites/jamesellsmoor/2019/07/23/77-of-people-want-to-learn-how-to-live-more-sustainably/>

Chapter 2: Food waste
Stat pack

Page 26: *Australians throw away one in every* ... Foodwise, 2024, Fast Facts on Food Waste <foodwise.com.au/foodwaste/food-waste-fast-facts/>

Page 26: *The average Australian household throws* ... Australian Government Department of Climate Change, Energy, the Environment and Water, 2020, A Roadmap for reducing Australia's food waste by half by 2030 <dcceew.gov.au/sites/default/files/documents/roadmap-reducing-food-waste.pdf>

Page 26: *If global food waste was a country* ... Food and Agriculture Organization of the United Nations, 2013, Food Wastage Footprint, Impact on Natural Resources <openknowledge.fao.org/server/api/core/bitstreams/1694038d-98f7-40f6-be4b-98782544b9f9/content>

Page 26: *The total greenhouse gas emissions* ... World Resources Institute, 2020, World Greenhouse Gas Emissions <wri.org/data/world-greenhouse-gas-emissions-2016>

Shop seasonally

Page 33: *It's estimated that transport accounts for* ... Nemecek, T. and Poore, J., 'Reducing food's environmental impacts through producers and consumers', *Science*, 2018, vol. 360 no. 6392, pp. 987–992 <doi.org/10.1126/science.aaq0216>

Pick imperfect produce

Page 33: *Did you know that perfectly good*

... British Government Environment, Food and Rural Affairs Committee, 2017, Food Waste in England, Eighth Report of Session 2016–17 <publications.parliament.uk/pa/cm201617/cmselect/cmenvfru/429/429.pdf>

Protein predicament

Page 35: *Average greenhouse gas impact* ... Nemecek, T. and Poore, J., 'Reducing food's environmental impacts through producers and consumers', *Science*, 2018, vol. 360 no. 6392, pp. 987–992 <doi.org/10.1126/science.aaq0216>

A meaty issue

Page 36: *It can take up to 15,000–20,000 litres* ... Food and Agriculture Organization of the United Nations, Livestock's Long Shadow: Environmental Issues and Options, 2006 <fao.org/4/a0701e/a0701e00.htm>

Page 36: *People who eat meat are responsible for* ... Barthelmie, Rebecca J., 'Impact of Dietary Meat and Animal Products on GHG Footprints: The UK and the US', *Climate*, 2022, vol. 10 no. 3, p. 43 <mdpi.com/2225-1154/10/3/43>

Page 36: *Livestock production accounts for roughly* ... Stoll-Kleemann, S., 'Reducing meat consumption in developed and transition countries to counter climate change and biodiversity loss: A review of influence factors', *Regional Environmental Change*, 2017, vol. 17 no. 5 <doi.org/10.1007/s10113-016-1057-5>

Page 36: *Meat production is also responsible for* ... Jacquet, J., Lazarus, O. and McDermid, S., 'Correction: The Climate responsibilities of industrial meat and dairy producers', *Climate Change*, 2021, vol. 165 no. 30 <doi.org/10.1007/s10584-022-03330-1>

Page 36: *A study published in* Scientific Reports *found* ... Eshel, G., Shepon, A., Stainier, P. and Swaminathan, A., 'Environmentally Optimal, Nutritionally Sound, Protein and Energy Conserving Plant Based Alternatives to U.S. Meat', *Scientific Reports*, 2019, vo. 9 no. 10345 <doi.org/10.1038/s41598-019-46590-1>

Page 36: *Here's a fact to consider: the vegan diet* ... Heller, M.C. and Keoleian, G.A., 'Greenhouse Gas Emission Estimates of U.S. Dietary Choices and Food Loss', Journal of Industrial Ecology, vol. 19 no. 3, pp. 391–401 <doi.org/10.1111/jiec.12174>

Page 36: *On the other hand, eating a vegetarian* ... Aleksandrowicz L., Joy, Edward J.M., Green, R., Haines, A. and Smith, P., 'The Impacts of Dietary Change on Greenhouse Gas Emissions, Land Use, Water Use, and Health: A Systematic Review', *Ecological Impacts of Climate Change*, 2016, vol. 11 <doi.org/10.1371/journal.pone.0165797>

Here, fishy, fishy

Page 37: *Every year approximately 650,000 whales* ... Lent, R. and Squires, D., 'Reducing marine mammal bycatch in global fisheries: An economics approach', *Deep–Sea Research II*, 2017, vol. 140, pp. 268–77 <doi.org/10.1016/j.dsr2.2017.03.005>

Page 37: *In 2022, as much as 37.5 per cent of all seafood* ... Food and Agriculture Organization of the United Nations, *The State of World Fishers and Aquaculture, Towards Blue Transformation*, 2022 <doi.org/10.4060/cc0461en>

Page 38: *According to the journal* Frontiers in Ecology and the Environment, ... Banobi, J., Hall, S. J., Hilborn, R., Pucylowski, T. and Walsworth, T.E., 'The environmental cost of animal source foods', *Frontiers in Ecology and the Environment*, 2018, vol. 16 no. 6, pp. 329–35 <doi.org/10.1002/fee.1822>

Page 39: *Milk vs. 'Milk'* ... Nemecek, T. and Poore, J., 'Reducing food's environmental impacts through producers and consumers', *Science*, 2018, vol. 360 no. 6392, pp. 987–992 <doi.org/10.1126/science.aaq0216>

Chapter 3: Breaking up with plastic
Stat pack

Page 56: *In 2019, plastic production generated* ... Organisation for Economic Co operation and Development, 2022, Plastic leakage and greenhouse gas emissions are increasing <oecd.org/environment/plastics/increased-plastic-leakage-and-greenhouse-gas-emissions.htm>

Page 56: *1580 kg (3483 pounds) of plastic enters our oceans* ... World Economic Forum, 2016, How much plastic is there in the ocean? <weforum.org/agenda/2016/01/how-much-plastic-is-there-in-the-ocean/>

Page 56: *By 2050 there will be more plastic than fish* ... World Economic Forum, 2016, The New Plastics Economy, Rethinking the future of plastics <www3.weforum.org/docs/WEF_The_New_Plastics_Economy.pdf>

Page 56: *Australians eat 1 teaspoon (5 g/⅙ oz) of microplastics* ... World Wildlife Fund, 2019, Revealed: plastic ingestion by people could be equating to a credit card a week <wwf.mg/en/?348337/Revealed-plastic-ingestion-by-people-could-be-equating-to-a-credit-card-a-week>

Page 56: *50 per cent of the plastic we use is thrown* ... Plastic Oceans, 2024, Plastic Pollution Facts <plasticoceans.org/the-facts/>

Page 57: *There are eighteen to twenty-four shopping bags* ... 'Hidden Beneath the Ocean's Surface: Nearly 16 Tonnes of Plastic Waste', 2016, *The New York Times* <nytimes.com/2020/10/07/world/australia/microplastics-ocean-floor.html>

Microplastics

Page 58: *A study by Australia's Newcastle University* ... World Wildlife Fund, 2019, 'No Plastic In Nature: Assessing Plastic Ingestion from Nature to People' <awsassets.panda.org/downloads/plastic_ingestion_press_singles.pdf>

Page 59: *A study completed by the Environment Agency* ... Harvey, F. and Watts, J., 'Microplastics found in human stools for the first time', *The Guardian*, 2018 <theguardian.com/environment/2018/oct/22/microplastics-found-in-human-stools-for-the-first-time>

Page 59: *Several global studies have also found ...* Cox, K. D., Covernton, G.A. et al., 'Human Consumption of Microplastics', *Environmental Science and Technology*, 2019, vol. 53 no. 12, pp. 7068–74 <doi.org/10.1021/acs.est.9b01517>

A circular economy

Page 65: *According to the Ellen Macarthur Foundation ...* Ellen Macarthur Foundation, 2024, What is a Circular Economy? <ellenmacarthurfoundation.org/topics/circular-economy-introduction/overview>

Forget tea bags

Page 68: *A study by Montreal's McGill University found that ...* McGill University, 2019, Some plastic with your tea? <mcgill.ca/newsroom/channels/news/some-plastic-your-tea-300919>

The plastic demise

Page 69: *Here are the length-of-stays in landfill ...* Science Learning Hub, 2024, Measuring biodegradability <sciencelearn.org.nz/resources/1543-measuring-biodegradability>

Chapter 4: Swap 'n' save in your kitchen
Stat pack

Page 74: *67 per cent of US consumers ...* Lindner, J., 'Sustainability in Food Service Statistics: Latest Data & Summary', Wifi Talents, 2024 <wifitalents.com/statistic/sustainability-in-food-service/>

Page 74: *In 2023, 53 per cent of Australians stated ...* NAB Business Insights, 2023, The growing importance of sustainability as a consumer issue & are SMEs ready? <https://business.nab.com.au/wp-content/uploads/2023/03/NAB-Business-Insights-Sustainability-report-MARCH-2023.pdf>

Page 74: *63 per cent of people have already ...* Ruiz, A., '52 Huge Environmentally Conscious Consumer Statistics', The Roundup, 2024 <theroundup.org/environmentally-conscious-consumer-statistics/>

Chapter 5: Clean 'n' Mean
Stat pack

Page 92: *Washing clothes releases, on average ...* Resnick, B., 'More than ever, our clothes are made of plastic. Just washing them can pollute the oceans', *Vox*, 2019 <vox.com/the-goods/2018/9/19/17800654/clothes-plastic-pollution-polyester-washing-machine>

Page 92: *A 2018 study found that the regular use ...* Svanes, Ø. and Bertelsen, R.J., 'Cleaning at home and at work in relation to lung function decline and airway obstruction', *American Journal of Respiratory and Critical Care Medicine*, 2017

<doi.org/10.1164/rccm.201706-1311OC>

The microplastic problem with laundry

Page 103: *A 2015 study found that a staggering ...* Hartline, N.J. and Bruce, N. J., 'Microfiber Masses Recovered from Conventional Machine Washing of New or Aged garments', *Environmental Science & Technology*, 2016 <doi.org/10.1021/acs.est.6b03045>

Pillows

Page 105: *The average person sheds 4 kilograms of ...* Kids Health, 2024, Your Skin: What Does Skin Do? <kidshealth.org/en/kids/skin.html>

Chapter 6: Mirror, mirror on the wall
Stat pack

Page 114: *It is estimated that the beauty industry ...* Zerowaste, 2024, The Zero Waste Home <zerowaste.com/zero-waste-home-guide/>

Page 114: *95 per cent of beauty products ...* British Beauty Council, 2024, Packaging <britishbeautycouncil.com/ppbg/packaging/>

Page 114: *Only 14 per cent of beauty plastic ...* British Beauty Council, 2024, Packaging <britishbeautycouncil.com/ppbg/packaging/>

Page 114: *In Australia we throw away over 30 million ...* Healthy, Clean and Green, 2022, 'Three Switches to Help the Planet and Have Clean, Healthy Teeth'

Page 114: *Buying a refillable product reduces carbon ...* Gatt, I. J. and Refalo, P., 'Life cycle assessment of recyclable, reusable and dematerialised plastic cosmetic packages', IOP Conference Series: Materials Science and Engineering, 2021, vol. 1196 <doi.org/10.1088/1757-899X/1196/1/012022>

Palm oil: the great pretender

Page 116: *One substance lurking in a staggering ...* World Wildlife Fund, 2024, Which Everyday Products Contain Palm Oil? <worldwildlife.org/pages/which-everyday-products-contain-palm-oil>

Page 116: *Palm oil yields are also high in comparison ...* World Wildlife Fund, 2024, 8 Things to Know About Palm Oil <wwf.org.uk/updates/8-things-know-about-palm-oil>

Sunscreen

Page 119: *But, with 14,000 tonnes of sunscreen ...* Smithsonian National Museum of Natural History, 2022, 'The Truth About Corals and Sunscreen' <ocean.si.edu/ecosystems/coral-reefs/truth-about-corals-and-sunscreen>

Page 119: *Hawaiian lawmakers recently passed a bill ...* National Library of Medicine, 2018, 'Hawaii Bans Sunscreens That Harm Coral Reefs', <www.ncbi.nlm.nih.gov/search/research-news/3474/>

The problem with parabens

Page 118: *Evidence is growing to support the claim that ...* Vale, F., Sousa, C. A., Sousa, H., Santos, L. and Simões, M., 'Parabens as emerging contaminants: Environmental persistence, current practices and treatment processes', *Journal of Cleaner Production*, 2022, vol. 347 <doi.org/10.1016/j.jclepro.2022.131244>

Microbeads

Page 125: *Microbeads are small, solid, manufactured ...* Australian Government Department of Climate Change, Energy, the Environment and Water, 2024, Plastic Microbeads <dcceew.gov.au/environment/protection/waste/plastics-and-packaging/plastic-microbeads>

Page 125: *These tiny plastics have a damaging impact ...* Australian Governmnent Department of Climate Change, Energy, the Environment and Water, 2024, Plastic Microbeads <dcceew.gov.au/environment/protection/waste/plastics-and-packaging/plastic-microbeads>

Page 125: *Fortunately, microbeads are being phased out in Australia ...* Australian Government Department of Agriculture, Water and the Environment, 2020, 'An assessment of the presence of microbeads in rinse-off personal care, cosmetic and cleaning products currently available within the Australian retail market, <dcceew.gov.au/sites/default/files/documents/microbeads-rinse-products-survey-report.pdf>

Chapter 7: It's fashun, darling
Stat pack

Page 139: *In 2017–19, the secondhand fashion industry ...* Fashion For Good, 2024, The Future of Circular Fashion: Assessing the Viability of Circular Business Models <fashionforgood.com/wp-content/uploads/2019/05/The-Future-of-Circular-Fashion-Report.pdf>

Page 139: *Globally it is estimated that 35 per cent ...* European Environment Agency, 2023, Microplastics from textiles: towards a circular economy for textiles in Europe <eea.europa.eu/publications/microplastics-from-textiles-towards>

Page 139: *The fashion industry is responsible for producing ...* Niinimäki, K., Peters, G., et al., 'The environmental price of fast fashion', *Nature Reviews Earth & Environment*, 2020, vol. 1, pp. 189–200 <doi.org/10.1038/s43017-020-0039-9>

Page 139: *Between 80 and 100 billion items ...* Naclerio, M., 'Sustainable Beauty', University of Connecticut, 2020 <sustainability.uconn.edu/2020/09/11/sustainable-beauty/>

Page 139: *Wearing a garment for nine months longer ...* Ro, C., 'Can fashion ever be sustainable?', BBC, 2020 <bbc.com/future/article/20200310-sustainable-fashion-how-to-buy-clothes-good-for-the-climate>

Fabrics fable

Page 143: *I've divided up fourteen of the most common* ... Textile Exchange, 2018, Global Material Production <store.textileexchange.org/wp-content/uploads/woocommerce_uploads/2019/11/Textile-Exchange_Preferred-Fiber-Material-Market-Report_2019.pdf>

Duck, duck, goose

Page 144: *Around the globe, there are increasing concerns* ... Turner, J., 'Animal Down in Clothing', Ethical Consumer, 2024 <ethicalconsumer.org/fashion-clothing/animal-down-clothing>

Silky story

Page 144: *Silk thread is made from silkworm larvae cocoons* ... Agricultural Holdings International, LLC, 2024, Silkworm Farming <ahi-intl.farm/post/silkworm-farming>

Page 144: *Not only do people have issues with the boiling* ... Hogeboom, R. J. and Hoekstra, A. Y., 'Water and Land Footprints and Economic Productivity as Factors in Local Crop Choice: The Case of Silk in Malawi', *Water*, 2017, vol. 9 no. 10, p. 802 <doi.org/10.3390/w9100802>

Page 144: *There are also human rights concerns* ... Collective Fashion Justice, 2024, Issues in the Silk Supply Chain <collectivefashionjustice.org/silk>

Semi-synthetic fabrics

Page 145: *For example, 200 million trees are logged every* ... Rollscane, C., Burley, H. and Williot, D., The Climate and Nature Risks Hidden in Viscose Fabric, 2022 <forest500.org/analysis/insights/climate-and-nature-risks-hidden-viscose-fabric>

Devilish denim

Page 153: *It sounds like a bold statement, but I will never* ... Levi Strauss, 2015, The Life Cycle of a Jean <levistrauss.com/wp-content/uploads/2015/03/Full-LCA-Results-Deck-FINAL.pdf>

Chapter 8: How to shop and sell secondhand

Stat pack

Page 160: *Since 2017, there has been a 31 per cent increase* ... Harding, N., 'Is Sustainable Fashion Only for the Rich?', *Cosmopolitan*, 2020 <cosmopolitan.com/uk/fashion/style/a32609106/sustainable-fashion-cost/>

Page 160: *Over 85 per cent of Aussies have unwanted* ... Fear, J., 'Stuff Happens: Unused Things Cluttering Up Our Homes', Research Paper No. 52, The Australian Institute Ltd, 2008 <australiainstitute.org.au/wp-content/uploads/2020/12/WP112_8.pdf>

Page 160: *The average household could make $7000* ... Statista, 2024, Estimate

Earning from Selling Secondhand Items in Australia from 2019 to 2020 <statista.com/statistics/1330177/australia-earnings-from-selling-second-hand-items/>

Chapter 9: Utilise your utilities and vote with your dollar

Stat pack

Page 172: *Washing your clothes at a cooler temperature* ... Help for Households, 2024, Make summer savings <helpforhouseholds.campaign.gov.uk/summer-savings/>

Page 172: *It's estimated that LED lightbulbs last* ... Energy.gov, 2024, Lighting Choices to Save You Money <energy.gov/energysaver/lighting-choices-save-you-money>

Let's gas bag about gas

Page 177: *Plus, a study by the University of New South Wales* ... University of New South Wales, 2023, A heated debate – how safe are gas stoves? <unsw.edu.au/newsroom/news/2023/02/a-heated-debate--how-safe-are-gas-stoves-->

Fridge

Page 179: *The average Aussie spends 10.4 hours* ... A Guide to the Food Safety Standards, Safe Food Australia, 2023 <foodstandards.gov.au/sites/default/files/2023-11/Safe%20Food%20Australia_edn%204%20whole%20book%20-%20271123_0.pdf>

Top washing tips

Page 181: *90 per cent of a washing machine's energy* ... Direct Energy, 2023, How much energy does my washing machine use? <directenergy.com/en/learn/home-energy-management/how-much-energy-washing-machine-use#:~:text=Water%20heating%20can%20account%20for,pump%20in%20hot%20water%20directl>

Chapter 10: Go to work without the waste

Stat pack

Page 190: *It's estimated that cars are responsible* ... Climate Council, 2024, Fact Sheet: Transport Emissions: Driving Down Car Pollution in Cities <climatecouncil.org.au/wp-content/uploads/2017/09/FactSheet-Transport.pdf>

Page 190: *Australians use, on average, a whopping* ... Adarsh Fibre, 2022, Australia's Recycling Crisis – How to Recycle Paper Properly! <adarshfibre.com.au/post/how-to-recycle-paper>

Page 190: *Over 8000 companies worldwide* ... TravelPerk, 2024, 60+ Business sustainability statistics (relevant in 2024) <travelperk.com/blog/business-sustainability-statistics/>

Plastic-free lunches

Page 192: *It is estimated that the average worker could save* ... The Australian HR Institute, 2017, So, which country spends the most money on work lunch? <hrmonline.com.au/performance/country-spends-money-work-lunch>

The communal challenge

Page 193: *Removing individual bins in offices decreased* ... D'Onfro, J., 'How Getting Rid of Individual Trash Cans Changed E-Commerce Company Etsy's Culture', Business Insider, 2014 <businessinsider.com/why-etsy-got-rid-of-individual-employee-trash-cans-2014-9>

Chapter 11: Build a thriving garden and a blooming bank account

Stat pack

Page 200: *40 per cent of your household waste* ... Foodwise, 2024, Fast Facts on Food Waste <foodwise.com.au/foodwaste/food-waste-fast-facts/>

Page 200: *Organically active material contributes a* ... Department of Primary Industries and Regional Development, 2022, Composting to avoid methane production – Western Australia <agric.wa.gov.au/climate-change/composting-avoid-methane-production-%E2%80%93-western-australia>

Chapter 12: Travel the world but leave no footprint

Stat pack

Page 224: *Australians spend more than $900 million a year* ... Budget Direct, 2023, Holiday Costs Survey and Statistics 2023 <budgetdirect.com.au/travel-insurance/research/average-holiday-cost-statistics.html>

Chapter 13: Relationships: with you, the planet and your loved ones

Dating

Page 245: *In a term coined by Mintel, the creators of Barbie,* ... Mintel, 2018, The eco gender gap: 71% of women try to live more ethically, compared to 59% of men <mintel.com/press-centre/the-eco-gender-gap-71-of-women-try-to-live-more-ethically-compared-to-59-of-men/>

Index

Published in 2025 by Murdoch Books,
an imprint of Allen & Unwin

Murdoch Books Australia
Cammeraygal Country
83 Alexander Street
Crows Nest NSW 2065
Phone: +61 (0)2 8425 0100
murdochbooks.com.au
info@murdochbooks.com.au

Murdoch Books UK
Ormond House
26–27 Boswell Street
London WC1N 3JZ
Phone: +44 (0) 20 8785 5995
murdochbooks.co.uk
info@murdochbooks.co.uk

For corporate orders and custom publishing,
contact our business development team at
salesenquiries@murdochbooks.com.au

Publisher: Alexandra Payne
Editorial manager: Justin Wolfers
Design manager: Sarah Odgers
Designer and illustrator: Michelle Mackintosh
Editor: Andrea O'Connor
Production manager: Natalie Crouch

*Murdoch Books acknowledges the Traditional
Owners of the Country on which we live and
work. We pay our respects to all Aboriginal and
Torres Strait Islander Elders, past and present.*

ISBN 9 781 76150 001 5

 A catalogue record for this
book is available from the
National Library of Australia

A catalogue record for this book is available
from the British Library

Printed by 1010 Printing International
Limited, China

OVEN GUIDE: You may find cooking times
vary depending on the oven you are using.
For fan-forced ovens, as a general rule, set
the oven temperature to 20°C (35°F) lower
than indicated in the recipe.

TABLESPOON MEASURES: We have used
20 ml (4 teaspoon) tablespoon measures. If
you are using a 15 ml (3 teaspoon) tablespoon
add an extra teaspoon of the ingredient for
each tablespoon specified.

10 9 8 7 6 5 4 3 2 1